Behavioral
Finance

Behavioral Finance

Understanding the Social,
Cognitive, and Economic Debates

EDWIN T. BURTON
SUNIT N. SHAH

WILEY

Published by John Wiley & Sons, Inc., Hoboken, New Jersey.
Published simultaneously in Canada.

For general information on our other products and services or for technical support, please contact
our Customer Care Department within the United States at (800) 762-2974, outside the United
States at (317) 572-3993 or fax (317) 572-4002.

Wiley publishes in a variety of print and electronic formats and by print-on-demand. Some material
included with standard print versions of this book may not be included in e-books or in print-on-
demand. If this book refers to media such as a CD or DVD that is not included in the version you
purchased, you may download this material at http://booksupport.wiley.com. For more information
about Wiley products, visit www.wiley.com.

Library of Congress Cataloging-in-Publication Data:

Burton, Edwin T.
  Behavioral finance : understanding the social, cognitive, and economic debates / Edwin T. Burton
  and Sunit N. Shah.
     pages cm.—(Wiley finance series)
  Includes index.
  ISBN 978-1-118-30019-0 (cloth); ISBN 978-1-118-33410-2 (ebk);
  ISBN 978-1-118-33521-5 (ebk); ISBN 978-1-118-33192-7 (ebk)
  1. Investments—Psychological aspects.   2. Capital market—Psychological aspects.
  3. Decision making.   I. Title.
  HG4521.B837 2013
  332.01'9—dc23
                                                                        2012041904

Printed in the United States of America.
10 9 8 7 6 5 4 3 2

Contents

Preface

This book was the product of five years of teaching "Behavioral Finance" to over 1,800 undergraduates at the University of Virginia. The course never had a textbook. In fact, the course was originally intended to be limited to, at most, 15 students due to the difficulty of the reading. By a strange quirk of the registration process, the course limit in the online registration system was altered to 300 and was quickly filled by eager students. It remains one of the most sought after courses at the University of Virginia. Who would have guessed?

When I first decided to offer Behavioral Finance as a course, I was driven by the amount of space that the subject was occupying in the leading finance journals. There was no book that I could find suitable for such a course, so the initial reading list was comprised solely of original sources—professional, academic journal articles. Somehow, this worked, and students continue to pack into this course that is offered every spring at the University of Virginia.

It dawned on me that if this course proved useful to our students, perhaps I should write a book summarizing my thoughts on Behavioral Finance in book form so that others might consider offering a similar course at their institution. In this spirit, I dedicate this book to all of my students—past, present, and future.

I would especially like to thank my co-author, Sunit Shah, whose brilliance and attention to detail has hopefully made up for much of my unintended carelessness. I would also like to thank my students Francesca Archila, Mu Chen, Qichen Wang, Grace Chuang, Samantha Rivard, and Patrick Glading for help with this book. I would also especially like to thank my daughter Lindsay Burton Sheehan for her help with numerous aspects of the final version. My wife, Trish, and my daughter Elizabeth Burton have been a constant source of encouragement toward the completion of this enterprise. Finally, I am grateful to Wiley for their patience and support in getting this book to print.

Edwin T. Burton

My fascination with financial markets was born with the execution of my first trade at age 17. From that point forward, through forecasting macro trends, to conducting actuarial analysis on life settlements, to creating predictive models around movements of credit spreads, that interest has evolved into an ever-present curiosity as to how one might "beat the market." Its juxtaposition against my academic training at the University of Virginia, presented mainly through the lens of the Efficient Markets Hypothesis, provided the contrast between the two sides of the Behavioral Finance debate. As such, this book has served as the perfect transition in my life in finance, from academic setting to practice, from theory to application, from avocation to full-time vocation.

To Ed's sentiments, I'd simply like to add my heartfelt appreciation: to Ed for the opportunity to join him on this endeavor, and for setting the structure and organization to the topic that allowed our ideas to flow; to all of the aforementioned students for all of their assistance in this book's creation; and to all of my friends and family, including my parents, Nitin and Suhasini Shah, my sister, Vaishali Shah, and my niece, Kirsi Shah Chinn, for their continued support along this journey, and throughout my life in general.

Sunit N. Shah

Introduction

Behavioral finance is a subtopic of the broader subject of behavioral economics. The *behavioral* in the name means that the behavior of participants in the actual economy is fundamentally different than what most academic theorizing normally assumes. Behavioralists argue that the predictions of economics, finance in particular, must be modified to account for how people actually behave in economic situations.

What is "commonly assumed" in economics and finance? The answer, in a word, is *rationality*. The usual implementation of rationality is to assume that individuals in the economy have a utility function that serves as a guide to what makes them happy, happier, and less happy. That utility function values various choices that a person could make subject to wealth, income, or whatever constrains expenditures for a particular person. The rational person maximizes utility (satisfaction, happiness, whatever the utility function is presumed to measure), staying within the bounds of what is possible as constrained by wealth and liquidity.

The utility-maximizing exercise by agents (persons, businesses, etc.) leads to predictable behavior and provides predictions about how markets function in the real world. For example, rational behavior by individuals, along with some other assumed conditions, implies that resources are allocated efficiently by the price mechanism both for the broader economy and for financial markets in particular. Prices perform a signaling function for the economy and, under these conditions, the prices direct agents to produce the "right amounts" and to buy and sell the "right amounts." "Right amounts" means, roughly, that the economy does not waste resources. The result of the free interplay of market forces leads to results that are "right" in the sense that it is not possible to make anyone better off without making someone else worse off. This is the meaning of efficiency in economics and in finance.

This does not mean that the result of free markets is the best of all worlds—even in this highly theoretical exercise. The resulting income distributions might be "unfair," and such unfairness requires a separate discussion. Behavioral economics and finance attack the foundations of the argument that markets allocate resources efficiently, long before arguments arise about fairness or the lack thereof. The behavioralists argue that markets may not produce efficient resource allocation, and it is generally possible to improve the economic position of some individuals without harming the economic position of other individuals.

Behavioral finance specifically questions the efficiency of financial markets. The prices of assets—usually the discussion is about stock prices—may not really reflect value, argue the behavioralists. Even simple ideas in finance, such as the idea that identical assets should sell at identical prices, have been called into question by the behavioralists. The critique of received finance theory by behavioral finance advocates is broad, deep, and extensive. Events in the real world of finance, such as the 1987 stock market crash and the 2008 financial collapse in Western economies, have added fuel to the fire. These events are difficult to reconcile with the efficient market point of view.

What follows is an effort to summarize the developments to date in the behavioral finance debate. Numerous behavioral finance books have been written for popular audiences in recent years, but they are mostly written by true believers who are attempting to persuade the reader that behavioral finance is the winner in its debate with more traditional finance. This is not such a book. We are not sympathetic to the behavioral finance position and this book takes a skeptical look at behavioral finance. But even skeptics, such as ourselves, are today overwhelmed by the mountain of evidence that is piling up for those who support the behavioral finance point of view and the unexplained stock market behavior that is increasingly difficult to reconcile with the efficient market view.

Thus, this book represents a skeptic's view with a grudging acceptance that, at this point, the advocates of behavioral finance seem to have the upper hand in the ongoing debate. This debate revolves around three main discussions: (1) noise trader theory and models; (2) research in psychological behavior pioneered by Kahneman and Tversky; and (3) serial correlation patterns in stock price data. There are other discussions in behavioral finance not captured in the three categories mentioned above, but the three topics above are all on center stage in the ongoing debate.

We begin with a discussion of the efficient market hypothesis, which is the central paradigm that behavioral finance seeks to attack. Then we move on to consider each of the three main areas of attack set out in the preceding paragraph. Finally, we conclude with thoughts about where this debate will go from here.

Additional resources for professors can be found on Wiley's Higher Education website.

Introduction to Behavioral Finance

What Is the Efficient Market Hypothesis?

The efficient market hypothesis (EMH) has to do with the meaning and predictability of prices in financial markets. Do asset markets "behave" as they should? In particular, does the stock market perform its role as economists expect it to? Stock markets raise money from wealth holders and provide businesses with that money to pursue, presumably, the maximization of profit. How well do these markets perform that function? Is some part of the process wasteful? Do prices reflect true underlying value?

In recent years, a new question seems to have emerged in this ongoing discussion. Do asset markets create instability in the greater economy? Put crudely, do the actions of investment and commercial bankers lead to bubbles and economic catastrophe as the bubbles unwind? The great stock market crash of October 19, 1987, and the financial collapse in the fall of 2008 have focused attention on bubbles and crashes. These are easy concepts to imagine but difficult to define or anticipate.

Bubbles usually feel so good to participants that no one, at the time, really thinks of them as bubbles; they instead see their own participation in bubbles as the inevitable payback for their hard work and virtuous behavior—until the bubbles burst in catastrophe. Then, the attention turns to the excesses of the past. Charges of greed, corruption, and foul play accompany every crash.

If the catastrophe and the bubble that precedes it are the result of evil people doing evil things, then there is no reason to suppose that markets are themselves to blame. Simple correctives, usually through imposition of legal reforms, are then proposed to correct the problem and eliminate future bubbles and catastrophes. Casual empiricism suggests this approach is not successful.

What if markets are inherently unstable? What if bubbles and their accompanying catastrophes are the natural order of things? Then what? If prices do not, much of the time, represent true value and if the markets themselves breed excessive optimism and pessimism, not to mention fraud and corruption, then the very existence and operation of financial markets may cause instability in the underlying economy. Prices may be signaling "incorrect" information and resources may be allocated inefficiently. The question of whether asset markets are efficiently priced, then, is a fundamental question. The outcome of this debate could shed light on the efficiency of the modern, highly integrated economies in which a key role is played by financial institutions.

It is important to agree on a definition of market efficiency, but there are many such definitions. Practitioners in the everyday world of finance often use market efficiency in ways that are different than the textbook definitions. We delimit the most common definitions in the next two sections of this chapter.

INFORMATION AND THE EFFICIENT MARKET HYPOTHESIS

The EMH is most commonly defined as the idea that asset prices, stock prices in particular, "fully reflect" information.[1] Only when information changes will prices change. There are different versions of this definition, depending on what kind of information is assumed to be reflected in current prices. The most commonly used is the "semi-strong" definition of the EMH: *Prices accurately summarize all publicly known information.*

This definition means that if an investor studies carefully the companies that he/she invests in, it will not matter. Other investors already know the information that the studious investor learns by painstakingly poring over public documents. These other investors have already acted on the information, so that such "public" information is already reflected in the stock price. There is no such thing, in this view, as a "cheap" stock or an "expensive" stock. The current price is always the "best estimate" of the value of the company.

In particular, this definition implies that knowing past prices is of no value. The idea that past stock price history is irrelevant is an example of the weak form of the EMH: *Knowledge of past prices is of no value in predicting future stock prices.*

The semi-strong form implies the much weaker version of the EMH embodied in the weak form of the EMH. It is possible that the weak form is true but that the semi-strong form is false.

The weak form of the EMH is interesting because it directly attacks a part of Wall Street research known as "technical" research. In technical

---

[1] See Eugene Fama's definition in "Random Walks in Stock Market Prices," *Financial Analysts Journal* 21, no. 5 (May 1965):55–59.

research, analysts study past prices and other historical data in an attempt to predict future prices. Certain patterns of stock prices are said by "technicians" to imply certain future pricing paths. All of this means, of course, that by studying past prices you can predict when stock prices are going to go up and when they are going to go down. Put another way, technical research is an attempt to "beat the market" by using historical pricing data. The weak form says that this cannot be done.

Unlike other versions of the EMH, the weak form is especially easy to subject to empirical testing, since there are many money managers and market forecasters who explicitly rely on technical research. How do such managers and forecasters do? Do they perform as well as a monkey randomly throwing darts at a newspaper containing stock price names as a method of selecting a "monkey portfolio"? Do index funds do better than money managers who utilize technical research as their main method of picking stocks? These questions are simple to put to a test and, over the years, the results of such testing have overwhelmingly supported the weak form version of the EMH.

The semi-strong version of the EMH is not as easy to test as the weak form, but data from money managers is helpful here. If the semi-strong version is true, then money managers, using public information, should not beat the market, which means that they should not beat simple indexes that mirror the overall market for stocks. The evidence here is consistent and overwhelming. Money managers, on average, do not beat simple indexes. That doesn't mean that there aren't money managers who seem to consistently outperform over small time samples, but they are in the distinct minority and hard to identify before the fact. Evidence from institutional investors, such as large pensions funds and endowments, are consistent with the view that indexing tends to produce better investment results than hiring money managers.

If this were all we knew, then the EMH would be on solid ground. But we know more. There is growing evidence that there are empirical "regularities" in stock market return data, as well as some puzzling aspects of stock market data that seem difficult to explain if one subscribes to the EMH.

We can identify three main lines of attack for critics of the semi-strong form of the EMH:

1. Stock prices seem to be too volatile to be consistent with the EMH.
2. Stock prices seem to have "predictability" patterns in historical data.
3. There are unexplained (and perhaps unexplainable) behavioral data items that have come to be known as "anomalies," a nomenclature begun by Richard Thaler.[2]

---

[2]See Richard Thaler, *Winner's Curse: Paradoxes and Anomalies of Economic Life* (New York: Free Press, 1992).

The evidence that has piled up in the past 20 years or so has created a major headache for defenders of the EMH. Even though money managers don't necessarily beat the indexes, the behavioralists' research suggests that perhaps they should.

There is a third form of the EMH that is interesting but not easy to subject to empirical validation. The third form is known as the strong form of the EMH: *Prices accurately summarize all information, private as well as public.*

The strong form, of course, implies both the semi-strong and the weak forms of the EMH. However, both the semi-strong and weak forms can be true while the strong definition can be false. The strong form includes information that may be illegally obtained—or, perhaps, information that is legally obtained but illegal to act upon. Needless to say, those breaking the law are not likely to provide performance data to researchers attempting to ascertain whether they are beating the market.

There seems to be a general consensus that the strong form of the EMH is not likely to be true, but one should not rush to such a conclusion simply because relevant data may be hard to come by. What little data we have from those who have obtained illegal information and then acted upon it is mixed. Sometimes crooks win, sometimes they appear to lose. When Ivan Boesky, probably the most famous insider information trader in history, concluded his investment activities and was carted off to jail, it was clear that investors who owned index funds made better returns than investors in Boesky's fund, even before the legal authorities got wise to Boesky's activities. If Boesky couldn't beat the market with inside information, it does give one pause.

Of the three informational definitions of the EMH, it is the semi-strong hypothesis that commands most interest. It is widely believed that the weak form is likely to be true, it is commonly assumed that the strong form is not likely to be true, so interest focuses mainly on the semi-strong hypothesis. Information determines prices and no one can really exploit publicly known information—that is the content of the semi-strong EMH hypothesis.

RANDOM WALK, THE MARTINGALE HYPOTHESIS, AND THE EMH

There is an alternative, mathematical view of the stock market related to the EMH. The mathematical version begins with the idea that stock prices follow a process known as *random walk*. The idea of the random walk is sometimes taken by wary observers as the idea that stock price behavior is simply arbitrary, but that is not what random walk means.

Imagine a coin flip where the coin is completely "fair" in the sense that a heads or tails flip is equally likely to occur. Suppose you start with $100 in wealth before beginning a series of coin flips. Suppose further that if you flip a heads, you receive $1, and if you flip a tails, you have to give up $1. After the first flip, for example, you will have either $101 (if you flip a heads) or $99 (if you flip a tails). Your total wealth over time, in this simple example, is following a process known as a random walk. A random walk is a process where the next step (flip outcome, in this example) has a fixed probability that is independent of all previous flips.

What does random walk rule out? If knowing the results of previous coin flips is useful in predicting future coin flips, then the process is not a random walk. Imagine that there have been five flips of heads in a row with no flips of tails. Does this mean it is more likely that the next coin flip will be tails? If so, then the process is not a random walk. The likelihood of a heads or a tails on the next coin flip must be independent of the history of previous flips for the process to be a random walk.

Does this mean, as some assume, that the results are arbitrary? No. We know a lot about this process. What we can't do, however, is predict the next coin flip with any high degree of certainty. If the coin is a fair coin, the heads or tails are equally likely on the next flip regardless of its history.

The coin-flipping game is a good example of a *martingale*. A martingale has the following property:

$$E[X_{t+s} \mid X_1, X_2, \ldots, X_t] = X_t \text{ for any } t, s > 0 \tag{1.1}$$

What does the above equation mean? X_t is the value at time t of some variable X. It might be helpful to think of X as your wealth, so that X_t is the value of your wealth at time t. X_{t+s} is then your wealth at some future date, $t+s$. The E in the equation is the expectation operator. The simplest way to think about E is that $E[X_{t+s} \mid X_1, X_2, \ldots, X_t]$ is what, on average, you expect the value of your wealth to be at a future date, $t+s$, given your knowledge of your wealth historically.

So, back to our example. You start on date t with $100 and you flip a coin that is equally likely to be a heads flip as a tails flip. What do you expect your wealth to be s periods from today, t? Since you are just as likely to gain $1 as to lose $1 on each flip, your wealth at any future period is expected to be the same as is today. Thus, this process satisfies the martingale property. If your wealth is totally in stocks, and if stocks follow a martingale, so will your wealth. On average, you will neither make nor lose money.

But this is not a very satisfying theory of how stocks behave. Why would anyone own stocks if, on average, they could not be expected to increase their wealth? We need to modify our simple coin-flipping experiment to allow for wealth to increase, but in a way consistent with our martingale assumption. Suppose your wealth grows at \$0.20 per period on average, so that $E[X_{t+s} \mid X_1, X_2, \ldots, X_t] = X_t + \$0.20 \times s$. Then, your wealth is no longer a martingale.

To transform it into a martingale, define a new variable, Y_t:

$$Y_t = X_t - \{t \times \$0.20\} \tag{1.2}$$

Y_t is a martingale since:

$$E[Y_{t+s}] = E[X_{t+s}] - \{(t + s) \times \$0.20\}$$

$$= X_t + \{s \times \$0.20\} - \{(t + s) \times \$0.20\}$$

$$= X_t - \{t \times \$0.20\} = Y_t \tag{1.3}$$

Even though wealth is growing over time, we have converted the wealth variable into another variable that is a martingale.

If stock prices follow a random walk, then past stock prices cannot be used to predict future stock prices. Random walk doesn't mean we know nothing or that the result of the process is arbitrary. Instead, one of the implications of random walk is that the outcome on any specific future date cannot be known with certainty. By a simple conversion, similar to what was shown earlier, we can convert the wealth accumulation process into a martingale.

Why all the effort? A martingale is a process whose value at any future date is not predictable with certainty. While X_t is the best estimate of any future value of X after X_t, we still cannot know with any degree of certainty what that value will be.

The idea of a martingale captures the informational definitions given in the previous section in a mathematical statement. Given the information available today, the best estimate of a future stock price is today's price (possibly with a risk-adjusted trend over time).This process is described in Figure 1.1.

Of course, the actual prices will not be on the solid line in Figure 1.1. Instead, they will bound around randomly, but trend upward in a pattern suggested by the bold solid line. The actual price movement might appear (or be expected to appear) as the lighter line that bounces around the solid line in Figure 1.2.

What makes the martingale an appropriate model for the EMH is that on any date, past information offers no real clue to predicting future prices. It is the absence of predictability that is the single most important feature of the martingale process.

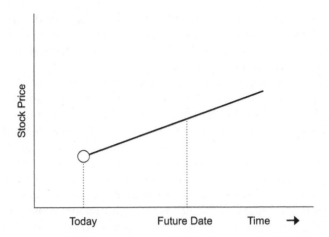

FIGURE 1.1   Expected Future Stock Price

FALSE EVIDENCE AGAINST THE EMH

There are always, at any point in time, legendary money managers who have arguably beaten the market over their respective lifetimes. Warren Buffett comes to mind as one of the more prominent examples. Is the existence of money managers with long track records of having beaten indices evidence against the EMH? To give this question some perspective, conduct a simple thought experiment. Imagine a group of 10,000 people engaged in a

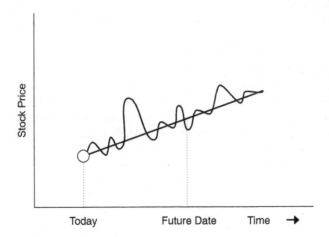

FIGURE 1.2   Actual Future Stock Price

coin-flipping experiment. In each period, each of these 10,000 people flips a coin and notes the result. What would we expect if the coins were, in all cases, fair coins? The likelihood of heads or tails is identical and equal to 50 percent on each and every coin toss.

In the first trial, you would expect, on average, about half of the 10,000 folks to flip heads and about half to flip tails. This would mean 5,000 flipped heads and 5,000 flipped tails. This wouldn't be the exact outcome, but it serves as a useful approximation to the actual outcome. Now, flip again. After the second trial, you would expect about one-fourth of the participants (2,500) to have flipped two heads in a row and one-fourth (2,500) to have flipped two tails in a row. Continue on in this manner through eight coin flips and what would you have? On average, you would expect about 39 flippers to have flipped eight heads in a row and about the same to have flipped eight tails in a row. Are these 39 flippers evidence that there is something to the science of coin flipping?

What about the number of folks who flipped heads seven out of eight times? There should be about 312 of those folks on average. That makes over 350 people who flipped heads at least seven out of eight times. Isn't that evidence that these people are good head flippers?

No, clearly such evidence is useless. If coin flipping is completely random, with a 50 percent chance each time of either flipping heads or tails, you will still get a significant number of extreme outcomes, even after repeated trials. In fact, failure to get the extremes of eight in a row or seven out of eight a reasonable number of times would be evidence that the flipping was not truly random. The same is true of evidence from money management. If money management outcomes are completely random and no one is really any good at stock picking, then a small percentage of money managers will, nevertheless, appear to be good on the basis of their track records.

One of the anomalies the behavioralists have uncovered is that things that are random often appear not to be random.[3] That is, they don't look random. There seems to be an expectation by observers that if a random process is creating a data series, then that data series should have a random appearance. It turns out that there are many more ways for the outcome of a randomly generated data series to look like a pattern than there are ways for it to look random. Put another way, output from a randomly generated process will typically exhibit trends, repetition, and other patterns even though the results are generated by a truly random process.

---

[3] See Chapter 12 for a broader discussion of this topic.

WHAT DOES IT MEAN TO DISAGREE WITH THE EMH?

Behavioral finance argues that the EMH is false and that academic finance needs to rethink its foundations. What does it mean for the EMH to be false? There are three different ways that behavioralists have waged warfare against the EMH: the first is logical, the second is psychological, and the third is empirical. The logical argument is what economists call *economic theory*. The psychological arguments are derived mostly from experiments in human psychology that throw doubt on the realism of the assumptions that underlie finance theory. Finally, the empirical arguments exhibit patterns of "predictability" in financial data that belie the assumed "nonpredictability" of future asset prices.

The three different ways to confront the EMH correspond to casual observations that have persisted and echoed through financial markets since their beginning. These observations were dismissed just as casually by finance economists as minor and unscientific. Until very recently, the preponderant view among finance economists was that markets were efficient and that casual observers were wrong. Sometimes, it was argued the casual observers had a vested interest in their assertions that the market was inefficient. After all, virtually the entire money management industry is built on the proposition that intelligent and diligent research and thinking can produce investment returns that exceed random stock picking or indexing, contrary to the semi-strong hypothesis of the EMH.

In the chapters that follow, we consider each of the three ways that the EMH has been challenged in the academic literature. A natural question is: if not the EMH, then what? What paradigm would supplant the EMH if the behavioralists succeed in undermining it? We look at that question after considering the behavioralist critique.

CHAPTER 2

The EMH and the "Market Model"

RISK AND RETURN—THE SIMPLEST VIEW

If stocks don't earn positive returns over time, why would anyone own them? This commonplace observation suggests that stocks with high risk, however that may be defined, should earn higher returns than stocks with lower risk. This observation leads to a fairly simple model of stock prices. Under this simple view, stock prices should be such that riskier stocks, over time, make higher returns on average than less risky stocks. Some of those risky stocks will blow up, but the risky stocks that do well will compensate owners for taking the risk by producing larger returns. This theory is interesting as far as it goes, but it doesn't tell us much about what we should own in a portfolio of stocks. It suggests that folks who like to take on risk should buy the riskier stocks and more conservative investors should own less risky stocks.

A number of economists tackled this "portfolio" problem in the 1950s and 1960s. Harry Markowitz formulated the portfolio problem as an optimization problem for an individual investor.[1] Markowitz assumed that each stock could be described by the mean and variance of its returns. Consequently, any portfolio of stocks could be considered an asset itself based on its mean and variance of returns. A stock's return in each period consists of the gain or loss in price plus any dividends received during the period. This sum was then divided by the price at the beginning of the period to give the percentage return during the period.

It is assumed that all investors prefer a portfolio with higher mean returns but are averse to higher variance in return. This latter property is known as *risk aversion*. It is also assumed that all investors have identical

---

[1] Harry Markowitz, "Portfolio Selection," *Journal of Finance* 7, no. 1 (March 1952): 77–91.

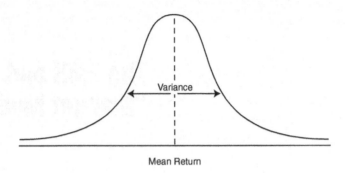

FIGURE 2.1   A Normal Return Distribution

information. That means that each investor is looking at the same set of stocks and has common information regarding the means and variances of these stocks. Implicitly, the Markowitz model was identified with normal distributions, such as that pictured in Figure 2.1.

Assuming that each stock can be characterized by such a return distribution, Markowitz was able to derive an optimal portfolio for any risk-averse investor that would be a combination of two fundamental portfolios. If at least one of the assets has a zero variance of return, then the Markowitz result has an investor always choosing one or both of only two assets: the asset with a zero variance of return (the riskless asset) and another portfolio of assets that contains risky assets (ones with nonzero variance of return).[2] This latter portfolio does not depend upon the investor but results strictly from a consideration of the assets. In this sense, this risky portfolio is an outcome of the mathematics of the various asset combinations and is the most efficient combination of the risky assets. A simple diagram in Figure 2.2 shows the Markowitz result when at least one of the assets is riskless.

The two small dots in the diagram represent the two portfolios that all investors will own. Each investor owns some combination of the risk-free asset and the efficient portfolio of risky assets. The thick line that begins at the risk-free asset and passes through the efficient portfolio of assets is the collection of possible outcomes for different investors who differ only by their preferences (how they feel about return versus risk). Those who want little or no risk end up near the vertical axis, owning mostly the risk-free

---

[2]This result was first pointed out by James Tobin in "Liquidity Preference as Behavior Toward Risk," *Review of Economic Studies* 25, no. 2 (February 1958): 65–86.

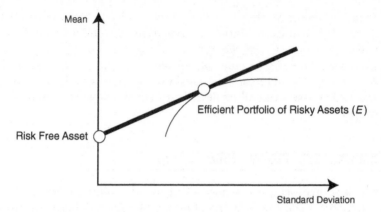

FIGURE 2.2 The Markowitz Result with a Single Riskless Asset

asset. Those who prefer more risk move accordingly up the heavy line, up and to the right. Once you pass the efficient portfolio, such investors are borrowing to buy even more of the *E* portfolio. In effect, portfolios to the right of the *E* portfolios are portfolios that employ an increasing amount of leverage. They are implicitly borrowing at the risk-free rate.[3]

The remarkable conclusion of Markowitz's analysis is that all risk-averse investors, with any tolerance for risk at all, should purchase identical portfolios of risky assets. Such investors should generally hold some cash (the riskless asset) and some of the *E* portfolio. This means that if one investor likes risk and the other doesn't, both should still hold the same "mutual fund" of risky assets (the *E* portfolio). The investor who doesn't like much risk should hold less of *E*, relatively, than the investor who prefers more risk. The significance of this conclusion cannot be overstated. What Markowitz is saying is that the common adage that folks who don't like risk should buy less risky stocks and folks who like more risk should by risky stocks is flat wrong. Both of these sets of investors should buy the identical portfolio of risky assets—it's just that one should buy relatively more of it than the other. This means that the portfolio *E* is the most efficient way to own risky assets, regardless of the investor's preference for risk. That makes *E* almost an engineering outcome that simply falls out of the mathematics.

---

[3]This assumption can be altered to provide for the more realistic assumption that borrowing rates will be higher than the risk-free rate, but that is a detail we can ignore for present purposes.

What is behind Markowitz's important result? In a word: diversification. The mathematics in Markowitz's analysis is combining assets into a diversified portfolio. *Given the riskless rate of interest (the return of the riskless asset), there will be only one efficient portfolio of risky assets and it will be the same for all investors.* That shows the power of diversification in a world where assets can all be described by a simple mean-variance characterization.

THE CAPITAL ASSET PRICING MODEL (CAPM)

Markowitz's analysis was extended to a general equilibrium setting by several economists. The names Sharpe, Lintner, Mossin, and Black are all associated with the general equilibrium version of Markowitz's analysis, known as the capital asset pricing model (CAPM). Imagine a large number of investors who face a Markowitz situation—a set of assets with normally distributed returns with known means and variances. The outcome is identical to the Markowitz solution. Each investor chooses between the risk-free asset and some portfolio, *E*, that is the most efficient portfolio of risky assets. (This portfolio *E* will be different if there is a different risk-free rate on the risk-free asset.)

The CAPM Equation

The CAPM asks the question: what happens in a world of many investors who are choosing assets in the manner of the Markowitz model, by looking at their statistical return distributions (which need not be assumed normal for the CAPM conclusions to hold). *Equilibrium* is defined as a situation where the total quantity bought equals the total quantity sold for each asset at its currently prevailing price. Equilibrium, then, means that there is no tendency for prices to deviate from current prices because investors are satisfied with their current portfolios given their wealth constraints. The conclusion that emerges is:

$$E[R_i] = R_f + \beta_i(E[R_M] - R_f) \qquad (2.1)$$

This forbidding-looking equation is actually fairly simple to interpret. Let's begin with the left hand side of this equation, $E[R_i]$. R_i is the return of the stock i and the $E[]$ simply means $E[R_i]$ is the expected future return (the average of what might occur in the future)—something like the statement, "On average, I expect stock i to have a return of 6 percent." This would mean that $E[R_i]$ is 6 percent, but that doesn't mean the actual future return in any particular period is 6 percent. It means the average of future returns is expected to be 6 percent. The actual return might be higher or lower. Equivalently, the "expected" number of head flips in two coin tosses is expected to be one, but could be zero or two.

What is R_f? R_f is the risk-free rate. It represents what an investor can earn without taking any risk. In the real world such an asset might be approximated by three-month U.S. Treasury bills. So far, the equation says that asset i will, on average, produce a return equal to what I can earn risklessly plus something else. This something else is known as the equity risk premium for stock i.

Let's look inside the brackets. What is the meaning of the following expression?

$$E[R_M] - R_f \qquad (2.2)$$

$E[R_M]$ is the expected return of M, a portfolio. What is contained in portfolio M? That we shall discover shortly, but for now, let's just assume we know what portfolio M is and proceed. What $E[R_M] - R_f$ represents is the average (future) return of portfolio M after deducting the certain return of the risk-free asset. This is also known as the risk premium of portfolio M. It is the average return in excess of the risk-free rate that is attributable to the risk of owning portfolio M.

Finally, what is beta for asset i?

$$\beta_i$$

β_i represents the relationship between the returns of asset i and the returns of the portfolio M. If the returns of asset i perfectly mirror the returns of portfolio M, then beta is equal to +1. If the returns of asset i are exactly the opposite of the returns of the portfolio M, then beta is equal to –1. In the case where the returns are completely unrelated to one another, beta is equal to zero.

Betas are different for different stocks (assets). Some stocks are perfectly correlated to portfolio M, but others are not. A stock's beta can be an arbitrary number. The interesting question is, what is the portfolio M?

Now let's repeat the fundamental equation of the CAPM:

$$E[R_i] = R_f + \beta_i \, (E[R_M] - R_f) \qquad (2.3)$$

We can now give a full interpretation to the CAPM equation. The equation says: the average future return of stock i will be the risk-free return plus the stock's beta multiplied by the amount by which the return on portfolio M exceeds the risk-free rate on average.

What is the mysterious portfolio M? M, in casual usage, is referred to as "the market portfolio," often approximated by a large stock index such as the Standard & Poor's (S&P) 500, the Wilshire 5000, or some international stock index. But in the theory, M has a very specific meaning: M consists of every single stock (asset) that has value (i.e., has a positive price). The proportions of M that each stock represents are determined by their *market capitalization*. That is, if you take the quantity of stock outstanding for a particular company and multiply that amount by the price of the stock, the result is the market capitalization of the company (the market value of the equity in the company).

Take all the stocks that have positive market capitalizations and add up all of their market capitalizations to get a total market capitalization:

$$\text{Total Market Capitalization} = P_1 Q_1 + P_2 Q_2 + \ldots + P_N Q_N = M \quad (2.4)$$

This portfolio is M and the weight of each stock in the portfolio is equal to its market capitalization divided by the total market capitalization of M:

$$\text{Weight of } i^{\text{th}} \text{ stock in the portfolio } M \text{ is equal to } \frac{P_i Q_i}{M} \quad (2.5)$$

The Interpretation of CAPM

The key variable in the CAPM equation is beta. Beta measures how much the individual stock's return is related to the return of the market. In mathematical terms:

$$\text{Beta (for stock } i) = \beta_i = \frac{cov(i, M)}{var(M)} \quad (2.6)$$

where $cov(i, M)$ measures how closely related the return of stock i is to portfolio M and $var(M)$ measures the volatility (or average fluctuations in value) of the market basket of all stocks, M.

If a stock behaves exactly like the market—goes up the same percentage as the market when the market goes up and goes down the same percentage as the market when the market goes down—then beta will equal 1. If a

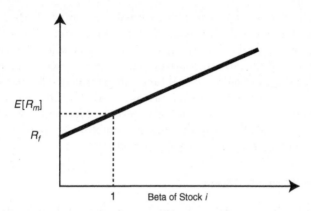

FIGURE 2.3 Expected (Future) Return of Stock *i*

stock's beta is greater than 1, then it tends to go up faster than the market when the market goes up and tends to go down faster than the market when the market goes down. Betas can be negative. Gold stocks are often cited as an example of a negative beta stock, since gold often goes up when the market goes down and vice versa. A beta of zero means that the returns of the stock behave in a way quite independent of the behavior of the overall market. The vast majority of stocks have betas between 0.5 and 1.5.

Now, let's repeat the fundamental CAPM equation:

$$E[R_i] = R_f + \beta_i \, (E[R_M] - R_f) \qquad (2.7)$$

What this equation says is that a stock's future return, on average, should be the risk-free return plus an additional amount for the risk taken in own-ing stock *i*. A graphic representation of this result is shown in Figure 2.3.

The higher the beta, the higher the future expected return of stock *i*. Notice that how volatile a stock's price may be is irrelevant. A stock's price might have wide fluctuations and be considered risky as an individual stock, but it will not necessarily be risky from a CAPM point of view. In CAPM, investors will choose to diversify and hold a fully diversified portfolio (*M*, in fact). Thus, the risk of an individual stock depends on how it influences the behavior of the portfolio, not how it behaves on its own. This is the heart of CAPM. That beta, not volatility, determines the risk of a single asset as well as its future expected return is a consequence of *diversification*.

Diversification is the true theme of CAPM. Diversification by individual investors leads them to own the entire market basket (think here of a mu-tual fund that is the entire market basket and individuals own shares in the mutual fund). An investor who likes risk will own more of M; an investor who doesn't like risk will own less of M. One of the principal conclusions of CAPM, in addition to the CAPM equation, is the conclusion that each investor's portfolio will turn out to consist of at most two assets: (1) the risk-free asset, and (2) shares in an M mutual fund. An extremely risk-averse investor might own only the risk-free asset and none of M. An extremely risk-loving investor would own more and more M, perhaps even more than his entire net worth (which would mean that investor employs leverage to own more M than his net worth would normally permit).

CAPM as an "Accepted" Theory

It should already be apparent to the reader that the CAPM, as a theory of how financial markets work, leaves a lot to be desired. To begin with, we don't see many investors owning the entire market, M. Instead, most households don't own stock, in the United States or anywhere else in the world. When households do own stock, they don't tend to own portfolios anywhere near as diversified or as universal as the M portfolio of the CAPM.

Yet the CAPM dominates the financial landscape as the "language" of modern finance. *Beta* is a widely used term to describe the risk of an individual stock and is commonly used to describe the exposure of a portfolio to broad stock market movements. Measures of covariance of returns with "the market" are used in asset allocation studies for institutional investors—pension funds, endowments, and foundations. Measures of portfolio performance are also thoroughly infused with CAPM terminology, techniques, and methodology. So, in a real sense, the CAPM rules.

However, the CAPM has never been validated empirically. There is simply no empirical support for the notion that a stock's beta can predict its future returns. There is a lot of evidence, in fact, that no such relationship exists between an individual stock's beta and its future returns. In 1977, Richard Roll published a critique of the CAPM, arguing that the theory was not even testable in practice.[4] Roll's argument was that the CAPM was a completely vacuous tautology that could not be tested unless one could successfully delineate all the assets that are theoretically contained in the portfolio M. Roll especially criticized the widespread use of the CAPM in portfolio management and in the performance measurement of money management.

---

[4]Richard Roll, "A Critique of the Asset Pricing Theory's Tests; Part I: On Past and Potential Testability of the Theory," *Journal of Financial Economics* 4, no. 2 (March 1977): 129–176.

The famous "Cross-Section" paper by Eugene Fama and Kenneth French put to rest any claims of validity of the CAPM.[5] Their analysis argued that other factors, such as book-to-market, were far more important than any CAPM measures. They noted that a stock's beta, the cornerstone of CAPM, appeared to be unrelated to future expected returns.

Summarily, the CAPM is a theory unsupported by evidence, and it may not even be possible to subject it to evidence. Nonetheless, the CAPM still controls the language and the methodology of much of practical day-to-day finance, especially in the arena of institutional investing.

WHAT IS THE MARKET MODEL?

The efficient market hypothesis (EMH) is the broad statement that information determines prices and that no one can predict future stock returns outside of the simple idea that risk creates reward. High expected returns can be achieved only by taking large risks. There is no simple arbitrage strategy that permits an investor to make returns (beyond the risk-free rate) without taking risk. We saw in Chapter 1 that there are a variety of ways of formally stating the EMH, but basically they all lead to the idea of information determining prices and an absence of predictability in asset prices.

A *market model* is a much more specific characterization of asset prices than that given by the broad EMH dictum. The CAPM would be one such model. The CAPM focused on the role of beta in determining expected returns (as opposed to a stock's own price-volatility) and reshaped and clarified the meaning of diversification in asset pricing theory. Another market model is that of Fama and French, which we discuss in a later chapter in some detail. Book-to-market plays a prominent role in the Fama-French market model. There are numerous other market models, mostly parented by the groundbreaking Fama-French 1992 paper.

Why do we care about the market model? In most tests of the EMH, we are forced to use some market model to describe the asset return-generating process. When testing the EMH and employing a market model, one can never be sure what is being tested—the EMH or the model? The tests tend to simultaneously test both the CAPM and the researcher's employed market model. This problem haunts much of the literature in later chapters.

---

[5] Eugene Fama and Kenneth French, "The Cross-Section of Expected Stock Returns," *The Journal of Finance* 47, no. 2 (June 1992): 427–465.

CHAPTER 3

The Forerunners to
Behavioral Finance

A cademics were reasonably content with the efficient market hypothesis (EMH) until sometime toward the end of the twentieth century. The year 1987 was critical in undermining faith in the EMH. U.S. stock market behavior in 1987 was bizarre. The year began with the Dow Jones Industrial Average at slightly above 2,200, and it ended the year in that general area. If all you knew were the beginning and ending stock market averages, then 1987 would seem to be a ho-hum type of year. But in between the beginning and ending averages, there was an incredible rally and a historic collapse. The market's behavior can be summarized in Figure 3.1.

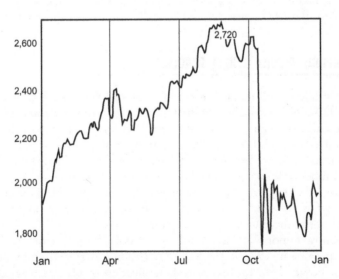

FIGURE 3.1   Summary of Market Behavior

The interesting question about 1987's stock market performance is: why? What news and information were there that led to a 30 percent rally in the first half of the year, followed by October 19, 1987, the worst single-day percentage loss in U.S. equity market history? The year 1987 should be called the "Rip Van Winkle" year. If you fell asleep in early January and awoke in late December, you would not know that much of anything had happened.

When you ask observers what happened to cause the big rally and big decline, almost everyone will provide an answer, especially those who consider themselves savvy about financial markets. But the answers are all over the map, and no single explanation has gained enough currency to gain widespread acceptance. There are plenty of one-off explanations, but none that command any real authority. The *Wall Street Journal* had a special edition the day after the 509-point, 22 percent historic sell-off on October 19, 1987. In that edition, they surveyed the various top executives of the largest and most prestigious Wall Street firms as to their opinions regarding the cause of the stock market crash. The opinions varied widely with no particular consistency. Even among market professionals who commune with one another regularly and drink at the same watering holes, there was no consensus as to what had happened and a blithering variety of different views espoused.

If you lived through the 1987 crash, then you are likely still wondering what happened. The very few who guessed that the crash was coming (and predictably there should be a few who guessed right) built careers and fortunes out of their prescient views. Paul Tudor Jones was one such individual and created the highly successful Tudor Management on the back of his accurate prediction of the 1987 crash. But did he really know what caused it? Perhaps.

THE FOLKLORE OF WALL STREET TRADERS

The first modern bull market in common stocks was in the United States in the 1920s. This was also the first time that nonprofessional investors, ordinary citizens, began to take an active participatory role in the public financial markets. A lot of speculative activity took place during this period and financial "traders" became mythic actors on the Wall Street stage. There were a number of books published during the 1920s that described "trading the market" that suggested that the market was "predictable," if one simply followed a few set and time-tested rules. Of course, different books had different rules, but there were some common themes.

The most famous of these books grew out of a series of articles that began appearing in 1922 in the *Saturday Evening Post* written by financial journalist Edwin Lefèvre. In 1923, the collection of articles was recast as a book published that year by Lefèvre entitled *Reminiscences of a Stock*

Operator.[1] The book chronicles the trading activity of a fictitious character named Lawrence Livingston. It has long been assumed that the real trader, whose activities are described in this book, was Jessie Livermore, known early in his career as the "Boy Plunger." The book described all sorts of trading activities including the use of short selling and conducting short squeezes. For our purposes, the significance of Lefèvre's book and others of this genre is that the book suggests that there are ways for the speculative trader to "beat the market." Some of the activities spelled out in this book became illegal under reform legislation in the 1930s. But many of the strategies discussed were based on understanding the emotional sentiment factors that, according to the book, create important stock market moves.

In the 1920s, there wasn't any real academic interest in the stock market, so ideas like the EMH were not discussed in any serious way. Indeed, one of the leading academic economists in the United States, Yale's Irving Fisher, published a book in 1929 (bad timing) that suggested that stocks were unlikely to ever go down again. John Maynard Keynes, one of the most famous economists in history, was, in the 1920s, busily speculating on currency markets, the metals markets, and stock markets. Keynes was to later describe the market as being dominated by "waves of pessimism and optimism" in his classic *The General Theory of Employment, Interest and Money,* published in 1935.[2] Even leading economists suggested, by their behavior, that financial markets were predictable. Behavioral finance did not exist as an academic discipline, nor did any particular finance curriculum exist anywhere in academia during this period, but it is clear from what economists were saying that the EMH would not have ruled the roost among academic economists.

What is interesting about all of this is that trading folklore and the activities of leading academic economists fit the behavioral finance point of view, not the EMH point of view. Economists who were actively discussing and acting in financial markets seemed of the opinion that markets were predictable, which is a key tenet of modern behavioral finance.

There were generally two trading strategies that circulated in the folklore. The first strategy was what we today call a *momentum* strategy. If you see a stock going up dramatically, then hop on board because it will likely continue going up. If everyone hops on board and you can perceive that everyone is on board, then you should hop off. The "hopping off" is more

---

[1] Edwin Lefèvre, *Reminiscences of a Stock Operator* (New York: John Wiley & Sons, 2006; originally published in 1923).

[2] John Maynard Keynes, *The General Theory of Employment, Interest and Money* (New York: Harcourt, Brace and World, Inc., 1935). See especially Chapter 12, pages 154 and 155.

akin to what we call today *mean reversion*. Mean reversion is the idea that if a stock has been doing really well for a long time and people seem to love the stock, then you should sell on the premise that the stock will not do well in the future. So, two trading strategies, mildly conflicting, permeated a lot of the folklore, including Lefèvre's book:

1. In the short term, stocks that are going up will continue that trend; stocks that are going down will continue that trend.
2. In the long run, stocks that have done well for a long time will do poorly in the future, and vice versa.

The first strategy is known today as *short-term momentum,* and the second strategy is still known as *mean reversion.* The central ideas behind these strategies were known and discussed openly by traders in the 1920s. Sixty and 70 years later, academic economists would pick up these ideas and begin to research their validity under the banner of behavioral finance. Because of the ready availability of data, by the time these researchers began to look at the data, it was relatively easy to document data trends such as those suggested by momentum and mean reversion. We look at this in some detail later in this book. Our point here is that Wall Street trading folklore had long believed in these strategies, even if there was no serious research to test their validity.

THE BIRTH OF VALUE INVESTING: GRAHAM AND DODD

In 1934, Benjamin Graham and David Dodd, both business school professors, coauthored a book entitled *Security Analysis*[3] that focused investor attention on the financial statements of public companies. The timing for publishing this book could not have been better. The Securities Acts of 1933 and 1934 required all public companies to publish detailed financial statements at least every three months (10-Q quarterly filings). This meant that investors had ready access to the data that Graham and Dodd were now saying could be used to beat the market.

Graham and Dodd argued in their famous book that investors could profit by studying a company's financial statements, income statements, and balance sheet statements to ascertain its value. They implicitly and explicitly decried the "horse race" character of the public markets and said the conscientious investor could beat the crowd by painstakingly studying the

---

[3] Benjamin Graham and David Dodd, *Security Analysis* (New York: Whittlesey House, 1934).

"true value" of a company, which could, they argued, be gleaned from the company's financial statements.

The Graham and Dodd approach came to be known as *value investing.* Many modern-day investors hearken back to Graham and Dodd as their inspiration. Warren Buffett is one such Graham and Dodd admirer. The idea is that an investor should buy out-of-favor stocks with strong "fundamentals." The fundamentals are ascertained by poring over income statements and balance sheets to uncover what could best be described as diamonds in the rough. The clear message was don't buy the stocks that other people like; buy the stocks that other people shun. Look for value among the stocks beaten down and overlooked.

This theme meant that markets could be beaten, which is the opposite of the theme of the EMH. Value investing also seemed to be similar to the message of mean reversion. Stocks that had not done well might be the best "values" because investors overreact emotionally to a string of bad news without necessarily considering the underlying fundamentals. Stocks that had done well for a long time were likely to not be good buys because market participants may not have looked closely at deteriorating fundamentals.

The 1930s destroyed much of the public's interest in the stock market, but when interest returned in the 1950s, value investing became a big business, with money managers professing adherence to Graham and Dodd's message. Over time, empirical support seemed to develop for value investing, culminating in a landmark research paper published in 1992 by two academic economists, Eugene Fama and Kenneth French. The research by Fama and French appeared to validate the idea that value investing could beat the market.[4]

The main message of Graham and Dodd reinforced the common perception in the 1930s and 1940s that there were ways to beat the market and that stock price movements were, in principle, predictable.

FINANCIAL NEWS IN A WORLD OF UBIQUITOUS TELEVISION AND INTERNET

In modern financial markets, there is constant news reporting on television and the Internet describing the ups and downs of individual securities and aggregated indices as well as all the news that seems relevant to their movements. Traders, eager to have the latest information, keep tuned minute-by-minute to the constant barrage of information that emanates from modern electronic sources. But what kind of information is being

---

[4] See Chapters 14 and 15 for a broader discussion of this research.

conveyed? Most often, the information is opinion as opposed to facts, and the facts that are reported are typically already publicly known facts. One word that could aptly fit the modern financial news that is reported is *noise*. What about the audience? No doubt, many in the audience could be described as "noise traders." If listeners rush out and buy and sell stocks based on outdated facts or random opinions, then such listeners are—by definition—noise traders, because they are not trading on true information but, much of the time, on stale and bogus information.

These news outlets are constantly trumpeting ideas such as "year-end rallies" and the like, which have no relationship to the fundamental drivers of company value. Rational traders would have no interest in year-end rallies. Notions of "support" and "resistance" levels of prices permeate the daily drumbeat of financial news. But a rational trader would find no meaning in these concepts. Yet someone is listening, and no doubt, someone is trading off the noise that is ever-present in the financial news reporting media.

PART
Two

Noise Traders

CHAPTER 4

Noise Traders and the Law of One Price

One of the very first things a student learns in beginning economics is that if two commodities are identical, then they will command identical prices in the marketplace. If the price of the two commodities should ever diverge, buyers will buy the cheaper of the two, and sellers will sell the more expensive of the two, pushing the divergent prices toward each other. It is likely that someone will try to buy the commodity in the cheap market and sell it in the more expensive market and earn an *arbitrage* profit. Thus, the *law of one price* emerges: two identical commodities must have the same price almost all the time.

THE LAW OF ONE PRICE AND THE CASE OF FUNGIBILITY

All of this seems simple enough, as long as we are comfortable with the definition of *identical*. What if two things are identical, but we refer to them by different names? Are they still identical? Do they still command the same price in the marketplace? Imagine a factory that produces baseballs. Suppose that every second baseball produced is called a *hardball*, whereas all others produced are called *baseballs*. But suppose in every respect there is absolutely no physical difference between a *hardball* and a *baseball*. They are the exact same thing except for their differing names. Can a *hardball* have a different price than a *baseball*? (See Figure 4.1.)

The two items above are not strictly identical because they have different names. This difference in name allows for the possibility that market participants may see them as truly different and that it may be possible for these two physically identical items to have different prices. If we think of these as assets, then we could say that the efficient market hypothesis (EMH) requires that these two items have identical prices since all information about them is the same. A *behavioral economist* might argue otherwise.

Baseball versus Hardball

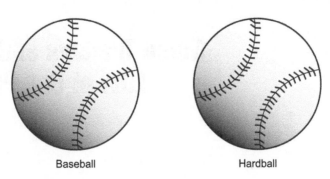

Baseball   Hardball

FIGURE 4.1   Can These Two Have Different Prices?

The different names might lead to different prices, even when the items themselves are physically indistinguishable.

Imagine a baseball-hardball machine that costlessly converts hardballs into baseballs and baseballs into hardballs, one for one in each case. If the price of baseballs and hardballs were to differ, then one should buy the cheaper of the two, feed it into the machine, and out would come the other, which could then be sold at a profit. This is a simple example of arbitrage. This type of costless conversion is known as *fungibility*.

There are many examples of fungibility in financial markets. Options in certain combinations and most futures contracts are completely fungible into the underlying instruments from which they derive their value. Owning a gold future is simply another way of owning gold, and if the owner of a gold future does not sell the future, then delivery of gold will take place on the future's delivery date. In this manner, the gold future owner becomes the owner of actual gold. This is an example of fungibility. The simple arbitrage of the baseball-hardball machine example is possible in the options and futures markets, though in a more complicated fashion.

What happens if the hardball and the baseball are not fungible? An easy way to make them not fungible is to put an indelible label on each. Each hardball would have the label *hardball* imprinted on it, and each baseball would have the label *baseball* imprinted on it. Then the arbitrage process might fail.

Suppose hardballs have the higher price. A buyer of hardballs might hold out for the product with the preferred label, even though, except for labeling, there is absolutely no physical difference. In the absence of fungibility, there is a clear possibility that the prices of two "identical" things might command different prices (almost all the time). There is no simple arbitrage that produces a guaranteed profit in finite time by buying one and selling the other. In principle, nothing forces the prices to equality, absent fungibility.

The reason fungibility is an important issue is that many seemingly identical pairs of securities are not fungible. The most famous example is the stock pair consisting of Royal Dutch common stock (a Netherlands corporation) and Shell common stock (a British corporation).[1] This pair represents different amounts of ownership in the same company. The former is entitled to 40 percent of all the earnings of the company, while the latter is entitled to 60 percent of all of the earnings of the company. The price of three shares of Royal Dutch should always be approximately equal to the price of two shares of Shell, if the law of one price holds. There simply is no difference between three shares of Royal Dutch and two shares of Shell regarding their economic claims on the company. But, as is well known, Royal Dutch and Shell rarely trade at a 1.5 ratio and can diverge from that ratio by substantial margins and for indefinite periods of time.

Why doesn't the law of one price work in this case? The answer is lack of fungibility. You cannot buy three shares of Royal Dutch Shell and convert those shares into two shares of Shell (British). If you buy shares in either company, the only available method of disposal is to sell them.

If you could convert the cheaper shares into the more expensive shares at a three-to-two ratio, then simple arbitrage would bring the prices together, but you cannot do the conversion. No machine is available. The only thing available is the marketplace. That lack of fungibility has, in practice, meant that those who purchase the cheaper of the Shell stocks and an offsetting position[2] in the more expensive (on a three-to-two ratio) have lingered in that transaction with no particular tendency for the prices to equalize.

If two commodities are identical and fungible (in the sense that one could be converted into the other and vice versa at minimal cost), then the law of one price should hold. But if fungibility is not present, then it is an open question whether the prices of two identical but not fungible assets will converge. The famous example of Royal Dutch and Shell is a very public example of identical things that lack fungibility for which the law of one price doesn't seem to hold.

---

[1] See the exposition of the twin Shell stocks by Andrei Shleifer in *Inefficient Markets* (New York: Oxford University Press, USA, 2000), Chapter 2.

[2] Offsetting position means a short sale, or borrowing the stock from a holder and selling it, planning to repurchase the stock at a later date and return it to its original owner.

What If Identical Things Are Not Fungible?

Now let us imagine two identical assets that cannot be transformed one into another except by selling one and buying the other. This is the truly interesting case for the EMH. The fungibility case has a mechanical way of resolving itself and is more an exception than the norm in financial markets. Things that seem almost identical in financial markets are typically not fungible one into the other.

Can prices of two identical, but not fungible, things, like our baseball and hardball, diverge and maintain that divergence for a significant period of time, perhaps even indefinitely? The EMH would say that the prices of two things, even if not fungible, should be identical or virtually identical most of the time. That sounds vague, but it is nonetheless a demanding requirement, as we shall see.

If prices in the marketplace are not right, then someone has to be buying and selling at these incorrect prices. There have to be buyers willing to pay too much or sellers willing to sell for too little in order to keep prices from being the right prices. What does the phrase "right prices" mean? It means the prices that rational, knowledgeable participants would be willing to buy or sell something for.

One can easily imagine that there might be individuals who think that our baseballs and hardballs are different things. Individuals perhaps lack the knowledge to know that the baseball and hardball are identical. But, in time, surely they would learn that they are not truly different. Then, it becomes hard to imagine that anyone would pay more for one than the other. But what if there were people that could never be convinced that these two identical items were identical? Perhaps they don't learn, or perhaps they think the fact that they are labeled differently is enough to constitute a true difference.

Can two identical things with different names be different? For our purposes, the answer is no. They should be considered the same thing. But the deeper question is: can they have different prices? If they cannot have different prices, then the EMH, at least for this case, is validated. If different prices can prevail for products that differ only by label, then much other economic theorizing, not just the EMH, could be challenged as well.

How could these prices be different? Someone has to be willing to pay a higher price for one than for the other.

The Friedman View

Milton Friedman provided an argument in the context of currency markets that amounted to a defense of the EMH:

Despite the prevailing opinion to the contrary, I am very dubious in fact that speculation in foreign exchange would be destabilizing. . . . People who argue that speculation is generally destabilizing seldom realize that this is largely equivalent to saying that speculators lose money, since speculation can be destabilizing only if speculators on the average sell when the currency is low in price and buy when it is high.[3]

Friedman was discussing whether speculators were a destabilizing influence in currency markets. He is arguing that speculators, traders who move prices away from efficiency, will lose money, suggesting that *smart* traders will push prices back toward efficiency while they take the opposite positions and that such speculators will eventually lose all of their capital.

The modern version of Friedman's argument introduces the notion of noise traders, which would include not only Friedman's speculators but other market participants as well. Friedman's argument, updated, would be that noise traders as a group would lose money as they foolishly buy at high prices and sell at low prices.

But Noise Traders, if Sufficiently Diverse, May Not Matter

Imagine some individuals who are irrationally willing to pay more for a baseball than a hardball. Isn't it reasonable to suppose that there may be other individuals who are irrationally willing to pay more for a hardball than a baseball? Perhaps degrees of irrationality are randomly distributed about the true rational outcome. Then, such irrational individuals may offset one another. A kind of law of large numbers might come into play that has the baseball lovers counterbalanced by the hardball lovers so that the prices of the two remain approximately identical—offsetting irrationality, we might suppose. Eugene Fama made precisely this argument in his defense of the EMH[4] against the argument that noise traders would disrupt matters.

The Noise Trader Agenda

It has long been known that there are many, often silly, reasons that people buy and sell stocks. No one pretends that all traders and investors are completely rational; common observation suggests that is not the case. But the very existence of noise traders is not sufficient to invalidate the EMH.

---

[3] Milton Friedman, *Inefficient Markets* (Chicago, University of Chicago Press: 1953), 175.
[4] Eugene Fama, "Efficient Capital Markets: A Review of Theory and Empirical Work," *Journal of Finance* 25, no. 2 (May 1970): 383–417.

In order to show that the EMH is in trouble, at least two conditions must be met. We will call these two conditions the *noise trader agenda*:

1. Noise trader behavior must be *systematic*. Noise traders must be shown not to simply cancel one another out. If some are too optimistic and others are too pessimistic, then one group may simply cancel out the effect of the other. Instead, there must be something like herd activity, such that a large group of noise traders, or a small group with a large amount of assets, behave in a similar manner.
2. Noise traders need to survive economically for a significant period of time. If all noise traders do is lose money through their noise trading, then their impact will be limited. Noise traders need to make substantial and persistent profits under some conditions. Otherwise, noise traders are simply cannon fodder, as Friedman suggests, for the smart traders.

NOISE

Where does the term *noise trader* come from, and what does it mean? Noise trading is normally defined by what it is not. A noise trader is not the rational, knowledgeable trader or investor who is commonly assumed in finance theory. The noise trader is doing something else. A noise trader could be as harmless as a year-end tax seller, paying no attention to values at the moment of sale. It could be a grandmother buying a present of stock for a grandchild, where the main interest in the stock is that the company produces something appealing to children, regardless of the inherent investment merits of the company itself.

Fischer Black's 1985 Presidential Address to the American Finance Association

The concept of noise in a financial market context has its first modern expression in Fischer Black's address to the American Finance Association meetings in December 1985. Black's talk on that occasion was simply entitled "Noise."[5] Noise, in a scientific context, almost invariably refers to "white noise" or "Brownian motion." Intuitively, this notion of noise is describing something that bounces around with no particular direction. But the bouncing around is stable. Figure 4.2 is a typical depiction of white noise.

---

[5] See Fischer Black, "Noise," *The Journal of Finance* 41, no. 3 (July 1986); Papers and Proceedings of the Forty-Fourth Annual Meeting of the America Finance Association, New York, NY, December 28–30, 1985, 529–543.

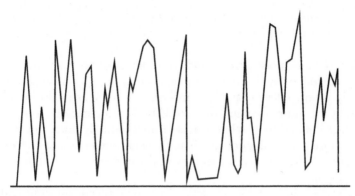

FIGURE 4.2   White Noise

Notice that the pattern is continuous but erratic. Modern financial theory uses white noise to characterize the pattern of stock prices,[6] so Black's lecture was aimed at an audience that was familiar with this notion of noise.

Fischer Black was both an academic and a practitioner. At least half of his working days were spent in Wall Street or Chicago security trading operations. Black was intimately familiar with the diversity of trader motives and activities. He describes a variety of different types of noise traders. The definition of a noise trader is elusive in Black's talk (as it is in the entire literature), but Black provides the following definition: "Noise trading is trading on noise as if it were information."[7] That definition begs the question as to what exactly is noise, which Black elsewhere in the talk describes as something characterized by "a large number of small events." It is not completely clear what Black means here, but the talk is descriptive of many aspects of trading markets that those who trade for a living would quickly recognize.

Following are the opening lines of Black's presentation:

I use the word "noise" in several senses in this paper. In my basic model of financial markets, noise is contrasted with information. People sometimes trade on information in the usual way. They are correct in expecting to make profits from these trades. On the other

---

[6]Salih Neftci, *An Introduction to the Mathematics of Financial Derivatives* (New York, Academic Press, 1996). Neftci gives a simple explanation of Brownian motion and its equivalent, a Wiener process, on pages 148–149. Neftci's book is an intuitive and easy-to-read description of the role that white noise plays in modern finance.
[7]Black, "Noise," 531.

hand, people sometimes trade on noise as if it were information. If they expect to make profits from noise trading, they are incorrect.[8]

Black defines noise traders indirectly by what they are not. A noise trader is someone who is not trading on *information*. By information, Black implicitly means relevant and true information such as might be useful in predicting the future earnings of a publicly traded company. It is not clear from Black's description what a noise trader actually does, but it is clear what a noise trader doesn't do. Black's noise trader is not the rational, information-seeking investor that is typically portrayed in the efficient market paradigm.

In the preceding section, we defined a noise trader as someone willing to buy or sell at "incorrect" prices. In the hardball/baseball story, a noise trader would be someone willing to pay a different amount for a hardball than for a baseball even though they are the same asset. Someone who doesn't use information would fit both Black's definition and our definition. There is no way around the idea that if you want the EMH to be violated, you will need to have models that incorporate noise traders. Without them, you simply can't get identical, nonfungible things to trade at different prices.

As the father of the noise-trading concept, Black seemed little bothered by the implications of noise trading: "Noise makes financial markets possible, but also makes them imperfect."[9]

But Black goes on to say, "With a lot of noise traders in the market, it now pays for those with information to trade. . . . Most of the time, the noise traders will lose money by trading, while the information traders as a group will make money."[10]

After a description of how information traders move prices back to their correct value, Black concludes: "I think almost all markets are efficient almost all of the time. 'Almost all' means at least 90 percent."[11]

Fischer Black's talk paradoxically introduced the notion of noise trading, but concludes that the EMH withstands the impact of noise traders. But Black was not the first to see things this way.

It is clear that Black shares the Friedman view, outlined earlier, and that his talk in 1985 can be interpreted as an update of the earlier Friedman position with one important caveat. Black left open the door to critics of the EMH when he observed: "In other words, I do not believe it makes sense to create a model with information trading but no noise trading where

---

[8] Black, "Noise," 529.
[9] Ibid., 530.
[10] Ibid., 530.
[11] Ibid., 533.

traders have different beliefs and one trader's beliefs are as good as any other trader's belief."[12]

Behavioral finance would look back to the following remark as a prescient preview of the direction noise trader research would take: "Noise makes financial markets possible, but also makes them imperfect."[13]

Friedman would not have agreed with Black that noise traders played a positive and essential role in financial markets. Friedman saw such activity as foolish and mostly as a nuisance. Friedman seemed to feel that noise traders were simply sitting ducks for rational traders to take money from. Other than that, noise traders need not be considered and could not influence asset prices in any significant way. It is clear that Black's presidential address moves away from Friedman by asserting that noise traders are essential to financial markets, that they impact prices constantly, and that they cannot be left out of any serious financial market theorizing.

The Friedman-Black Path for Noise Traders

The arguments advanced by Milton Friedman and Fischer Black suggest the pathway ahead for critics of the EMH. Inserting noise traders into models of the financial system, as Black insisted upon, and dealing with what we earlier referred to as the *noise trader agenda,* could enable the existence of noise traders to pose a challenge to the presumed efficiency of financial markets.

In the following chapter we consider a financial model developed by four academics that seeks to provide the *noise trader agenda* and pose a serious theoretical challenge to the EMH.

---

[12] Black, "Noise," p. 531.
[13] Ibid., 530.

CHAPTER 5

The Shleifer Model of Noise Trading

An article published in 1990 provided the first model of a financial market that squarely confronted both parts of the noise trader agenda:

1. Noise trader activity should be systematic.
2. Noise traders should be profitable for a significant period of time.[1]

In this chapter, we will refer to this model as the *Shleifer model,* though there were four authors in all. The article was later reprinted in a collection of papers by Andrei Shleifer,[2] and thus the model has become more widely associated with Shleifer's name than with his co-authors.

The Shleifer model incorporates two types of traders: rational traders and noise traders. The systematic behavior of noise traders is assumed. The first key result is that, under certain circumstances, two fundamentally identical assets can trade at different prices, and that the price differential can widen over time. The second key result is that under certain circumstances, noise traders can make money. It is even possible in the model for the rational traders to go bust.

The Shleifer model has a number of ingenious devices that enable the model to forecast the possibility of noise trader financial success, but nothing more striking than the definition of the assets. The assets are much like our hardball and softball described in the previous chapter. The assets differ mainly in name but are fundamentally the same asset. So can their prices

---

[1]J. Bradford DeLong, Andrei Shleifer, Lawrence Summers, and Robert Waldman, "Noise Trader Risk in Financial Markets," *Journal of Political Economy* 98, no. 4 (August 1990): 703–708.
[2]Andrei Shleifer, *Inefficient Markets: An Introduction to Behavioral Finance* (New York: Oxford University Press, 2000).

differ? Yes, in the Shleifer model, the prices of the two identical assets not only can differ, but the price gap can also widen with the passage of time!

Much is not explained by the Shleifer model. For example, there is no explanation as to why noise trader behavior should be systematic. Noise trader behavior is simply assumed to be systematic without much justification. The reader is referred to the other behavioral finance literature to uncover reasons why noise trader behavior should be systematic. Another example of what is left unexplained in the Shleifer model is the issue of what drives the relative proportions of noise traders and arbitrage traders. The Shleifer model shows that the proportions matter but does not delve into the determinants of the proportions.

THE KEY COMPONENTS OF THE SHLEIFER MODEL

There are two assets in the Shleifer model: a safe asset and an unsafe asset. Both assets provide the same fundamental economics because both provide an identical dividend per unit in each time period with certainty. The question becomes: how can these two assets that provide the owner with exactly the same dividend endure a sustained price difference over time?

The Assets

Asset s—*the safe asset*. The safe asset, s, is assumed to be costlessly convertible (fungible) into the consumption good. There is only one consumption good in the model, and all prices in this model are in terms of the consumption good. Thus, the price of s is always equal to 1. This means that one unit of asset s can always purchase one unit of the consumption good. This convertibility works both ways: a unit of the consumption good can be costlessly converted into asset s. This makes the safe asset available in *elastic* supply.

Asset u—*the unsafe asset*. The unsafe asset is assumed to be nonconvertible into the consumption good. To use the unsafe asset to purchase consumption, one must first sell some of it and then use the proceeds to purchase the consumption good. There is a fixed quantity of the unsafe asset u (unlike the situation with asset s), and price is determined in the marketplace. In principle, the price of asset u need not be the same as the price of asset s.

What both assets have in common is that they pay identical dividends, r, in each period. This dividend is assumed to be paid with complete certainty. The only uncertainty facing holders of u is its price in the following period.

There is no uncertainty facing holders of s, as both price and dividend are always known with complete certainty.

It must be emphasized that the two assets, s and u, have fundamentally identical claims to income. Both pay the same exact dividend period after period. There is simply no difference other than, potentially, a difference in price. These two assets are close to an exact analogue of the hardball and the baseball described in Chapter 4. They are identical except in name, but can they have different market prices?

The Market Participants

What kinds of people exist in the Shleifer model? Only two types of people exist: sophisticated investors and noise traders. The sophisticated investors are the rational agents of modern efficient market models. The noise traders are the creation of the Shleifer model builders. If there are no noise traders in the Shleifer model, then the prices of assets u and s must always be the same. The efficient market hypothesis (EMH) will prevail in the absence of noise traders, so the Shleifer model inserts them.

> *The sophisticated investors: the rational traders.* All of the sophisti-cated investors in the model are identical to one another. There is only one type. In each period, the sophisticated investors accu-rately perceive the future distribution of returns from holding the risky asset (they have perfect foresight[3] in the sense of the finance literature).The Shleifer model refers to the sophisticated investors as "arbitrageurs."

> *The irrational investors: the noise traders.* The noise traders are all iden-tical to one another as well. There is only one type. The noise trad-ers misperceive the true future distribution of returns from holding the risky asset. The mean of the distribution of future returns, as perceived by the noise traders, is different from the true mean.

What is being assumed here is a little complex. The rational traders perceive the correct future return distribution, which means they must be aware of the activities of the noise traders. The distribution of re-turns without noise traders is not going to be the same as the distribution of returns with noise traders present. Thus, the perceived risk to rational

---

[3] The rational investors' expectations of the return distribution will turn out to be true. But, as in the case of a coin flip, this does not mean they know in advance the actual outcome. They simply know the correct future distribution (the appropriate probabilities).

Market Participants

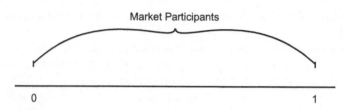

0   1

FIGURE 5.1   Investors in the Shleifer Model

traders will not simply be the fundamental risk, of which there is none in this model, but will include a risk arising from the activities of the noise traders. This additional risk will affect the behavior of not just the noise traders, but will also impact the behavior and future profitability of the rational traders as well.

Other Details of the Shleifer Model Structure

It is important to know how many rational traders (arbitrageurs) and how many noise traders populate the universe. If there is only one noise trader with insignificant assets, then the lone noise trader is not likely to have much of an impact. The Shleifer model has an infinite number of market participants, some of whom are rational traders, the rest of whom are noise traders. Imagine all of the real numbers between—and including—zero and one. There are infinitely many such numbers. The market participants in the Shleifer model are depicted in Figure 5.1.

Every participant is simply a point on the line that connects 0 to 1, as shown in Figure 5.1. If there are no noise traders, then all the points will be rational traders. Imagine cutting the line at some point and making all of those to the left of the cut rational traders, and those remaining, noise traders, as in Figure 5.2.

The model assumes that μ of all market participants are rational. 1 − μ represents the noise trader segment of the population. In the results, the percentage of traders that are noise traders will influence the outcomes.

Why the assumption of an infinite number of participants? You could assume a finite number of participants but nothing would be gained by such

rational traders, μ   noise traders,1 − μ

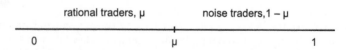

0   μ   1

FIGURE 5.2   Rational Investors versus Noise Traders

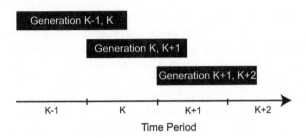

FIGURE 5.3 "Overlapping Generations" Model

an assumption. The mathematics are simpler with the infinite participant assumption. The assumption that is truly suspicious is not the infinity of participants, but the fact that there are only two types. This is not a very diverse group of participants even though there are a lot of them.

People live for only two periods in the Shleifer model. In any period, there are young people and there are old people. The young people are in the first stage of life, and the old people are in the second stage of life. This characterization is known as an "overlapping generations" model patterned after a famous construct by Paul Samuelson.[4] (See Figure 5.3)

The old folks are strictly consumers; they cash out whatever wealth they have at the beginning of the second period of their life and consume the proceeds. What about the young folks? They do not consume during the first period of their life—they work and invest. The old folks sell their holdings of s and u to the young folks. The old folks can costlessly convert s into the consumption good, so they are actually selling only their holdings of u to the young folks. The only asset market that is really functioning is the market for the unsafe asset, u.

Why this demographic structure? "The infinitely extended overlapping generations structure assures that each agent's horizon is short. No agent has any opportunity to wait until the price of the risky asset recovers before selling."[5]

The Limits to Arbitrage

Milton Friedman, Fischer Black, and Eugene Fama had long argued that arbitrageurs would take the money away from the foolish noise traders by

---

[4]Paul Samuelson, "An Exact Consumption-Loan Model of Interest with or without the Social Contrivance of Money," *Journal of Political Economy* 66 (December 1948): 467–482.

[5]DeLong et al., 713.

simply taking exactly opposite market positions and waiting patiently for market prices to correct. Critics of the EMH had argued in vain that it is not possible for the arbitrageurs to take unlimited positions to offset the foolish activity of the noise traders. There are *limits to arbitrage* that would prevent this simplistic correction from taking place; the arbitrageurs could go broke if the noise traders were able to move prices even further from the correct prices. The capital of the arbitrageurs may erode while waiting for market prices to correct. Prices that are too high or too low might become even higher or lower. Friedman, Black, Fama, and other EMH defenders considered this unlikely.

The Shleifer model puts the limits to arbitrage argument front and center. In the real world, arbitrageurs face fundamental risk that itself is a limit to how large a position a risk-averse arbitrageur is willing to take. But that risk is absent in the Shleifer model. The only risk that arises in the Shleifer model is due to the existence of noise traders. What if noise traders are available in sufficient numbers and with sufficient assets to move prices farther and farther away from the correct[6] prices? Wouldn't arbitrageurs take on a lot of risk and, in fact, lose money as prices diverged from the efficient prices that they are presuming would come about in a relatively short period of time? This possibility for a widening divergence away from price efficiency exists in the Shleifer model structure. It is also possible that arbitrageurs may lose money or not make money and the noise traders could prove more profitable than arbitrageurs. All of these things are possible, at least in principle, in the Shleifer model.

The EMH requires that market prices are efficient most of the time and that deviations from efficient prices tend to be corrected quickly. The limits to the arbitrage argument suggest that there may be no mechanism to provide this correction. Arbitrageurs could face serious losses if prices deviated farther and farther from efficient prices. This fear of losses will keep arbitrageurs from establishing the arbitrarily large positions that would be required to force prices to efficient levels quickly. The Shleifer model asks the question: Is it possible that noise traders actually make a profit in certain situations, and can they be more profitable in their trading activity than arbitrage traders? Can arbitrage traders lose money by betting that prices will return fairly quickly to efficient levels? Ultimately, it is the limits to arbitrage principle that provide an affirmative answer to the two preceding questions in the Shleifer model.

---

[6]The terms *correct prices* and *efficient prices* refer to the prices that would be established in the absence of the existence of noise traders. In the Shleifer model, the correct and/or efficient price for the unsafe asset is 1, the same price as for the safe asset.

RESULTS

The conclusions of the Shleifer model depend crucially on the role played by noise traders. While there are many ways to conceive of noise trading, it pays to look closely at the definition of noise traders used in the Shleifer model. Recall that there are only two types of investors (or traders) in this model: arbitrageurs and noise traders. Each type will form expectations about the subsequent price of the unsafe asset. No one has any interest in asset prices beyond the beginning of next period because, by assumption, no one lives more than two periods and there are no bequests to future generations. Imagine the following as a description of the views of the arbitrage traders regarding the next period price, P_{t+1}, of asset u (see Figure 5.4).

The arbitrageurs' expectation of the distribution of P_{t+1} is assumed to be a normal distribution with mean MP_{t+1}. This is the true distribution of P_{t+1} as viewed from time t. That doesn't mean that arbitrageurs know the actual value that P_{t+1} will take on when $t+1$ arrives, but it does mean that they know the probability distribution of P_{t+1}. The arbitrageurs are aware of the existence of the noise traders and of expectations and activities of the noise traders. Without such information, the arbitrageurs would not know the true distribution of P_{t+1}.

Notice that it is not just *fundamental* knowledge that is possessed by the arbitrage traders. The fundamental knowledge in the model is almost trivial: both assets pay a known, constant, and certain dividend r. Both noise traders and arbitrageurs are assumed to possess the same fundamental knowledge. There is not much to know about the fundamentals. It is the knowledge of

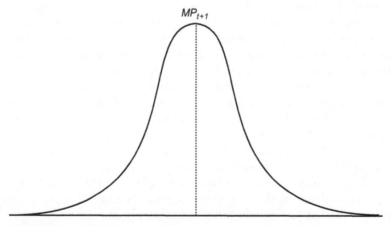

FIGURE 5.4   Probability Distribution of P_{t+1}

the noise traders' misperceptions and the nature of their future misperceptions that drives the arbitrageurs' decisions.

> *Conclusion 1:* The price of the two assets will generally not be the same. Overly optimistic or overly pessimistic forecasts by noise traders can lead to a higher price or lower price for the unsafe asset than the price for the safe asset.
>
> *Conclusion 2:* The expected return of the noise trader's portfolio can, in some circumstances, exceed the expected return of the arbitrageur's portfolio. This outcome happens only under certain conditions, including that noise traders have to be overly optimistic.

Much of the explanation for noise trader outperformance, when it occurs, is based on noise traders' taking on more risk than arbitrage traders because of their unjustified enthusiasm for the risky asset. The risk being taken by the noise traders is not, as Shleifer is careful to note, based on any fundamental risk related to the risky asset, of which there is none. The risk being borne arises solely from the existence and activities of the noise traders. Taking into account such risk should make markets less efficient, not more efficient.

WHY THE SHLEIFER MODEL IS IMPORTANT

As we discuss in the next chapter, there are many different ways that economists have characterized the concept of noise trader. The one common theme is that noise traders are people who are not acting rationally, though they might think they are. The Shleifer model has a particularly simple way of defining a noise trader. A noise trader in the Shleifer model is maximizing utility, just like the rational traders. But, unlike the rational traders, Shliefer's noise traders' expectations are biased, systematically, since there is only one representative noise trader, away from the rational and correct expectations of the arbitrage trader. This simple description carries a lot of power in the model, because in the overoptimistic case it creates the possibility for the noise trader to earn higher expected profits than the arbitrage trader, contrary to the Friedman argument.

What really drives the Shleifer model is the definition of the assets. The two assets in the Shleifer model are identical except in two respects: (1) the safe asset is available in totally elastic supply, and (2) the safe asset is costlessly convertible into the consumption good. Neither of these attributes applies to the risky asset, which is fixed in supply and not convertible into anything except through purchase and sale activities. What this means is that the two assets aren't fungible. Combined with overoptimistic expectations by the noise traders, the definitions of the two assets drive the result that the prices of the two assets can be different, even though the two assets have the same fundamental risk. This seems to capture the real-world aspect of the Royal Dutch–Shell pricing discrepancy.

That prices of two assets with the same fundamentals can be different is the main contribution of the Shleifer model. That noise traders can, in some situations, earn higher expected returns is the secondary contribution of the Shleifer model and provides an argument for why noise traders will always exist. Obviously, when noise traders are successful, even over relatively short periods of time, it will attract attention and swell the ranks of future noise traders. This suggests that noise traders will always exist.

RESOLVING THE LIMITS TO ARBITRAGE DISPUTE

The debate over whether or not arbitrage activity would quickly or reasonably quickly eliminate inefficient pricing is the linchpin issue in the debate between behaviorists and the adherents of the EMH. The article by Shleifer and his co-authors seems to have settled the question of whether a logical (theoretical) basis exists for the market mispricing of essentially identical assets in a world in which all traders are utility maximizers. Unexplained is why traders become too optimistic and what determines how many overly optimistic traders there might be. One also might wonder about the dynamics. Can bubbles result?

While Shleifer and his co-authors left a number of issues yet to be resolved, the article seems a milestone in its representation of the logical foundations of market mispricing of identical assets. In the real world, there are not many examples of identical assets, but there are a large number of similar assets. The Shleifer model would seem to apply with equal force in dispelling the notion that similar assets must necessarily always be priced similarly in the marketplace.

CHAPTER 6

Noise Trading Feedback Models

Supporters of the efficient market hypothesis (EMH) would argue that firms need not worry about noise traders creating short-term price movements that do not reflect underlying fundamentals because those mispricings would quickly get corrected by rational agents in the market. However, the Shleifer model discussed in the previous chapter demonstrated conditions under which rational traders may not be able to correct prices enough to truly reflect fundamentals, disrupting the implications of the EMH.

Feedback models attack the same EMH conclusion but from a different angle. In these models, movements in a firm's price affect the decisions of other rational agents related to the firm, such as suppliers, customers, or employees, which changes the underlying value of the firm itself. Such models would not argue that a firm's price might not revert back to fundamentals; instead, they argue that the fundamental value to which it reverts back may be different than it was before the stock price moved at all. In other words, price movements "feed back" into the underlying value of the firm.

One such model is the Hirshleifer model, in which feedback effects from noise trading not only impact financial markets, but also have real economy effects, such as on production effort and resource allocation. The second model explored here examines feedback effects that impact a firm's affiliates, which have a degree of complementarity across them. In this model, a change in a firm's price can cause some of its affiliates to change their relationships with the firm, which can in turn cause a cascade of changes from other such confederates, resulting in large changes in the firm's underlying value.

THE HIRSHLEIFER MODEL

The mid- to late-1990s brought about an unprecedented era in stock market trading. With the advent of the Internet rose an entirely new business model: the dot-com. The nature of this model was such that most analysts felt traditional valuation methods did not apply to these firms. Historically, companies were often valued on multiples of the profit they earned; however, many dot-com companies, even those favored by Wall Street analysts, had negative earnings. Traditional valuation techniques would therefore imply that these firms had negative value—in other words, that the owners would have to pay another entity to take the business off their hands.

As a result, much uncertainty existed around the valuation of these firms. Analysts came up with new ways to value them, such as multiples of revenue instead of profit, or based on number of viewers or users, and so on. Time would reveal that these valuation techniques were often grossly inaccurate, but Internet companies were in vogue with investors at the time, so techniques such as these allowed these firms' market values to be bid significantly above the values implied by their fundamentals.

A natural question that arises from this experience is: Do the grossly unjustified prices have any positive or negative effects on the underlying firm? That is, does the effect of seemingly aberrant price behavior feed back into the value of the firm itself, despite its inaccurate representation of firm value? Whether through a signal to prospective employees, or through an increased ability to raise capital, the experience of the Internet bubble raises the question of whether a change in stock price could have real effects on the underlying firm, and if so, what these effects would look like. Research by David Hirshleifer and colleagues[1] aims to answer that question.

Action in the Hirshleifer model takes place over three time periods. There are three main types of entities in the model: the firm, the investors, and the stakeholders.

The Firm

There is one representative firm in the Hirshleifer model, which represents an investment opportunity for the economic agents. There exists a fixed amount of equity in the firm, and it is traded at the end of the first two time periods at prices P_1 and P_2, respectively. At the end of the third period, the firm pays out an amount:

$$F = \theta + \varepsilon + \delta \tag{6.1}$$

for each share, where θ and ε are independent mean-zero random variables that follow a normal distribution, and δ is determined by the action of the

[1] David Hirshleifer, Avanidhar Subrahmanyam, and Sheridan Titman, "Feedback and the Success of Irrational Investors," *Journal of Financial Economics* 81, no. 2 (2006):311–338.

stakeholders after the second period. One can think of θ as the base value of the firm that savvy investors come to know, whereas ε represents some aspect of the firm value that no one can know ahead of time.

Note that the amount paid out by the firm could be negative, but the actual value the firm pays out does not matter in an absolute sense. The payouts only matter relative to one another in an ordinal sense,[2] meaning only that more money is better than less. In other words, while one might think of the scenario $F = 0$ as representing some real-world phenomenon such as bankruptcy or breakeven, the number zero has no special meaning here.

The Investors

There are two kinds of investors: rational investors and irrational ones. These two types differ in two important ways—the information they each receive and their perceptions of the terminal payout by the firm, F. Rational investors are aware of the true makeup of F and are endowed with knowledge of the base firm value, θ. Irrational investors, on the other hand, mistakenly believe that $F = \eta + \varepsilon$, where η is a mean-zero normally distributed variable that is unrelated to the other parameters of the model. Instead of learning θ, these investors learn η instead. Since they are unaware of the existence or effect of δ, they do not incorporate potential stakeholder actions into their decisions.

The volume of each type of investor is the same in the model, so that no one side can dominate the market. However, each type is split into two subtypes based on when they learn their private information. M of the rational investors are called early informed traders and learn θ in period one; the rest are late informed and learn θ in period two. N of the irrational investors are early irrational traders and learn θ in period one, while the rest are late irrational traders and learn η in period two.

The Stakeholders

The final important agent type in the model is the stakeholder. The term *stakeholder* here is meant to represent any resource provider to the firm— the authors provide suppliers, customers, and employees all as possible examples of stakeholders. The most natural interpretation in the model is that the stakeholders are employees, and hence that is how they will be thought of here.

Only one stakeholder exists in the model as a representative agent, so that his actions represent those of all stakeholders in the firm. The

---

[2] See Chapter 8 for a broader discussion on ordinal functions.

stakeholder has but one decision to make—how much effort to invest in the firm itself. How much of a return the stakeholder receives on his effort investment depends on the base value of the firm, θ, representing the idea that firms that do well provide better advancement and educational opportunities for their employees. The stakeholder does not observe θ though; in fact, the stakeholder has no private information on the firm. However, the stakeholder does get to observe P_1 and P_2 before making a decision, both of which are affected by θ, and hence needs to infer his best guess of θ given observed prices. Mathematically, he needs to determine $E(\theta \mid P_1, P_2)$.

The assumption that the stakeholder determines his effort output based solely on what he can read into the firm value based on observed stock prices is a tenuous one at best. One would think that if there exist rational investors who can do research to acquire knowledge of θ based on publicly available information, there would also be some rational stakeholders who could perform the same tasks to acquire the same information. An individual searching for a job during the dot-com bubble doubtfully made his decision based solely on which firm's stock price was high; more likely, he did research on the firm and some due diligence into what it is like to work there, and this information is likely what drove his decision.

The authors define a new variable

$$\mu_\theta = E(\theta \mid P_1, P_2) \tag{6.2}$$

and explicitly specify the stakeholder's utility so that his optimal investment choice is simply this conditional expectation times a constant. They further stipulate that δ is proportional to stakeholder investment so that δ is also simlpy a constant times this conditional expectation. This implies that when the stakeholder acts optimally, the firm's terminal payout is:

$$F = \theta + \varepsilon + k\, E(\theta \mid P_1, P_2) \tag{6.3}$$

where k is a constant.

Timing

The authors also incorporate a liquidity shock in each period, which can be thought of as additional irrational trades that are uncorrelated with any of the other parameters. Prices are then set by risk-neutral market makers in the open market. This simply means that price each period is the expected value of the firm's terminal payoff conditional only on public information (i.e., the prices themselves).

Incorporating all of the various pieces, the timing of the game is as follows:

1. θ, ε, and η are drawn from their distributions.
2. Early rational traders learn θ, and early irrational traders learn η, which they mistakenly believe drives the firm's terminal payoff through the relationship $F = \eta + \varepsilon$.
3. All traders submit their stock demands.
4. The first liquidity shock, z_1, is drawn.
5. The first-period price, P_1, is set by risk-neutral market makers, and equity claims change hands at this price.
6. Late rational traders learn θ, and late irrational traders learn η.
7. All traders submit their stock demands.
8. The second liquidity shock, z_2, is drawn.
9. The second-period price, P_2, is set by the market makers, and equity claims change hands at this price.
10. The stakeholder makes his effort investment decision based on P_1 and P_2, and this determines δ.
11. The firm delivers its payout per share, F, to each shareholder.

The tenth step incorporates the feedback loop inherent in the model. Consider a case in which the irrational information, η, is high. Irrational traders become very enthusiastic about the stock and bid its price up in both periods. The stakeholder sees the rising price but cannot tell if it is a result of the actual firm value, θ, or the irrational information, η, being high. Seeing only the prices, his best guess is that it is a little of both, so he mistakenly invests more effort into the firm than he would otherwise. But this effort increases the value of the firm, so that essentially the irrational traders bidding up the price causes the value of the actual firm to increase through this feedback mechanism.

Results

The authors show that under certain conditions, it is possible for the irrational traders to acquire a positive expected return in total. The early irrational traders are able to make some money off of their late counterparts, as the former know exactly how the latter are going to bid once they learn η, and they are able to take advantage of that. Consequently, the late irrational traders always lose money. However, the early irrational traders are sometimes able to make enough money to counteract those losses, in part due to the feedback effect that causes an irrational bidding up of the price to increase firm value (and an irrational bidding down of it to decrease firm value).

Further, it is even possible for the irrational traders to have a higher expected return than the rational ones. This occurs in other models of irrational traders but generally only occurs due to the increased risk those traders are taking on. That is not the case here. In a sense, irrational traders in this model have some relevant information that the rational traders do not have because η does feedback into the prices and because early irrational traders can take advantage of the late ones in a way that the early rational traders cannot, since they do not see η.

The authors then adapt the model to examine what happens in the context of an equity issuance, in which the firm offers shares to raise capital for an investment, and find similar results. The irrational investors are still able to turn a higher expected profit than the rational investors under certain conditions.

The highly specified nature of the model detracts from the results to a large extent. Functional form assumptions are made throughout the model, and it is possible that these are driving the results more than the basic intuition explored above. The nature of the feedback mechanism, that stakeholders make their decisions about how much to invest in the firm based solely on the stock price and not based on any other information about the firm related to its fundamentals, also gives one pause. However, the model does display what can happen when irrational investors bidding the price in one direction or another feeds back into the actual value of the firm, and it demonstrates how this can actually lead to a profit for the investors making the irrational decisions in the first place.

THE SUBRAHMANYAM-TITMAN MODEL

Two of the authors from the Hirshleifer paper, Avanidhar Subrahmanyam and Sheridan Titman, had examined a different version of feedback five years earlier.[3] This earlier model aimed to reconcile the observation that firms spend considerable resources on investor relations to mitigate short-term dips in their stock prices with the traditional finance theory that stock price movements unrelated to company fundamentals should quickly get corrected by the market.

Such fluctuations might matter to firms if the fluctuations themselves damage a company's underlying fundamentals. If a short-term price drop affects how entities related to the firm choose to interact with it, the company's underlying value may be reduced as a result of the drop itself. Further,

---

[3] Avanidhar Subrahmanyam and Sheridan Titman, "Feedback from Stock Prices to Cash Flows," *Journal of Finance* 56, no. 6 (2001): 2389–2413.

if the benefit to each stakeholder from associating with the firm is affected by the number of other stakeholders that associate with it, that same price drop could trigger a cascade in which a few stakeholders terminate their relationships and then several more follow suit. The Subrahmanyam-Titman model incorporates these potential outcomes to consider the impact of such feedback on a firm's value.

The Basic Model

The basic model consists of a single firm, which has assets in place and a potential growth opportunity, as well as N stakeholders, each of whom is to decide whether or not to interact with the firm. The term *stakeholder* is used here in much the same way as in the Hirshleifer paper; the authors define stakeholders as "agents who receive a benefit from being associated with the firm, such as the firm's employees, customers, lenders, and suppliers."[4]

The benefit to each stakeholder for associating with the firm increases based on the number of other stakeholders that also associate with the firm. This represents scenarios such as an operating system being more valuable to additional customers when a higher number of other customers have already adopted it. Specifically, the benefit to each stakeholder from adoption is:

$$\Pi = \rho_1\left(\bar{F}+\delta\right)+\rho_2\left(\bar{G}-mr\right),\qquad(6.4)$$

where $\bar{F}$ is the mean value of the firm's assets in place, δ is a mean-zero normally distributed random variable, $\bar{G}$ is the maximum value of the growth opportunity, m is the number of stakeholders that do not associate with the firm, and r is the degree of complementarity across stakeholders, with $r > 0$ and $\bar{G} > mr$. Each stakeholder will only associate if the benefit exceeds his reservation price. The stakeholders are ordered by the reservation prices at which each would associate with the firm, $\bar{w}_1$ to $\bar{w}_N$, with $\bar{w}_1$ being the highest.

Cascades

Consider a scenario in which the stakeholder with the second-lowest reservation wage does not want to associate with the firm unless at least one other stakeholder does so. That implies

---

[4]Subrahmanyam and Titman, 2391.

$$\rho_1\left(\overline{F}+\delta\right)+\rho_2\left(\overline{G}-(N-1)r\right)<\overline{w}_{N-1} \tag{6.5}$$

However, if it is also true that

$$\rho_1\left(\overline{F}+\delta\right)+\rho_2\left(\overline{G}-(N-2)r\right)>\overline{w}_{N-1} \tag{6.6}$$

then this stakeholder will associate so long as at least one other stakeholder does. If, in addition,

$$\rho_1\left(\overline{F}+\delta\right)+\rho_2\left(\overline{G}-(N-1)r\right)>\overline{w}_N \tag{6.7}$$

then the stakeholder with the lowest reservation wage is willing to associate unilaterally, which triggers the second-to-last to do so as well.

More generally, if it is true that

$$\rho_1\left(\overline{F}+\delta\right)+\rho_2\left(\overline{G}-(N-k-1)r\right)>\overline{w}_{N-k} \tag{6.8}$$

for $k=1,\ldots,N-1$, then each stakeholder will associate one by one as those in front of them each decide to do so in turn. In the end, all stakeholders will associate with the firm, even though only one would have associated in isolation. When the last stakeholder makes his decision, he triggers an avalanche of other stakeholders to associate as well. This is an example of a positive cascade.

A similar cascade can happen in the other direction, with one stakeholder jumping ship, causing all others to follow. Consider a firm that pays each of its employees' wages that are dependent on the firm's success. As more employees join the firm, its overall prospective success increases and the expected payment to each employee goes up; conversely, if one employee decides to leave the firm, this reduces expected future payments to the others and hence they might follow suit.

If

$$\rho_1\left(\overline{F}+\delta\right)+\rho_2\overline{G}>\overline{w}_1 \tag{6.9}$$

then all employees will want to stay. However, if

$$\rho_1\left(\overline{F}+\delta\right)+\rho_2\overline{G}<\overline{w}_1 \tag{6.10}$$

then the highest reservation wage employee will quit. Then, if

$$\rho_1\left(\overline{F}+\delta\right)+\rho_2(\overline{G}-r)<\overline{w}_2 \tag{6.11}$$

employee 2 will also quit, even if he would have stayed had employee 1 decided to stay. In a similar way to the positive cascade above, if

$$\rho_1\left(\overline{F}+\delta\right)+\rho_2(\overline{G}-(k-1)r)<\overline{w}_k \tag{6.12}$$

for $k=2,\dots,N$, a negative cascade will occur here in which all employees decide to quit even though all but one would have decided to stay unilaterally.

The Feedback Effect

The previous two subsections have explored how the actions of each stakeholder might affect the decisions of his confederates, but how do movements in the firm's stock price affect the decisions of the stakeholders? The model incorporates a mechanism very similar to that from the Hirshleifer paper to represent how stakeholder decisions might be driven by movements in the price of the firm's stock.

The stock market model is split into two time periods. In the first period, rational investors in the market learn the true value of δ and submit demands for the firm's stock based on this information. The authors examine two versions of the model, one in which the number of rational traders is fixed, and another in which anyone who wants to can learn δ but only by paying a cost (e.g., buying a trade periodical or spending time doing research). The market maker, who may or may not be risk-averse, receives these demands, as well as a noise demand, which is a mean-zero normally distributed variable, and from these demands he sets the market price.

At the end of the first period, stakeholders see this market price and then choose whether or not to associate with the firm in the second period. However, they do not get to see δ. Instead, they must infer something about δ from the price they see in a manner similar to the decision process of the stakeholders in the Hirshleifer model. If they see what they perceive to be a high market price, they cannot know if this was a consequence of a very high noise demand or a high value of δ that drove the rational investors to become excited about the stock. Either case is possible, but the latter cannot be entirely ignored. The high market price will therefore cause the stakeholders to guess that δ is higher than they likely would have guessed otherwise. Similarly, a low price would cause stakeholders to reduce their expectations of δ to some extent. Based on their best guess of δ, stakeholders with the most extreme reservation prices make their decisions, after which other stakeholders may follow suit as a result.

Subrahmanyam and Titman find that the probability of a cascade increases with the underlying stock's volatility, but decreases with the cost of information. The more volatile a stock's price, the more likely it is to have large movements that stakeholders would read as a big change in δ, which therefore might trigger a cascade. Conversely, if information is more difficult to obtain, stakeholders know that movements in the stock price are less likely to be a function of rational investing and more likely to be a function of noise, and hence are less apt to make decisions based on swings in the price.

The authors then consider what might happen if the firm itself has some control over the precision of the information the public sees. Changing this precision will change both the firm's upside and downside risks, and hence its preferences will rest on whether the potential benefits of a positive cascade outweigh the potential costs of a negative one. They find that nascent firms that have a strong need to get their products out and become known have a stronger incentive to release information and try to attract market analyst attention, whereas well-established firms would worry more about the downside risk of losing potential stakeholders and hence may choose to scale back their transparency to the market.

This model of feedback effects suffers from some of the same concerns that haunt the Hirshleifer paper, namely that the functions that drive the agents' decisions are highly specified, so it is difficult to feel confident that the results are driven by the underlying intuition. However, the paper does demonstrate how stock price movements might feed back into the intrinsic value of a firm in an environment with network externalities. In such a setting, firms must worry about short-term movements in price, not for fear that these prices will never revert back to underlying fundamentals, but for fear that those movements may negatively impact the fundamentals themselves based on the resulting actions of the firm's stakeholders.

CONCLUSION

Both models discussed here demonstrate how movements in a firm's stock price might alter the behavior of its stakeholders and therefore feed back into its underlying fundamentals. However, one of the fundamental questions raised by the existence of noise traders is, do noise traders adversely affect resource allocation? Nothing in the literature thus far seems to provide a credible interpretation of the resource allocation issues that might arise in the face of noise traders. The strong suspicion is that distortions are likely to occur due to stock price inefficiencies, but there is no satisfactory treatment of such issues in the current literature.

If prices are distorted by noise traders, then some firms are likely to raise capital at the wrong prices. More deserving firms, neglected by noise trader optimism, may receive less capital than they should based on fundamentals. Most feedback models contain only a single firm, but a single firm model cannot really address this issue. To develop a theory of resource allocation distortion, a model must contain multiple firms over which these resources are to be allocated.

The Shleifer noise trader model may suggest the way ahead for studying resource allocation impacts from noise trading. Imagine a Shleiferesque setup with two firms with identical fundamentals but different stock prices, even though they are identical in every way. The creative side of a model of this type would be to describe the differential impact that different stock prices can generate. In this setting, the resulting impact of the issues raised in these two models can be studied.

CHAPTER 7

Noise Traders as Technical Traders

When watching contemporary news accounts of financial market activity, one frequently hears expressions that have no explicit role in traditional finance theory but seem to mean something to the audience of the news commentators. Examples include:

"The market is forming a bottom."

"A very oversold market rallied today."

"The market broke through resistance today."

"The market dropped through support today."

"The market acts well."

"The market looks tired."

These expressions have meaning in the trading world, but they are not part of the received financial theory, and the efficient market hypothesis (EMH) predicts that none of these remarks has any real truth embodied in them. All of these expressions and many more like them are descriptions of technical analysis. If *fundamental analysis* can be defined as basing stock analysis on things taken from accounting statements and projections of accounting statements, then *technical analysis* is based on things that explicitly eschew considerations of profits, cash flow, dividends—any of the tools of fundamental analysis.

The most popular form of technical analysis is the charting of stock prices. There is a big business in providing investors with stock price charts both in printed form and in computer-accessible online form. Armed with pricing history, many traders base their stock buys and sells on how they interpret stock price patterns from historical data. An example of a stock price chart is given in Figure 7.1.

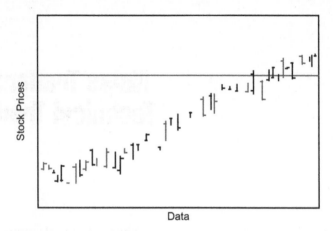

FIGURE 7.1   Stock Price Chart

Dates are plotted on the horizontal axis and stock prices are plotted vertically. The horizontal line indicates a particular stock price that the charting pattern suggests is significant. That stock prices have surpassed the value indicated by the horizontal line is taken to be important in determining the future path of the price of the stock.

Academics once scoffed at technical traders as akin to believing in voodoo dolls, but technical trading by the turn of the twenty-first century had gone mainstream. The Market Technicians Association (MTA), by 2012, boasted a membership of 4,500 "market analyst professionals in over 85 countries around the globe."[1] The MTA boasts that it offers a certification program to become a Chartered Market Technician (CMT), achievable by passing a set of examinations that test applicants on their knowledge of technical analysis. It has three levels of the CMT exam, much like its much revered ancestor, the Chartered Financial Analyst certification, pioneered by the CFA Institute.[2]

Besides attracting the interest of individual traders, technical analysis was available from mainstream stockbrokers for their clients' usage. Large pools of hedge fund money, by 2012, were invested in trading strategies solely based on past stock price histories. The National Futures Association counts among its members 4,500 firms and 55,000 associates, the vast majority of whom are actively involved in some form of technical trading. All of this activity, of course, runs counter to the EMH, which says that

---

[1] Information taken from www.mta.org on June 9, 2012.
[2] Details available at www.cfainstitute.org.

technical analysis activity represents wasted motion and wasted money. But regardless of the calumny heaped upon technical analysis by adherents of the EMH, it is an undeniable fact that technical trading underlies a very large amount of actual trading in modern financial markets.

Many common strategies in technical trading involve projecting past pricing trends into the future. This type of trading, if widespread, can create and sustain a pricing bubble. We will refer to such occurrences as *herd instinct* trading. In the latter part of this chapter, we consider some examples of the herd instinct and bubble literature.

TECHNICAL TRADERS AS NOISE TRADERS

Since technical traders are not rational traders in the sense of the EMH, they can instead be thought of as a specific type of noise trader. To simplify matters, think only about that subset of technical analysis that involves nothing more than the use of stock price charts. There are two things that are intriguing about stock price chart analysis: (1) stock price charting is widely used, and (2) users tend to agree on what many stock price chart patterns mean. The first of these considerations implies that noise traders who are price chart traders represent a significant part of the actual trading community. The second suggests that their behavior in the marketplace may be systematic.

Trend-Following Noise Traders

One of the most widely believed patterns observable in stock price charts is that if a trend is portrayed by the chart, the trend will continue. If the stock price has been rising over time, then the prediction is that it will continue to rise. If the stock price has been falling over time, then the prediction is that it will continue to fall. This idea that price trends, once in place, will continue seems to be a prevailing view in other markets besides financial markets. Many participants in the housing market seem to have expectations of future prices that are a straightforward projection of recent pricing trends.

One simple way to model a noise trader would be an extrapolative model that forecasts future prices as a straightforward projection of the trend implicit in most recent prices (see Figure 7.2). A noise trader using the extrapolative expectations, such as depicted in the Figure 7.2, might pay little or no attention to fundamentals. Bad news would not matter to such a noise trader, unless the bad news changed the pattern of stock prices so the extrapolation would lead to some different forecast.

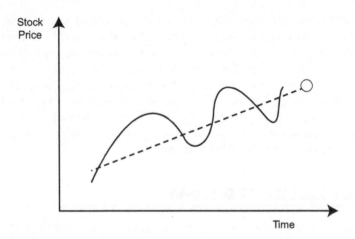

FIGURE 7.2   Predicted Stock Price Based on Trend Projection

If there is a large number of noise traders defined in this way, then one would expect some self-fulfilling aspect of such trading behavior. Expecting current trends to continue could lead to a higher or lower demand for a stock than might be warranted by the fundamentals. This characterization of a noise trader is consistent with the Shleifer model since overoptimism or overpessimism could easily result from trend following. Such traders might even be more profitable than rational traders, at least for a while, for the reasons given in that model.

Reversal Patterns in Stock Prices

Somewhat more complicated is what stock price charts might tell us about market reversals. A market reversal takes place when a rising (falling) price trend becomes a falling (rising) price trend. What stock price patterns predict reversals? There are many.

One of the most interesting stock price patterns that technical traders subscribe to is known as the *island reversal*. The island reversal requires that a stock price jumps from one price to a substantially different price either immediately or during a trading halt, which could be nothing more than close of market on one day and the opening of the market on the next trading day. The gap in the price creates an island, as shown in Figure 7.3.

According to some versions of the island reversal signal, whenever a stock price gaps it must go back and fill in the gap, so that some future reversal in price is predicted by the island reversal phenomenon.

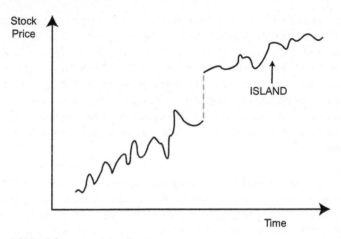

FIGURE 7.3   Price Island

Another popular reversal pattern is the *head-and-shoulders* pattern. Sometimes this is called either a head-and-shoulders top or a head-and-shoulders bottom, depending on whether it is forecasting a fall in future stock prices or an increase in future stock prices. A head-and-shoulders top is pictured in Figure 7.4, together with its forecast of declining prices. In Figure 7.4, the head-and-shoulders pattern has formed and is now suggesting

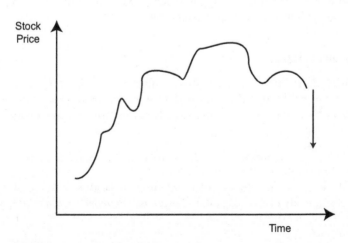

FIGURE 7.4   A Head-and-Shoulders Top

that stock prices will fall, reversing the previous uptrend in prices that had been in place before the formation of the head-and-shoulders pattern.

Head-and-shoulders patterns were studied extensively by Carol Osler[3] and later by Osler and Kevin Chang.[4] Osler's 1998 study reported that strategies based on head-and-shoulders patterns in U.S. equity markets proved to be unprofitable. The Osler-Chang results, published a year later and based on data from currency markets, found the opposite. Head-and-shoulders trading in currency markets was profitable, according to Osler and Chang.

> *The head-and-shoulders trading rule appears to have some predictive power for the German mark and yen but not for the Canadian dollar, Swiss franc, French franc, or pound. Taken individually, profits in the markets for yen and marks are also substantial when adjusted for transactions costs, interest differentials, or risk. These results are inconsistent with virtually all standard exchange rate models, and could indicate the presence of market inefficiencies.*[5]

A final example of reversal patterns are the twin concepts of *base building* and *forming a top*. Base building occurs when a stock has dropped over a period of time but seems to have stabilized at a lower level and has traded in a narrow range around that lower level (see Figure 7.5).

The dotted line represents the base that is forming. Forming a top is a similar pattern, flipping the chart upside down so that forming a top is ultimately predicting a future decline in prices, while base building is suggested to lead to prices headed higher at some future date.

The Systematic Issue

Stock price charts are easy to construct and the simple patterns that we just discussed can be discerned from the data with minimal effort. Simple algorithms can be employed—not necessarily all identical—to take advantage

---

[3] Carol Osler, "Identifying Noise Traders: The Head-and-Shoulders Pattern in U.S. Equities," Federal Reserve Bank of New York, 1988.

[4] Kevin P. H. Chang and Carol Osler, "Methodical Madness: Technical Analysis and the Irrationality of Exchange-Rate Forecasts," *Economic Journal* 109, no. 458 (October 1999): 636–661.

[5] Ibid., abstract.

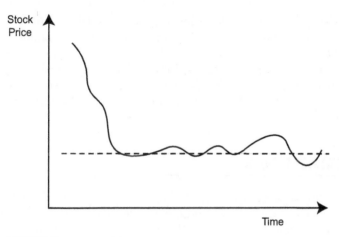

FIGURE 7.5   Base Building

of any profit opportunities that stock price charts might have embedded in them. Trend following can be seen as a version of herd mentality. A price is going up rapidly, and everyone jumps on board and buys the stock whose price is rising. A frenzy develops as the price rises higher and higher, and future prices are extrapolated to be even higher still. This line of reasoning suggests that trend following is likely to be systematic. Defenders of the EMH argue that noise traders will tend to cancel one another out, and something like the Law of Large Numbers will take hold, so that, in the aggregate, noise trader activity won't matter. But if the noise traders are all doing pretty much the same thing, then the cancel-out argument no longer applies.

Technical trading is a broader approach than simply stock price charting. Besides other stock market information such as volume, various trading statistics, seasonal trading patterns, and the like, technical trading also encompasses many other considerations with the common characteristic that none of these considerations involve fundamental company information such as dividends, earnings, and so forth. Since there is such a variety of different things that are encompassed under the umbrella of technical trading, the cancel-out criticism is likely to apply to much of technical trading. But the cancel-out phenomenon will not apply to strategies that are widely followed by a large number of traders and investors and for which there are not some obvious counterstrategies that seek to do the opposite.

The term *herd instinct* has been applied to models that have systematic behavior. This could be one application of the technical trading strategies, when such strategies are characterized by a large number of investors and traders pursuing similar strategies. Robert Shiller developed a herd instinct model in 1984 that was overlooked until much later, when the idea of systematic noise trading behavior found a more accepting home in the finance literature.

HERD INSTINCT MODELS

Herd instinct models[6] are motivated by observing financial market booms and busts. They are typically highly aggregative, and the herd behavior is usually summarized by a single-agent model representing the herd. Market practitioners have observed cycles in financial markets that are often described as a "feeding frenzy." A price of a particular asset begins to rise then develops a momentum of its own, seemingly independent of any real fundamental change in the things that should determine its price.

The Shiller Model

Shiller builds his model of stock returns on the back of two different observations. First, he notes that the prevailing thought at that time (the mid-1980s) was that the lack of forecastability in stock returns implied investor psychology could not have much impact in financial markets. The logic was that investor fads should be predictable, so if they impacted stock prices, price movements should be somewhat predictable as well.

Second, he notes that firms generally announce dividend movements in advance, implying that dividend movements are somewhat forecastable. Since dividends should certainly have some impact on stock prices, but price movements are not very forecastable, the prices themselves must anticipate future dividend movements. With investor psychology already ruled out as a factor, that leaves an optimal forecast of dividends as the only possible determinant of stock prices.

---

[6] These models are normally part of bubble models. For an excellent account of what we know and don't know about bubbles, see Rodney Sullivan, "Taming Global Village Risk II: Understanding and Mitigating Bubbles," *Journal of Portfolio Management* 35, no. 4 (2009): 131–141.

Consequently, he models returns on stock prices as:

$$E_t R_t = \delta \qquad (7.1)$$

where δ represents a constant, E_t represents the mathematical expectation conditional on all known information at time t, and R_t is defined as

$$R_t = \frac{P_{t+1} - P_t + D_t}{P_t} \qquad (7.2)$$

with P_{t+1} and P_t representing next period's and this period's prices, respectively, and D_t representing this period's dividend. The fact that δ is a constant reflects the idea that, in equilibrium, prices adjust so as to equate all stocks' expected returns.

One can solve this equation recursively to obtain a representation of a given stock's price at any time t:

$$P_t = \sum_{k=0}^{\infty} \frac{E_t D_{t+k}}{(1+\delta)^{k+1}} \qquad (7.3)$$

In other words, Shiller argues that the EMH implies that the price of a stock at any point in time is simply an optimal forecast of the future stream of dividends. Consequently, if the price of a given stock moves, more often than not that movement should reflect movement in future dividends from that stock.

However, the data does not bear out such a finding. If investor psychology cannot be a factor in price movements according to the EMH, Shiller argues that that leaves only anticipation of dividend movements as a driver of stock prices, so that stock price movements should generally be followed by changes to dividends. The fact that empirical evidence does not support that conclusion, he argues, casts doubt on the EMH as a complete model of stock price movements.

In response, Shiller proffers a slightly adapted version of the EMH that includes irrational investors. This model has rational, or smart-money, investors, as well as investors Shiller calls "ordinary," which represent noise traders. Smart-money investors have the following demand for a given stock as a proportion of total shares outstanding:

$$Q_t = \frac{(E_t R_t - \rho)}{\varphi} \qquad (7.4)$$

where $E_t R_t$ is defined as above, ρ is the expected return level at which there is no smart-money demand for the asset, and φ represents the risk premium smart-money investors would require to hold all the shares of the given stock.

Ordinary investors, however, are assumed to demand a total value of stock defined as Y_t. Market equilibrium requires that

$$Q_t + \frac{Y_t}{P_t} = 1 \qquad (7.5)$$

from which one can solve recursively to arrive at the expression for the price of the stock:

$$P_t = \sum_{k=0}^{\infty} \frac{E_t D_t + \varphi E_t Y_{t+k}}{\left(1 + \rho + \varphi\right)^{k+1}} \qquad (7.6)$$

This is simply an adjusted form of equation (7.3). Noise traders have their impact through the Y_t terms, so that as φ goes to zero, noise traders have no impact and the formula reverts to (7.3), and as φ goes to infinity, noise traders drown out smart-money investors and the market price is $P_t = Y_t$.

Shiller then goes through several specifications for Y_t and examines the resulting effect on price. First, he postulates what would happen if ordinary investors are driven by fads for stocks. Y_t would then have a hump-shaped pattern, rising as the stock comes into fashion, leveling off for a while, and then tapering back down towards its original level. The effect on price would depend on the how long the pattern takes to evolve. A relatively short fad would have little effect, since price includes a weighted sum of all future ordinary investor demands, so that a brief fad would get attenuated significantly in its effect on price. Essentially, smart-money investors would simply take the opposite position of ordinary investors, selling the stock high while it is in vogue and then buying it back at lower prices as it goes out of style, so that overall price movements would be minimal.

However, a long-developing fad would have a significant impact on price, with smart-money investors slowly buying in as Y_t rises toward its peak, knowing prices will be higher in the future. The price would peak shortly before Y_t does, then decline as future Y_t values are set to decline as well. Shiller argues that such a phenomenon could explain the lack of forecastability in stock prices.

He then looks at a couple of extreme views on Y_t, namely that Y_t respond directly to either past returns or current and past dividends, and argues that both would imply that a stock's price might overreact to dividends relative to what the EMH would predict. To test this theory, he looks at historical data on the relevant metrics for the Standard & Poor's Index, and finds that stock prices have historically overreacted to dividends. The excess volatility of prices relative to dividends could therefore be explained by an irrational investor model such as this one.

Shiller does, however, caution about reading too much into his results. The specifications of his model are rather restrictive and make strong assumptions about the impact of irrational investors. Further, even if the model's assumptions are correct, Shiller admits that the observed relationship could have other explanations, such as firm dividend behavior responding to the same social dynamics that influence the society at large. Regardless, it is difficult to look at the evidence presented and come away without some additional doubt about the validity of the EMH.

Abreu-Brunnermeier Model

Abreu and Brunnermeier (2003)[7] provide a noise trader model designed to deal specifically with bubbles and crashes. The Abreu-Brunnermeier (AB) model has the interesting feature that even arbitrage traders may find it in their interest to ride the wave of the bubble. Arbitrage traders, the so-called rational traders, are aware that there are noise traders out there and that they can impact prices, perhaps in the manner suggested by Shiller in his model. AB assume that prices begin to diverge from efficient prices without any particular reason and the arbitrageurs observe the divergence. Not all arbitrageurs notice the divergence at the same time. Once an arbitrageur observes the divergence, the arbitrageur will not necessarily trade against the divergence. Some will trade against it, but others might be tempted to ride the wave. The model permits the bubble to be burst by the combined action of the arbitrageurs, but it doesn't provide any certainty that the combined action of the arbitrageurs will ever successfully burst the bubble. Instead, AB use an arbitrary stopping time by which the bubble will burst, no matter what actions the noise traders and the arbitrageurs may be taking. The authors describe this arbitrary stopping date as based on "exogenous reasons." The interpretation of the arbitrary stopping date is that an unforeseen event of significance occurs that changes things and bursts the bubble.

The AB model is successful in capturing the idea that people join bandwagons and get off of bandwagons and such herding activity can prolong a bubble as well as end it. The model is less successful in explaining why this herding activity takes place. The model is descriptive more than insightful. The idea that arbitrageurs might ride the wave of the bubble even when they

---

[7] Dilip Abreu and Markus K. Brunnermeier, "Bubbles and Crashes," *Econometrica* 71, no. 1 (January 2003): 173–204.

are perfectly aware that the market is in a bubble phase is an interesting
feature of the AB model. There seems some casual evidence that even those
who are aware that market prices are beyond what can be supported by
fundamentals often will participate anyway on the grounds that they can
rationally expect the bubble to continue.[8] This changes the usual definition
of an arbitrageur in a way that could prove troublesome for supporters of
the EMH.[9]

AB assumes that a divergence between market price and efficient price
emerges and then is observed. An econometric study by Gurkaynak[10] suggests that such observations may be difficult to accomplish in practice. The
old adage that you only know you were in a bubble when it is over seems
borne out by Gurkaynak's statistical tests.

CONCLUSION

We will return to the subject of technical trading with contrarian investing and momentum in Chapters 15 and 16. Bubbles are still not well
understood. As Reinhart and Rogoff[11] note in their landmark work on
financial crises, most economists treat bubbles largely as narratives, as
if they are a part of economic history but not much a part of economic
theory. We don't really understand how bubbles begin or end, and we
are not sure how one can detect bubbles until after the fact. What we
do seem to know is that technical trading and herd instinct trading
likely play a role in bubbles. Technical traders who herd together and
follow simple trend-following strategies can serve to prolong a bubble
by simple feedback from price increases to expectations of future price
increases.

One of the most interesting questions about bubbles is whether bubbles are an inherent feature of modern financial systems. Are the seeds of
the next bubble ever present? Minsky[12] is the most well-known proponent

---

[8] For a discussion of experimental results on bubbles, see Chapter 21.

[9] A similar point is made in Taisei Kaizojiand and Didier Sornette, "Market Bubble
and Crash," reprinted in Rama Cont, *Encyclopedia of Quantitative Finance*
(Hoboken, NJ: Wiley, 2009).

[10] Refet S. Gurkaynak, "Econometric Tests of Asset Price Bubbles: Taking Stock,"
Journal of Economic Surveys 22, no. 1 (2008): 166–186.

[11] Carmen M. Reinhart and Kenneth Rogoff, *This Time Is Different: Eight Centuries
of Financial Folly* (Princeton, NJ: Princeton University Press, 2009).

[12] Hyman Minsky, "The Financial Instability Hypothesis," The Jerome Levy
Economics Institute of Bard College, Working Paper No. 74, May 1992.

of the view that bubbles inevitably arise from financial markets. Minsky argues that Keynesian economics, properly interpreted, is about bubbles and collapses and quotes Keynes extensively in his own research. Policy makers seem to have the opposite view. After bubble crashes, policy makers rush to enact reforms that will prohibit future bubbles. This may be foolhardy if Minsky's inevitability arguments are correct.

Three

Anomalies

CHAPTER 8

The Rational Man

Economic theory aims to model human behavior in a variety of contexts. How does someone choose which car to purchase? How does one select a mate? Between a stock with a high potential return and a lot of uncertainty and one with a low potential return but with little or no uncertainty, which would one pick?

Underpinning all of these questions is a basic inquiry on how people make decisions. Historically, economics has chosen to deal with these questions with a concept known as *utility theory*. However, behavioral finance has revealed some of the pitfalls of utility theory and some ways in which normal human behavior deviates from the predictions of this theory. In this chapter, we explore such issues.

CONSUMER CHOICE WITH CERTAINTY

Grace lives in a world with two goods—guns and butter—which are provided by the government at no cost to the consumer beyond taxes, which have already been collected. Grace has three options: she can choose 14 guns and 15 tubs of butter, 2 guns and 45 tubs of butter, or no guns and 50 tubs of butter.

How does Grace decide which bundle to choose? Economists assume Grace chooses the bundle that makes her the happiest, which does not seem like too big of a stretch for an assumption. But how do we measure whether one bundle makes Grace happier than another?

Economists use a concept called *utility* to represent the happiness a consumer derives from a bundle of goods. Each bundle is given a number, or utility "score," that represents how happy that bundle makes the consumer. Therefore, the goal of choosing the best bundle equates to the goal of maximizing utility. The mapping of every potential hypothetical bundle a consumer might enjoy to each bundle's resulting utility is called the *utility function*.

In our example, the utility function need only address the utility Grace receives from those three specific bundles of goods in order to predict her behavior; whichever bundle provides the most utility is her optimal choice.

What happens as her choice set expands? Assume markets are available for guns and butter, and Grace has $100 to spend, with prevailing market prices of $5 per gun and $2 per tub of butter. Grace faces a number of options—an infinite number, in fact. She could spend all of her money on guns and purchase 20 guns, or all of her money on butter and purchase 50 tubs of butter. Or she could spend some money on guns and some on butter, such as 10 guns and 25 tubs or 4 guns and 40 tubs, and so on. To predict her behavior, the utility function must map from every possible bundle in Grace's choice set to her utility derived from consuming that bundle. We can determine which bundle out of all of the bundles that are possible for her to purchase would make her the happiest, and this would be her optimal purchase.

Not just any mapping will allow us to do that. In order for a utility function to be valid in this context, it must have the following three characteristics:[1]

- *Universality.* Every possible bundle must have a utility associated with it.
- *Comparability.* For any two bundles A and B, it must be the case that $U(A) > U(B)$, $U(B) > U(A)$, or $U(A) = U(B)$.
- *Transitivity.* For any three bundles A, B, and C, if $U(A) \geq U(B)$ and $U(B) \geq U(C)$, it must be the case that $U(A) \geq U(C)$.

These three characteristics are common to the preference specification of a rational individual in theoretical economics. The first assumption requires that all bundles can be evaluated. The second ensures that any two bundles can be ranked, even if that ranking reveals a tie. The last assumption rules out the possibility of a set of bundles in which the bundle which seems optimal depends on the pairwise comparisons you make within that set.

An infinite number of utility functions meet these three criteria. If G represents the number of guns Grace consumes, and B represents the tubs of butter she consumes, the following utility functions are all valid:

- $U(G,B) = G+B$
- $U(G,B) = \max[G,B]$

---

[1] $U(X)$ is a real valued function, where X is a commodity bundle and $U(X)$ is the utility value assigned to the commodity bundle.

- $U(G,B) = G^{\alpha}B^{1-\alpha}$
- $U(G,B) = \alpha ln(G) + (1-\alpha)\, ln(B)$

These functions may look familiar from elementary microeconomics courses. The first represents perfect substitutes, in which one unit of one good substitutes perfectly for one unit of the other. The second represents perfect complements, in which you derive additional utility from more of one good only if you have at least the same amount of the other good. These are commonly used utility functions in economics that have desirable mathematical properties to make theoretical modeling simpler.

Note that the third and fourth examples are the same utility function—that is, they represent the same preference relationships over the two goods. That is because the fourth is simply a monotonic transformation[2] of the third; specifically, the fourth expression for utility is just the natural logarithm of the third. Since utility matters only insofar as the rankings it implies between any two bundles of goods, and any monotonic transformation on a utility function simply changes the utility of all bundles without allowing any one bundle to "pass" another, the resulting transformation represents the same preference ordering. For this reason, utility functions are called *ordinal* functions, as the utility numbers have no meaning in an absolute sense; the only relevance of the utility score itself is the way the numbers are ordered.

Not any function that one can write down can be a valid utility function in this context. For example, the utility function $U = \arcsin(GB)$ would violate the first assumption of universality, since any bundle for which $GB > 1$ would not return a value. A complex utility function such as $U = G + Bi$ would meet the first assumption but would violate the second and third since no two bundles with differing nonzero values of G and B would be comparable.

Consider an election with three candidates. It could be that the majority would prefer the first candidate to the second and the second to the third, but that most would still prefer the third to the first. This example, commonly referred to as the *voting paradox,* would violate the transitivity assumption.

Returning to Grace's decision, once we have a mapping from each possible bundle to her corresponding utility level for that bundle, we can determine her choice by finding the bundle that gives her the highest utility. Consider the utility function $U(G,B) = GB$. Figure 8.1 displays the "budget constraint," or the set of bundles Grace can choose from, as well as the optimal bundle given her utility function.

---

[2] A monotonic transformation preserves the ordering of the original function. If $U(X) > U(Y)$ and V is a monotonic transformation of U, then $V(X) > V(Y)$, for all X and Y.

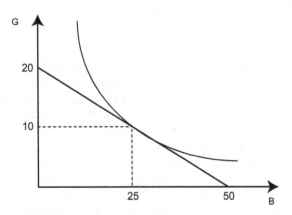

FIGURE 8.1   Grace's Optimal Choice

CONSUMER CHOICE WITH UNCERTAINTY

The previous section described consumer choice when the outcomes are deterministic;[3] we knew exactly how happy Grace would be for any given bundle she might purchase. Not all situations are like this. There is often a random chance involved in the eventual outcome, regardless of what bundle one might wish to purchase. Asset markets are an example of this. Aside from risk-free securities, one cannot know what the eventual outcome will be ahead of time, and therefore, choices are usually made in situations fraught with uncertainty.

Consider Grace's choice between two games—one game pays $100 with certainty and the other pays $10 with certainty. Which will Grace choose? The answer is probably obvious: Grace will choose the first game since it pays her more money. Implicitly, we're assuming that Grace prefers having a higher ultimate level of wealth to a lower one, which seems a reasonable assumption and is likely to be true for most people.

But what happens if Grace faces some uncertainty? Suppose in the first game there is a 5 percent chance she will receive $100 and a 95 percent chance she will receive $0, and the second game involves a 50 percent chance she will receive $10 and a 50 percent chance she receives $0.[4]

This choice is a little more complicated than the last. One might guess that Grace will choose the second game, the logic being that both games will

---

[3] A situation is deterministic if there is no uncertainty present. In the previous section, all commodity bundles were known with certainty.

[4] Assume away psychological affects like the thrill of the game itself and assume that Grace is making this decision strictly on a monetary basis.

pay off the same amount on average, namely $5, yet the first game involves more risk. The second game is more likely to pay some, albeit a smaller amount. In this case, we are implicitly assuming that Grace is averse to risk, a concept discussed further later in this chapter. This still might seem like a reasonable assumption, though other decision outcomes are certainly possible depending on what we assume about Grace's preferences.

Now tweak the first game slightly—there is a 10 percent chance it pays $100 and a 90 percent chance it pays $0, while the second game is still 50/50 that it will pay either $10 or $0. Now the decision might not be as clear. The first game still seems more risky, but it also pays out a higher amount on average. Consequently, Grace's decision will depend on how happy she might be at various levels of wealth.

Games like these are called *lotteries*. A lottery is any situation in which there are multiple potential payouts for the participant and the method in which the eventual outcome is chosen contains a random component. A lottery consists of a set of specific dollar payoffs, each with a specific probability of that particular payoff occurring. The probabilities in a lottery add up to one, so that all possibilities are accounted for. For example, imagine a roll of one die with a payoff equal to the roll:

The One-Die Lottery Example

Roll of the Die	Payoff	Probability
1	$1	1/6
2	$2	1/6
3	$3	1/6
4	$4	1/6
5	$5	1/6
6	$6	1/6

The question becomes: How do individuals make decisions when faced with a choice between different lotteries?

Economists typically deal with this issue by taking each individual's utility function over wealth, which maps every possible level of wealth to a utility score that represents that individual's happiness at that wealth, and assuming that each individual makes choices under uncertainty in such a way as to maximize their expected utility. This is the most common approach in economics to modeling what is known as *decision-making under uncertainty*. This will represent a core point of attack against traditional economics by behavioral economists.

Let's return to the three potential game pairings that Grace might face. Assume that her beginning wealth is $100 and that her utility at various levels of wealth is as follows:

- $U(100) = 10$
- $U(110) = 12$
- $U(200) = 18$

The answer to the first game pairing, receiving $10 with certainty or $100 with certainty, is straightforward. Grace's utility when receiving $10 is 12, lower than 18, her utility from receiving $100 with certainty.

The answer to the second game pairing is less straightforward due to the uncertainty. Now, we need to apply the concept of expected utility. The first option provides a 5 percent chance of receiving $100, which would leave her at an ending wealth of $200, and a 95 percent chance of receiving $0, in which case her wealth would end unchanged at $100. The expected utility from this option is therefore:

$$E_1[U] = 5\% \times U(200) + 95\% \times U(100)$$
$$= 5\% \times 18 + 95\% \times 10 = 10.4 \qquad (8.1)$$

The second option provides a 50 percent chance of receiving $10, leaving her with $110, and a 50 percent chance of leaving her wealth unchanged at $100, so her expected utility in this option is:

$$E_2[U] = 50\% \times U(110) + 50\% \times U(100)$$
$$= 50\% \times 12 + 50\% \times 10 = 11 \qquad (8.2)$$

Since her expected utility is higher with the second option, classical economics would predict she would choose that option.

Finally, in the third pairing:

$$E_1[U] = 10\% \times U(200) + 90\% \times U(100)$$
$$= 10\% \times 18 + 90\% \times 10 = 10.8 \qquad (8.3)$$

while the expected utility of the second option remains the same:

$$E_2[U] = 50\% \times U(110) + 50\% \times U(100)$$
$$= 50\% \times 12 + 50\% \times 10 = 11 \qquad (8.4)$$

Grace will still choose the second option.

The intuition behind why Grace chooses as she does follows the logic given in the earlier example. When both payouts are guaranteed, Grace chooses the higher payout. When the higher payout is less likely, but the lotteries pay the same on average, Grace will choose the lower maximum payout option because it's a safer play. In fact, she'll even choose this option in some instances in which the other option has a higher expected payout, as demonstrated by the third pairing.

One can solve for the payout probabilities in the first option of the third pairing that would make Grace indifferent between the two lotteries:

$$p \times U(200) + (1-p) \times U(100) = 11 \tag{8.5}$$

$$18p + 10 \times (1-p) = 11$$

$$8p = 1$$

$$p = 1/8$$

For values of p less than 1/8, Grace prefers the lower maximum payout option, whereas for values of p above 1/8, Grace prefers the higher maximum payout option.

Grace's preference for the safer option is evidence that this utility function demonstrates *risk aversion*. Risk aversion is defined as the condition in which an individual prefers receiving a fixed amount of money with certainty over a lottery with the same expected value but a positive probability of receiving some amount lower than the fixed amount of money.

One can also define a continuous utility function that exhibits risk-averse behavior. As it turns out, a continuous utility function is risk-averse if and only if it is concave. As an example, consider $U(x) = ln(x)$. Figure 8.2 demonstrates what this utility function looks like graphically as well as how concavity implies risk aversion. Consider a lottery in which you have a small chance of obtaining b and a large chance of obtaining a, which is less than b. The expected utility one receives from the lottery will be the weighted average of the utility one would receive from each of the two amounts separately, and therefore will lie on the straight line that connects those two utility outcomes. Alternatively, the utility one would receive from the expected value of the lottery lies on the curve itself at the x-coordinate of the relevant point on that line, which, because the curve is concave, will always be above the line itself. As a result, the utility one would get from receiving the expected value of a lottery will always be higher than the expected utility one receives from the lottery itself.

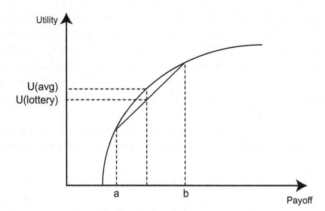

FIGURE 8.2   Example of Risk Aversion

Risk aversion is a common assumption that economists make when they model human behavior. In these models, economic agents need to be compensated for taking on risk in the sense that they would have to receive a higher-than-expected-value amount in order to prefer an option with some uncertainty around the outcome.

Imagine that Fran has $50,000 to invest. As she considers various stocks in which to invest, she might find some that have the possibility of providing a very large return but could also provide a very small return or even create a large loss, as well as some that will provide a small return with near certainty and have virtually no chance of providing a large gain or loss. If Fran expands her search to other types of assets, she might also consider U.S. Treasury bills, which are considered to provide a fixed return with virtual certainty.

When looking at her various options, Fran will have to decide whether the risk associated with a given stock or a portfolio of stocks is worth the extra potential return. The way this behavior has been modeled historically in economics is by means of a utility function representing how happy Fran is at each given level of wealth. Economists assume Fran acts so as to maximize her expected utility in each decision she makes.

Arrow[5] draws an interesting connection between utility functions that are bounded from above and risk aversion. Arrow notes that an individual with a utility function that is bounded from above must exhibit risk aversion over most of the wealth possibilities he or she faces. The basic logic is

---

[5] Kenneth J. Arrow, "The Theory of Risk Aversion." In *Essays in the Theory of Risk Bearing*, Chapter 3, (New York: Elsevier, 1971).

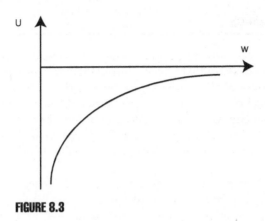

FIGURE 8.3

that if a utility function is bounded from above, the marginal utility must tend to zero, meaning that with relatively few exceptions, marginal utility is generally decreasing. In other words, the utility function itself is generally concave.

These utility functions need not exhibit positive utility everywhere; in fact, they need not be positive anywhere. One salient example comes from the article by Shleifer and colleagues[6] covered in Chapter 5. In that paper, all investors are assumed to have the utility function:

$$U = -e^{-(2\gamma)^w} \tag{8.6}$$

Where w represents the individual's wealth, γ is a parameter that represents aversion to risk, and e represents Euler's number, a mathematical constant approximately equal to 2.718. In this case, all investors are assumed to have negative utility at all levels of wealth. Figure 8.3 depicts this utility function graphically. Since e raised to any exponent—positive or negative—is always positive, this utility function is always negative, as shown in the graph.

Economists have traditionally modeled human behavior, when facing uncertain outcomes, this way—that is, individuals have utility functions and they behave so as to maximize the expected value of their utility. Behavioral finance has challenged this and other utility maximization assumptions as inconsistent with ordinary human behavior. The next section discusses one famous example of these criticisms.

---

[6] J. Bradford DeLong, Andrei Shleifer, Lawrence Summers, and Robert Waldman, "Noise Trader Risk in Financial Markets," *Journal of Political Economy* 98, no. 4 (August 1990): 703–708.

THE ALLAIS PARADOX

Probably the most famous counterexample to classical utility theory is known as the Allais Paradox, which evolved in an interesting way. Leonard Savage, a leading utility theorist at the time, had created four axioms for choosing among bets that strictly defined rational behavior in the choice of uncertainty. Maurice Allais, another leading utility theorist, disagreed with his friend and colleague Savage's synopsis of what makes for rational behavior, and he set out to show Savage that rational individuals could violate his assumptions.

As the well-known story goes, one day, when Allais and Savage were having lunch, Allais laid out two different choices between two lotteries (see Table 8.1). Savage picked his favored choices—A in the first set and B in the second—and these choices violated his own axioms on what defines rational behavior.

This is known as the Allais Paradox. The second set of lotteries is the same as the first, but with an 89 percent chance taken away from winning $1 million and shifted to winning $0 for each lottery. Given the assumption that individuals maximize expected utility, an equivalent shift such as this could not change an individual's optimal choice *regardless of the specification of his or her utility function.* That is, no matter what an individual's utility function looks like, under the assumption that everyone maximizes expected utility, choosing A in the first set implies that he or she must prefer A in the second, and choosing B in the first set implies that he or she must prefer B in the second.

TABLE 8.1

Lottery A		Lottery B	
Winnings	Probability	Winnings	Probability
$1 million	100%	$1 million	89%
		$0	1%
		$5 million	10%
Lottery A		Lottery B	
Winnings	Probability	Winnings	Probability
$0	89%	$0	90%
$1 million	11%	$5 million	10%

A mathematical proof of this is straightforward; if one's initial wealth is w, choosing A in the first set implies that:

$$U(w + 1M) > 0.89U(w + 1M) + 0.01U(w) + 0.1U(w + 5M) \qquad (8.7)$$

which implies that

$$0.11U(w + 1M) > 0.01U(w) + 0.1U(w + 5M)$$

$$\Rightarrow 0.11U(w + 1M) + 0.89U(w) > 0.9U(w) + 0.1U(w + 5M) \qquad (8.8)$$

which means that same individual prefers A to B in the second choice set as well. Note that this logic required no specification of the actual utility function $U(\cdot)$ nor any assumption about the initial wealth level w.

If individuals would choose A in one set and B in the other, that implies, when faced with uncertain choices like these, those same individuals do not act in a way consistent with the maximization of expected utility.

Another, perhaps even more straightforward, example of this comes from Kahneman and Tversky.[7] The two lotteries are shown in Table 8.2. In this experiment, most people pick B in the first choice but A in the second. This contradicts expected utility theory for the same reason as in the last example—the second choice is the same as the first, except for a 66 percent chance shifted from $2,400 to $0 in each lottery. Therefore, any individual who picks A in the first choice should also pick A in the second, and anyone

TABLE 8.2

Lottery A		Lottery B	
Winnings	Probability	Winnings	Probability
$2,500	33%	$2,400	100%
$0	1%		
$2,400	66%		
Lottery A		Lottery B	
Winnings	Probability	Winnings	Probability
$2,500	33%	$2,400	34%
$0	67%	$0	66%

---

[7] Daniel Kahneman and Amos Tversky, "Prospect Theory: An Analysis of Decision under Risk," *Econometrica* 47, no. 2 (March 1979): 263–292.

who picks B in the first choice should pick B in the second, assuming they are maximizing expected utility. The fact that most people do not choose in the manner indicated is evidence that expected utility maximization does not always accurately predict human behavior.

CONCLUSION

The Allais Paradox demonstrates that expected utility theory is a flawed representation of how humans make decisions under uncertainty, but behavioral finance has struck at classical economic utility theory on an even deeper level. Even the simple idea of modeling utility as a function of wealth has been put to question.

Consider a scenario in which Jack and Jill, each with the same preferences, have $5 million each. Are they equally happy? Classical economic utility theory would say that they must be, and, with no supplemental information, most would likely agree. But what if you were told additionally that yesterday Jack had $1 million and Jill had $9 million—would it still seem that they are equally happy today? Most would conclude in this case that Jack is enthralled to have quintupled his money while Jill is likely devastated at having lost almost half of hers.[8]

This has implications that impact the decisions humans make in varying contexts. Consider a gamble in which Jack and Jill can each either take a 50/50 chance of ending with a wealth of $1 million or of $4 million, or take the certain outcome of ending with a wealth of $2 million. What would each choose? Utility theory would predict they would make the same choice regardless of current wealth levels, but what if, in millions, Jack currently has 1 and Jill currently has 4? One can see how they are likely to make different decisions given their different starting points. These examples demonstrate that it is not only ultimate wealth levels that matter in decision making but historical and current wealth levels as well.[9]

This is where behavioral finance picks up the debate. Behavioral finance attempts to analyze how human behavior deviates from the usual ways that economists have attempted to model choices that individuals make. It attempts to discover how such choices are actually made in real-world settings. This topic is explored further in the next chapter.

---

[8] Daniel Kahneman, *Thinking, Fast and Slow* (New York: Farrar, Straus and Giroux: 2011), 275.

[9] Ibid., 275–276. The relevance of prior history is sometimes described as *path-dependent utility*.

CHAPTER 9

Prospect Theory

Chapter 8 examined the methods economists historically have used to model human behavior in the face of uncertainty. Economists assume each individual has a function that maps from every possible relevant level of wealth to a number that represents his or her happiness, and that under uncertainty each individual acts to maximize the expected level of happiness. That chapter considered one objection to expected utility known as the Allais Paradox.

A second problem with expected utility maximization lies in the assumption that individuals make decisions under uncertainty based solely on the eventual levels of his or her wealth. One simple way to see that this is unlikely to be a good approximation of human behavior is to realize that most individuals are unable to report their levels of wealth in a short amount of time within a reasonable degree of accuracy. Consumers could not be acting based on anticipated levels of wealth if they are not even aware of current wealth levels.

So if wealth isn't the issue, what is?

THE REFERENCE POINT

Consider the following set of choices, taken from Kahneman:[1]

In addition to what you already own, you receive $1,000 for sure and either:

- Another $500 for sure, or
- A 50 percent chance of nothing and a 50 percent chance of $1,000.

Second, consider this alternative set of choices.

---

[1]Daniel Kahneman, *Thinking, Fast and Slow* (New York: Farrar, Straus and Giroux, 2011), 280.

In addition to what you already own, you receive $2,000 for sure and either:

- Lose $500 for sure, or
- Face a 50 percent chance of losing nothing and a 50 percent chance of losing $1,000.

A large majority of respondents picked the first option in the first choice set and the second option in the second choice set. Note, however, that the two choice sets represent exactly the same ending levels of wealth—what you own plus $1,500 versus what you own plus a 50 percent chance of $1,000 and a 50 percent chance of $2,000.

What is different in the two examples is the reference point. In the first example, individuals use an initial wealth of $1,000 as their beginning reference point. When considering their choices, they exhibit risk aversion, preferring the certain gain of $500 over a risky choice with an identical expected value.

In the second choice set, individuals consider $2,000 as their reference point and see a decision between a certain loss or a risky alternative with the identical expected value. In this case, the majority of individuals choose the latter option—the risky one—even though there is no risk premium to compensate them for the expected risk. In this second choice situation, individuals tend to be risk seekers, not risk averters, as in the first choice.

Economists generally would have ruled this possibility out entirely because agents would have been assumed to be risk averse in levels of wealth, and this risk aversion would apply regardless of the reference point. In contrast, what this example demonstrates is that individuals may be risk averse when considering gains but risk seeking when considering losses.

THE S-CURVE

Consider another choice between two lotteries:

- Get $900 for sure, or
- Have a 90 percent chance of getting $1,000.

Now consider this alternative set of choices:

- Lose $900 for sure, or
- Have a 90 percent chance of losing $1,000.[2]

---

[2] Kahneman, 280.

In the first choice set, the expected value of each option is $900. Since the latter option carries more risk, a risk-averse individual would choose the first option, while a risk-loving individual would choose the second. In the latter choice set, both options have an expected value of –$900 (i.e., losing $900). The second option carries more risk, and hence would be chosen only by a risk-loving person, whereas a risk-averse individual would choose the first option.[3]

In practice, most individuals choose the first option in the first choice set as expected. However, most choose the second option in the second choice set. In other words, when facing potential losses, individuals become risk loving rather than risk averse. This occurrence is irrespective of their initial levels of wealth—all that matters is that they take their current levels of wealth as their reference points and face losses from there.

This behavior is not particular to this example; it is typical of the way people make choices when facing potential losses, which is fundamentally different than the way people make choices when facing potential gains. Figure 9.1 summarizes this phenomenon graphically.

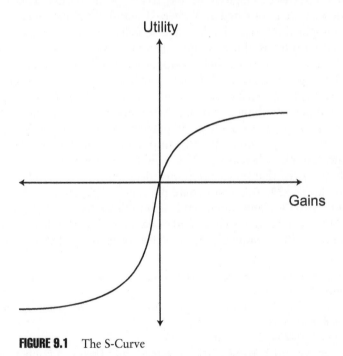

FIGURE 9.1   The S-Curve

---

[3] See Chapter 8 for a more detailed discussion of risk aversion.

For gains, an individual's utility function is concave,[4] representing his or her risk aversion. Conversely, for losses, the utility function is convex, representing risk-loving behavior.[5]

But there is more to the graph in Figure 9.1 than that observation.

LOSS AVERSION

The segment of the curve representing losses is steeper than that representing gains. This reflects the fact that for the representative individual, losses hurt much more than commensurate gains help.

As an example, consider choosing whether to take a gamble in which you have a 50 percent chance of getting $150 and a 50 percent chance of losing $100. Despite the positive expected value, most people find this lottery unappealing because the psychological cost of losing $100 is greater than the psychological gain of earning $150. This phenomenon is called *loss aversion*.[6] In the previous example, some may need a potential gain of $200 or so, or about twice as high as the loss, to accept the gamble. This loss aversion ratio has been estimated at between 1.5 and 2.5 in practice.

One might think that this loss-averse behavior could be explained by traditional wealth-based utility functions. However, in a now-famous theorem by Matthew Rabin,[7] such attempts yield ludicrous implications for human behavior in the face of other gambles. For example, Rabin shows that any individual with a concave utility function in wealth that rejects the gamble "50 percent chance of losing $100 and 50 percent chance of gaining $200" also rejects the gamble "50 percent chance of losing $200 and 50 percent chance of winning $20,000." In practice, many people might reject the former gamble, whereas very few would reject the latter.

Rabin showed that under traditional decision theory, an individual with initial wealth of $290,000 who would reject a 50/50[8] gamble of losing $100 or gaining $110 for any initial level of wealth under $300,000 must also reject a 50/50 gamble of losing $1,000 or gaining $718,190. Finally, one who would reject a 50/50 gamble of losing $100 or gaining $125 for any initial

---

[4] Concave means the second derivative is negative, as shown in the portion of the curve above the gains axis.

[5] Convex means the second derivative is positive, as depicted in the segment of the curve below gains axis.

[6] Kahneman, 283–284.

[7] Matthew Rabin, "Risk Aversion and Expected-Utility Theory: A Calibration Theorem," *Econometrica* 68 , no. 5 (September 2000):1281–1292.

[8] 50/50 means there is a 50 percent chance of each alternative outcome occurring.

level of wealth must also reject a 50/50 gamble of losing $600 or gaining any positive amount of money, regardless of how large the potential gain is.[9]

It is not likely that these implications would hold up in practice. One could envision an individual rejecting a 50/50 gamble of winning $100 or losing $110, but it is hard to envision someone rejecting a 50/50 gamble of losing $600 or winning $10 million.

Loss aversion has an important implication for utility theory—specifically, that decisions in the face of uncertainty are *path dependent*. If an individual gains $500 and then loses $500, traditional wealth-based utility theory would predict that there was no change in the individual's happiness after both transactions took place. However, under prospect theory,[10] if there were enough time between the two transactions that the individual reset her reference point to the wealth level after the gain, she would feel an overall loss in happiness over the two transactions. Initially, she feels a benefit from the gain, but under loss aversion, the disutility she feels from the subsequent loss outweighs that benefit so that the net change is negative.

This feature of prospect theory has important consequences for utility theory. When looking at the decisions an individual makes over time, traditional wealth-based utility theory looks at the net change in wealth over the course of all decisions to assess the overall impact on utility. Under prospect theory, one must look at each of the movements in wealth in turn because the path one takes to get from initial wealth to ending wealth impacts the overall change in happiness.

This path dependence complicates the task of examining human behavior when facing various choice decisions. An econometrician who wishes to model the behavior of agents under prospect theory needs to acquire a data set complete with every decision the agent makes over time as well as the outcome of each such decision. In the case of modeling stock-trading behavior, this data set would not only need the outcome of each trade executed, but also the paper gains or losses at each time when the trader checked his or her portfolio, and the econometrician would need to approximate the trader's thoughts on the distribution of possible returns at each time the portfolio is checked as well. This is a rather onerous task, unnecessary for applications that rely on traditional utility theory, which would require data only on trades that were executed or possibly even just on the beginning and ending portfolio contents and values. Acquiring end-of-period data is a significantly easier task than acquiring much

---

[9] Rabin, 1284–1285.

[10] Prospect theory was introduced by Daniel Kahneman and Amos Tversky in 1979. Prospect theory is an attempt to formalize a utility function approach that captures the concept of loss aversion. Daniel Kahneman and Amos Tversky, "Prospect Theory: An Analysis of Decision Under Risk," *Econometrica*, 47(1979): 263–291.

of the data within periods and part of the reason why traditional utility theory
has remained a much more attractive modeling technique for finance theory.

PROSPECT THEORY IN PRACTICE

Prospect theory has been tested in a variety of experimental settings, even
in contexts outside of finance. List[11] looked at the behavior of individuals
in a well-functioning marketplace and found that newcomers to the marketplace behaved in better accordance with prospect theory than with traditional utility models. Bleichrodt and colleagues[12] examine the behavior of
individuals when the payoffs are in states of health rather than in monetary
amounts and also finds that prospect theory explained the agents' behavior
better than traditional expected utility theory did. Similar implications have
been found outside of the experimental setting.

The implications of prospect theory for finance are profound. If investors consider paper gains and losses each time they check their portfolios,
then not only will loss aversion tend to drive their choices, but the frequency
with which they check their portfolios will greatly affect the decisions they
make as well. How frequently one checks one's portfolio will lead to different levels of utility and to different investment decisions. Such behavior
could account for a significant premium in markets with more active investors despite any risk factors for which such a premium should be rewarded.[13]

DRAWBACKS OF PROSPECT THEORY

Despite the benefits of prospect theory in modeling how humans make
decisions, the theory is not complete. There are many aspects of human
behavior that are inconsistent with the implications of prospect theory.
Consider the following prospects:

- A one in a thousand chance to win $1 million.
- A 90 percent chance to win $10 and a 10 percent chance to win nothing.
- A 90 percent chance to win $1 million and a 10 percent chance to win
  nothing.

---

[11] John A. List, "Neoclassical Theory Versus Prospect Theory: Evidence from the
Marketplace," *Econometrica* 72, no. 2 (2004): 615–625.
[12] H. Bleichrodt, J. M. Abellan, J. L. Pinto, and I. Mendez, "Resolving Inconsistencies
in Utility Measurement under Risk: Tests of Generalizations of Expected Utility,"
Management Science 53(2007): 469–482.
[13] See Chapter 18 for a broader discussion of this in the context of the equity
premium puzzle.

The possibility of winning nothing exists in each choice, but it would be difficult to argue the impact of winning nothing would be the same in each case. In the first case, winning nothing is the expected outcome. In the second, it's not expected, but it would not be too harmful a result, since the individual only missed out on winning $10. However, in the last case, winning nothing would be devastating to most, since the alternative involved winning a large sum and the chances of its happening were so great the individual was probably already planning what he or she would do with the money.

In other words, prospect theory does not deal with the effect of disappointment. Winning nothing is not that disappointing when the alternative involves a modest sum, but it is extremely disappointing when one expects to win a much larger amount. Realizing you are not going to have a job on Monday is not that painful when you have been unemployed for a while, but it is much more painful when you lost your job on the previous Friday.[14]

To see a second drawback of prospect theory, consider the following gamble choice:

- A 90 percent chance to win $1 million and a 10 percent chance to win nothing, or
- Receiving $10 with certainty

versus this one:

- A 90 percent chance to win $1 million and a 10 percent chance to win nothing, or
- Receiving $100,000 with certainty,

and consider how one would feel after choosing the gamble and receiving nothing in each case. Most people would think receiving nothing would be much more painful in the latter case than in the former, but prospect theory is incapable of assigning a different value to receiving nothing in the two cases. That is, it cannot account for regret. Receiving nothing in the latter case is so painful because one is faced with the reality that he or she could have received a large sum; in the former case, the alternative was not much better than receiving nothing anyway. It is this regret that drives the increased negative value associated with receiving nothing in the second case versus the first.[15]

---

[14]Kahneman, 287.

[15] Ibid.

CONCLUSION

Traditional wealth-based utility theory falls short in a number of areas, such as the Allais Paradox pointed out in Chapter 8, as well as the even more foundational assumption that individuals make decisions based on prospective levels of wealth. A more realistic assumption is that each person makes decisions based on gains and losses from a given starting point, and that after these gains and losses are realized, he or she resets the reference point to the current situation. That people make decisions based on the prospects available to them from a given starting point underlies the dynamics of prospect theory.

A more detailed analysis of how humans behave reveals that they also exhibit loss aversion—that is, they feel a larger pain from losses than they realize a benefit from commensurate gains. An implication of this is that utility outcomes are path dependent. Traditional utility theory implies that a trader that starts out with a wealth of $1,000, makes five trades, and ends with a wealth of $1,500 has a particular known level of happiness at the end. However, under prospect theory, one cannot know his or her ending utility without knowing the outcomes of each trade and hence the path that the portfolio value took along the way. This model of human behavior corresponds more closely to observation, but it also complicates the business of analyzing such behavior in practice.

Prospect theory formalizes the decision process in a way that corresponds more closely to how people behave than the utility approach of traditional economics. There are limitations, however, to the use of prospect theory. The biggest single limitation is its inability to provide insight into general asset pricing theory. Prospect theory has a distinctly dynamic flavor to it because of its implicit path dependence. No one has yet constructed a satisfactory asset pricing theory based on prospect theory utility functions. Other problems with prospect theory have been emphasized by Kahneman and referenced in this chapter. The failure to deal with the emotions of disappointment and regret are major limitations of prospect theory's descriptive power.

For whatever weaknesses there may be with prospect theory, it is unquestionably a step forward in our ability to generalize actual human decision-making and provides a convenient formalization of loss aversion as well.

CHAPTER 10

Perception Biases

A perception bias arises when an individual has difficulty figuring out what the problem is that needs to be solved. Perception biases come in many forms. We look at several perception biases in this chapter, including saliency, framing, anchoring, and sunk-cost biases. All four of these biases have been extensively studied by Kahneman and Tversky and others and are well established. While the four perception biases that we discuss in this chapter do not exhaust the list of perception biases, these four appear to be the most important.

SALIENCY

When we have not encountered something recently, we have a tendency to ignore that thing even if it is important to an upcoming decision. No one seems interested in buying flood insurance unless there has been a recent flood. Airplane accident insurance is almost never purchased except in airports just prior to boarding a flight, though it is available to be purchased from the moment travel plans are made. When the economy has been strong and vigorous for a long time, fears of an economic slowdown recede almost to the point of being completely ignored.

Saliency works in two ways. If an event has not occurred recently, then that event tends to be perceived as having zero or negligible probability of occurring in the future. However, if the same event has occurred very recently, the perceived probability of a future occurrence becomes overstated. A dramatic example of saliency seems to take place when financial crises occur. During an economic boom, people forget that crashes can occur and underweight their likelihood of occurrence.

Gennaioli, Shleifer, and Vishny (GSV) have constructed a theory of financial intermediation[1] based upon the idea that the occurrence of "bad" economic states seems to be perceived as almost impossible when the economy is strong and the demand for credit is high. This theory then uses an overweight of the probability of the "bad" economic state once the crisis has passed. Shleifer's theory formalizes the idea that credit standards for commercial lending seem to decline dramatically during periods of economic prosperity and then during economic recovery credit standards are tightened up to extreme levels. The opposite pattern would be more favorable to the economy, but saliency drives policy makers and market participants to incorrectly perceive the true environment in which they are operating.

The authors state their formalization of saliency in their model in the following way:

> [W]e assume that both investors and financial intermediaries do not attend to certain improbable risks when trading new securities. This assumption captures what we take to be the central feature of the historical episodes we describe: the neglect of potentially huge defaults in the housing bubble and of the sensitivity of AAA-rated securities to these defaults, the neglect of the possibility of massive prepayments in the early 1990s, or the neglect of the possibility that a money market fund can break the buck.[2]

GSV describes this as "formalization of the notion that not all contingencies are represented in the decision maker's thought process."[3]

The authors find that their model fits the financial crisis well and that attempts to account for the crisis without incorporating this element of surprise into their model significantly hinder its accuracy. They also address other research efforts that attempt to model the financial crisis. Much of this research models the crisis as an extremely low probability event that agents do rationally incorporate into their decision making. GSV find that these models do not fit the financial crisis as well as a model incorporating saliency. They conclude that the agents involved in the crisis used incorrect investment models that assigned a zero probability to a potential financial crisis. A correct model would assign a very low, yet nonzero, probability to the chances of a prospective financial collapse.

---

[1] Nicola Gennaioli, Andrei Shleifer, and Robert Vishny, "Neglected Risks, Financial Innovation and Financial Fragility," *Journal of Financial Economics* 104(2012); 452–468.

[2] Ibid., 453.

[3] Ibid., 453.

FRAMING

The correct answer to a question should not depend on how the question is phrased. Unless the alternative way of asking a question is truly different, the answer should be independent of phrasing, or *framing*, as it has come to be known in the behavioral finance literature. The simplest setting for framing is the consideration of alternative policies that involve an unavoidable loss of life. Kahneman and Tversky pose the following example.[4]

Problem 1

Imagine that the country is preparing for the outbreak of an unusual disease, which is expected to kill 600 people. Which of the following programs would you favor?

Program A: Has the effect of saving 200 people.

Program B: Has a 1/3 chance of saving 600 people and a 2/3 chance that no one will be saved.

Most people will choose Program A when given the choice. This is the risk-averse choice since 200 people are saved for certain as compared to the risky option in which 200 people are saved on average but it is possible that no one is saved.

Now consider the same problem phrased slightly differently.

Problem 2

Program C: 400 people will die for certain.

Program D: 1/3 chance that no one will die and 2/3 chance that 600 people will die.

In Problem 2, most respondents, when offered the choice, will opt for Program D. Program D is riskier than Program C, so risk-preferring behavior characterizes those who choose Program D over Program C.

---

[4]Daniel Kahneman and Amos Tversky, "Choices, Values, and Frames," reprinted from *American Psychologist* 39, no. 2(1984). In Daniel Kahneman and Amos Tversky, *Choices, Values and Frames* (Cambridge, UK: Cambridge University Press, 2000). The example of Problems 1 and 2 are taken, in slightly altered form, from this publication.

Note that Programs A and C are identical and that Programs B and D are identical. So why are over 70 percent of respondents choosing A over B and nearly 80 percent of respondents choosing D over C? The choices are inconsistent. Kahneman and Tversky use the expression *invariance* to capture the idea that the same answer should be given to questions that vary only in phrasing but are substantively identical. Here, there seems to be a clear violation of invariance. "The failure of invariance is both pervasive and robust. It is as common among sophisticated respondents as among naïve ones, and it is not eliminated even when the same respondents answer both questions within a few minutes."[5]

What seems to drive this particular example is the reference point.[6] Problem 1 is written in the context of saving lives, while Problem 2 is written from the viewpoint of people dying. Respondents consider saving zero people the reference point in the former and zero people dying the reference point in the latter. The outcome choices are of course the same in both problems, just written from a different standpoint. But that different standpoint motivates people to make different decisions.

In Problem 1, respondents think of each person they save as a gain, and therefore make the risk-averse choice—saving 200 people for sure is more palatable than taking the chance that everyone might die. In Problem 2, respondents think of each person that dies as a loss, so they make the risk-loving choice. Sending 400 people to their deaths seems rather Draconian when the other option presents a reasonable chance that all might live.

Kahneman and Tversky[7] also provide a simple choice among lotteries that verified the failure of invariance in settings that most directly apply to finance.

Problem 3

Program E: 25 percent chance to win $240 and 75 percent chance to lose $760.

Program F: 25 percent chance to win $250 and 75 percent chance to lose $750.

---

[5] Kahneman and Tversky, 5.
[6] See Chapter 9 for a broader discussion on the effect of reference points on utility theory.
[7] Kahneman and Tversky, 6.

In Problem 3, virtually everyone will choose F over E since F dominates E.[8] The rational and proper choice is F. Now consider the following problem, Problem 4.

Problem 4

Imagine that you face the following pair of concurrent decisions. First, examine both decisions, then indicate the options you prefer.

Decision (i)—choose between:

A. A sure gain of $240.
B. 25 percent chance to gain $1,000 and 75 percent chance to gain nothing.

Decision (ii)—choose between:

C. A sure loss of $750.
D. 75 percent chance to lose $1,000 and 25 percent chance to lose nothing.

In Problem 4, 73 percent of respondents in Kahneman and Tversky's experiments chose A and D, while only 3 percent chose B and C. But B and C together equate to F from Problem 3, and A and D together are nothing more than E. Therefore, more than 70 percent of respondents are effectively choosing E over F. What is happening in this example is that identical options are presented to respondents and their choices will differ depending on the framing that surrounds the choices, even though the actual content of the choices presented is identical.

What framing is doing is exploiting our attitude toward bad events. In the first example, respondents do not wish to do harm. Therefore, when the choice is between saving people and rolling the dice, respondents want to save people. But when the identical choice set is presented and framed as if the respondent is choosing that 400 people will die with certainty, respondents go for the choice that presents the possibility of saving everyone, even though all 600 might die. Perception is the key.

In the monetary lotteries of Problem 3, the choice of F is obvious for almost all respondents. In Problem 4, C is where the real difficulty lies for most respondents who fail to choose the dominant B-C combination. C is a sure loss of $750 against D, which provides a way of avoiding the loss. Similarly, A is attractive because you are certain to win and avoid the possible loss entailed in choice B. Framing is taking advantage of loss aversion in

---

[8] Dominance is implied since the probabilities are identical but the payoffs are better in F than in E.

Problems 3 and 4. Most respondents choose A, expressing risk aversion, and D expressing risk seeking. Such choices are routine to loss aversion. What makes Problems 3 and 4 striking is that the choice combination in 4 seems unpalatable once it is reframed as Problem 3.

ANCHORING

Anchoring is a perception bias that arises when you are attempting to make a guess at something about which you have limited information. An *anchor* biases your guess in the direction of the anchor. A famous example of anchoring comes from attempting to guess the number of jellybeans in a jar. Staring at the jar, it would be difficult to imagine how to even begin to guess the number of jellybeans that can be stored in a jar. But imagine that just before you attempted to guess the number of jellybeans in a jar someone says: "Wow, there are a 1,000 stars in the sky!" Would that influence your guess? Would your guess be closer to 1,000 after such a comment was made? Suppose the comment were made, instead: "Wow, there are 10,000 stars in the sky!" Would your guess be significantly larger than if the anchor was 1,000?

Experiments using a single jar of jellybeans have been conducted numerous times using separated classrooms of responders. Very different estimates arise from the respondents in each room, and the average estimate for each room is biased in the direction of the anchor that applied to that room.[9]

A similar bias can occur in the context of historical guesses. Suppose one plans to ask what century Galileo lived in, but just before posing the question about Galileo, one says: "Columbus discovered America in 1492." If one compares respondent guesses when 1492 is the anchor to a different anchor such as: "The Magna Carta was signed in 1215," the group that hears 1492 will place Galileo closer to the end of the fifteenth century than the latter group, who will place Galileo's life much closer to the beginning of the thirteenth century.[10]

Anchoring can be characterized as an example of lazy thinking, but there is a possible reason for such lazy thinking. Often, limited observations can provide a reasonable basis for an estimate. One of the more famous

---

[9] For similar examples, see Paul Slovic, Baruch Fischolff, and Sarah Lichtenstein, "Facts versus Fears: Understanding Perceived Risk," reprinted in Daniel Kahneman, Paul Slovic, and Amos Tversky, eds., *Judgment under Uncertainty: Heuristics and Biases* (Cambridge, UK: Cambridge University Press, 1982).

[10] Galileo was born in 1564 and died in 1642.

examples of this is the Secretary Problem. Generally, this describes any situation where:

- There are n objects (prizes) drawn in succession.
- If all are seen together, they can be ranked from best to worst unambiguously.
- The order in which they are actually seen is random.
- Immediately after seeing each object, you must reject or accept the object most recently seen, and the decision is irreversible.
- The only information you have on the objects is the value of each object you've seen so far.
- The objective is to maximize the probability with which you select the best object.

Consider a situation where there are 10 monetary prizes available and you get to observe each prize, one by one. As you select one of the prizes and learn how much money there is, you are given a choice: You may take the money and then the game ends, or you can reject it, in which case that prize is discarded and you move on to the next prize. Once you get to the last prize, you must, of course, accept it as there are no other remaining prizes left to examine.

In this 10-prize situation, what is your best strategy? Remember that the only information you have are the prize values you have seen. Any arbitrary amount of money can be contained in each of the 10 prizes. Clearly, you need to gain some information—the question is how much information should you gain before making a selection. After all, each prize that you discard means that you can no longer have that prize, which may have been the largest of all the prizes.

This is a classic optimization problem and the optimal strategy is to select the first three prizes, observe the dollar amounts of each prize, and then discard each of them regardless of their values. Then consider the fourth prize. If its value is greater than what was observed in the each of the first three prizes, accept that prize and the game is over. If not, reject it and continue until you do find a prize of an amount greater than any of the first three. There is the possibility that one of the first three is the largest prize, in which case you will end up gaining the last of the 10 prizes selected, regardless of its dollar value.

Note that in some sense you are anchoring your ultimate choice by examining the first three prizes. In this process, you have constructed a "rational" anchor. It just might be that experience with rationally selecting anchors in the manner of this 10-prize example provides the backdrop for the effectiveness of seemingly irrelevant anchors in the biasing of estimates.

Irrelevant anchors are latched on to in the absence of any other information. This might be harmless if the irrelevant anchor itself is unbiased noise. But if the anchor is provided intentionally such as in a purchase-and-sale situation, the perception bias triggered by anchoring can lead to biased behavior that may be in the interest of the person providing the anchor.

SUNK-COST BIAS

Imagine that you paid $200 for a nonrefundable, nontransferable ticket to see a great country-and-western singer—your favorite—perform next Thursday. But when Thursday rolls around, you no longer want to go. You've decided you don't like that singer after all. You try to give away your ticket or sell it, to no avail. So do you go to the performance, even though you no longer think that you would enjoy it? Traditional economics says that a rational person will choose not to go to the performance. You might feel bad if you don't go to the performance because you will regret having wasted $200, but feelings of regret are not part of the makeup of the rational person typically assumed by economists. Utility is derived from consumption, not from wistful looks back about things you wish that you had done or not done. Feelings of regret play no role whatsoever in traditional economic analysis.

An economist normally argues that paying for something and then using it are two entirely separate decisions. The decision to pay for a ticket to attend a future event is based on expectations about the utility of that future event. Having paid for the ticket, once the future event arrives, you must make a new decision—should you attend or not? What you paid for the ticket earlier should be irrelevant, economists argue, to the decision to attend. The ticket is viewed as a *sunk cost* that is an entirely separate event from the attendance at the concert for which the ticket was purchased.

Classifying sunk costs as a perception bias is questionable. The sunk-costs bias involves something left out of the utility function, which most of us know probably does affect decisions—regret. People feel regret for things done and not done. But such things are in the past, and since they cannot be changed, they should not influence a current choice. Does having bought a ticket in the past make today's attendance at a concert more pleasurable? Not likely. But wasting the ticket one has paid for makes one regret a past decision. That regret can be avoided by going to the concert, even if you would rather not. If you had not bought a ticket and someone offered you a free one, you would likely say no. But, having paid, you wish to avoid the feeling of regret, and so you go. To an economist those two situations are identical and you should make the same decision in each.

A slight variation of the sunk-cost bias is the situation that arises if you lose your $200 ticket on the way to the concert and are faced with having to purchase or not purchase another ticket. Suppose in this case you really do want to attend the concert. If, along the way to the concert, you had lost $200, rather than the ticket that you purchased for $200, you might react differently about these two situations. Where money is lost, you might not associate the lost money with the concert and therefore you might be more likely to pay $200 for a ticket than if you had recently lost a ticket to the concert of exactly the same value. This example is usually classified as an example of mental accounting, but sunk costs are involved regardless of the classification.

Because sunk costs involve regret, the bias that results is similar to the bias an investor shows when reluctant to purchase a stock after missing the opportunity to buy the stock at a cheaper price. Investors who "go to cash" in the midst of a financial crisis are sometimes disappointed that, after they sell out, stocks rally to higher prices. Will they get back in? Often, the answer is no. The investor will wait and hope that stocks fall back to the levels at which they had made their earlier exit. What if that never happens? Then investors may wait until the regret they feel from not getting back in goes away. Once the feeling of regret is no longer present simply because of the passage of time, the investor might invest again, often at much higher prices.

CONCLUSION

Perception biases run counter to the normal utility maximization paradigm that permeates economic and finance theory. Emotions, to the extent they matter in traditional economics and finance, have their impact on the utility function, which is presumed to be a function only of expected consumption or expected net worth, where net worth is obviously a proxy for future consumption. But in real life, psychologists have found that emotions do play a role in how problems and the impact of choices are perceived. Those perceptions can be altered even when the plain substance of the problems or choices are unchanged. If a car is described as pink in color and later as rose in color, but the color has not changed, has the car changed? To the observer, it might be a different car, and that is the rub, if physically nothing has been altered.

Feelings of regret are real enough for most people and clearly affect choices that people make, but how can we take account of feelings of regret in economic or finance theory? If you choose X when Y was available, and Y turns out to be the better choice, do you feel a pang of regret? Where is that in the standard treatment of utility maximization? It is not easy to brush regret aside as of little importance when it influences investor behavior in important ways such as looking back and wishing it weren't so or worrying that if I do this, I might live to regret it. Major financial decisions seem potentially affected by feelings of regret. None of this bodes well for the efficient market hypothesis.

CHAPTER 11

Inertial Effects

Imagine two identical people making a choice between two options, option A and option B. The only difference between the two people is that the first starts at A and is asked whether or not he or she would like to move to B, whereas the second starts at B and is offered the ability to move to A.

It might be surprising to find that the majority of the time, individuals in these situations tend to stay where they start, regardless of the context around the decision choice or with which option they began. Experiments show that individuals tend to stick with the status quo, and that tendency persists across a variety of scenarios and in a variety of contexts. In this chapter, we explore the research that investigates such phenomena as well as the consequences of the outcomes such behavior elicits.

ENDOWMENT EFFECT

In *The Winner's Curse*, Richard Thaler tells the story of a wine-loving economist.[1] As the story goes, this particular oenophile purchased several bottles of exquisite Bordeaux wine at auction years ago at extremely low prices, $10 per bottle. The wine has since appreciated significantly in value, and now routinely sells for $200 per bottle at auction.

The economist enjoys one bottle from his collection each year. One day, the economist finds himself conversing with a student who shares his affinity for wine. The student asks why the professor does not purchase more of his beloved wine at auction, and the professor replies that the prices have grown too high for his liking. The student then asks if he could possibly buy a bottle from the professor's inventory at the auction price of $200, to which the professor replies that he cannot sell any from his stash—the bottles are simply worth too much to him.

---

[1] Richard Thaler, *The Winner's Curse: Paradoxes and Anomalies of Economic Life* (New York: Free Press, 1992), 63.

This example probably does not sound that surprising. However, the example flies directly in the face of traditional economic theory. In traditional economic theory, an individual must have a specific reservation price for a given good, such that he or she would be willing to sell some positive amount of the good for any price greater than the reservation price and buy some positive amount for any lesser price. If someone is not willing to sell a unit of a good for p_1 and is also not willing to buy one unit for p_2, with $p_2 < p_1$, according to traditional economic theory, that person would be acting irrationally.

One might argue that this is simply a question of sentimental value, but similar results have been observed in a number of experiments that eliminate such an effect. Kahneman, Knetsch, and Thaler[2] ran one experiment in which half the participants, chosen at random, were each endowed with a coffee mug (the "sellers") and the other half with nothing (the "buyers"). Each seller was asked to list his or her reservation price to sell the mug and each buyer to list his or her reservation price to buy the mug. Economic theory would predict the average selling price and buying price to be the same, but this was not the case—in fact, the average selling price was approximately twice as large as the average buying price.

In a further instantiation of the same experiment, a third group was included, called "choosers," who could receive either a mug or a sum of money. Individuals in this group were asked to list the amount of money that was as desirable as receiving the good. The reservation prices were as follows:

Buyers	$2.87
Choosers	$3.12
Sellers	$7.12

Sellers listed a reservation price approximately twice as high as both buyers and choosers. The contrast between sellers and choosers is striking, since both faced the choice of either having a mug or a commensurate amount of money—the only difference is whether they were given the mug at the outset or not. The results clearly show that the simple effect of owning the mug in the beginning nearly doubles the reservation price.

---

[2]Daniel Kahneman, Jack L. Knetsch, and Richard H. Thaler, "Experimental Tests of the Endowment Effect and the Coase Theorem," *Journal of Political Economy* 98, no. 6 (1990): 1325–1348.

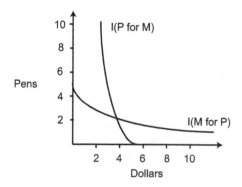

FIGURE 11.1   Crossing Indifference Curves

Jack Knetsch, one of the researchers from these experiments, performed a similar study[3] in which participants were chosen at random to receive either $4.50 or five ballpoint pens, and then were asked to accept or reject a series of offers that were designed to elicit their preferences for varying allotments of money and pens. From this data, Knetsch calculated indifference curves, or lines in two-dimensional space that represent allotments of the two goods (each corresponding to one of the two dimensions) such that the consumer is perfectly indifferent across those allotments.

Knetsch's results are displayed in Figure 11.1. The nearly vertical line represents the average indifference curve for those who were initially endowed with money. These individuals needed a lot of pens to compensate for the loss of a dollar. The nearly horizontal line represents the average indifference curve for those who started with pens—they required a lot of money to give up even a single pen.

The indifference curves on this graph violate one of the basic laws of traditional economics—namely, that indifference curves can never cross. Crossing indifference curves are ruled out by the definition of the indifference curve itself. An indifference curve is the collection of all bundles that a consumer prizes equally. If two separate indifference curves cross, the consumer must be indifferent between all bundles on each curve and the crossing point between the curves—but then it must be the case that he is indifferent between any bundle on either curve and any bundle on the other curve. This is a contradiction, since each curve was supposed to represent an exhaustive collection of bundles of indifference in the first place.

---

[3] Jack L. Knetsch, "Preferences and Non-Reversibility of Indifference Curves," *Journal of Economic Behavior & Organization* 17, no. 1 (1992): 131–139.

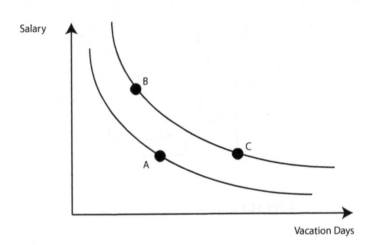

FIGURE 11.2

At the heart of the disruption lies the underlying assumption that an individual must be indifferent across the same exhaustive set of bundles regardless of his or her starting point. Traditional economic theory assumes the value an individual places on a bundle is unaffected by what he or she is endowed with to start; behavioral finance shows that, in practice, this need not be the case.

Consider two identical individuals with the indifference curves for salary and vacation days shown in Figure 11.2.[4] Both start at position A in the graph. Each receives an offer to get either an extra $10,000 in salary per year, ending in position B, or an extra 12 vacation days per year, ending in position C. As they are both indifferent between the two outcomes, they each flip a coin, and one takes the extra money while the other takes the extra vacation.

Some time passes and then their employers allow them to reconsider their decisions. Standard economic theory states that the starting point is irrelevant, and that both individuals should still find the two options equivalent and hence still be indifferent. However, from the point of view of the first individual, the choice is between:

- Stay at Position B: Incur no gain or loss.
- Move to Position C: Receive an extra 12 vacation days but lose $10,000.

[4] Daniel Kahneman, *Thinking, Fast and Slow* (New York: Farrar, Straus and Giroux, 2011), 289–291.

The second individual sees the choice as:

- Stay at Position C: Incur no gain or loss.
- Move to Position B: Receive an extra $10,000 but lose 12 vacation days.

It is not difficult to imagine that one might stay in his or her current position in both situations; in fact, it would be surprising if this were not the case. However, traditional economic theory would say that anyone in this situation should be indifferent between the choices regardless of the status quo.

Examples such as these show that indifference curves are not *reversible*—moving to another point and then back does not necessarily represent a net zero change in happiness. A movement from A to B along an indifference curve changes the indifference curve itself because the reference point changes.

Prospect theory[5] provides an explanation for this irreversibility. Regardless of the position each individual starts from, he faces a choice between a loss along one dimension plus a gain along the second and no movement at all. Since each was indifferent between the two points when starting at point A, the gain along one dimension is the same as the loss along the other. However, from prospect theory, a loss of a given size looms larger than a commensurate gain, so from a utility perspective, each individual sees the move as a net loss. Since the alternative involves no movement at all and therefore no change in happiness, neither individual will move, and both will remain at their current allocation.

The magnitude of the discrepancy in the coffee mug experiment is consistent with the results of prospect theory research—the average seller's reservation price was approximately twice as large as the average buyer's, the same two-to-one ratio that individuals exhibit when asked a question like, "How high would x have to be in order for you to accept a gamble of the following form: 50 percent chance of losing $100 and 50 percent chance of gaining x?" fMRIs[6] taken during the mug transactions have indicated that selling goods that have another use activated areas of the brain normally associated with disgust and pain, as did buying mugs at prices perceived to be too high, whereas buying mugs at low prices activated pleasure centers instead.[7]

---

[5] For a more extensive discussion of prospect theory, see Chapter 9.

[6] fMRIs (functional magnetic resonance imaging) are brain-wave measures used in neuroeconomics, a topic discussed in Chapter 20 (although fMRIs are not discussed there).

[7] Kahneman, 296.

The endowment effect does a better job of predicting human behavior than traditional economic theory, but it is worth noting that there are circumstances in which people do not succumb to this effect. This was shown as early as 1976, in a famous study by Vernon Smith.[8] Smith dispersed tokens, which had no alternative use outside of the experiment, as well as differing redemption values for the tokens themselves, to the various participants at random. Hence, a token may have been worth $1 to one participant and $3 to another. The participants were then allowed to publicly announce offers to buy or sell tokens which could be accepted or rejected publicly by the other participants. The results went as predicted by economic theory—the tokens ended up in the hands of those with the highest redemption values for them[9] and the market prices ended up as predicted by economic theory as well.

Similar results occur in more commonplace scenarios, such as when one changes a large bill for smaller ones or buys a product from a retail merchant in exchange for cash. Kahneman provides an explanation for such results. In such transactions, as in the token experiment by Smith, the item at hand serves as a placeholder for the other item in the exchange that will be received at a future point in time. When a lamp merchant trades a lamp for $20, the merchant feels no endowment effect from the lamp itself; mentally, the lamp served simply as a placeholder for the $20 that would be received for it in the future. Similarly, in the token experiment, the participants saw the tokens solely as a means to a monetary end; that the tokens had no alternative use outside of the experiment is key to the results. Along a similar vein, many of the results of experiments where the endowment effect does occur disappear when the participants are simply instructed to "think like traders" as they are making their decisions. Ironically, traders often do not think like traders themselves, as will be seen later in this chapter in the discussion of the disposition effect.[10]

STATUS QUO EFFECT

A similar result occurs when individuals are asked to choose among several options, with one option being the default, defined as the option implicitly

---

[8] Vernon Smith, "Experimental Economics: Induced Value Theory," *American Economic Review* 66, no. 2 (1976): 274–279.

[9] This is an example of the Coase Theorem, which states (in part) that, absent transaction costs and barriers to trade, resources will end up in the hands of those that place the highest value on them.

[10] Kahneman, 294.

chosen if no action is taken at all. In such situations, standard economic theory predicts that individuals should make the same choice regardless of which option is selected as the default. Experiments, however, show that individuals are influenced by which option is presented as the default one. The tendency to stick with the default option is known in the literature as the *status quo bias*.

Many experiments have demonstrated and explored this bias. Samuelson and Zeckhauser[11] asked a group of participants a series of questions phrased one of two ways, one providing a clear status quo default option and another providing no default option. For example, one question involved a decision about what to do with a significant sum of money that had been inherited. Two versions of the question appeared. Both listed investing in Company A as the first possibility. However, one version prefaced the explanation with the quote "A significant portion of this portfolio is invested in moderate-risk Company A." Samuelson and Zeckhauser found that a significantly higher percentage of individuals choose to invest in company A when it was listed as the status quo than would otherwise. Other research has consistently found the same effect.

Thaler and Sunstein have suggested that governments take advantage of such a phenomenon in the course of making policy decisions.[12] They argue for a school of thought they term *libertarian paternalism*.[13] They define this as a central body giving several options to its constituents with the one that it deems the best for the greatest percentage of people as the default (this is the *paternalism* part), while still giving individuals the right to opt out of the default and into another choice if they deem it appropriate for themselves (the *libertarian* part). At the heart of this philosophy lies the idea that people will tend to stick with the defaults except when they find them significantly unpalatable and that then and only then will they make a change. The government is able to nudge individuals in one direction or another without giving them a hard shove.

This might seem surprising as a regulatory philosophy, but such a strategy has been observed in practice. One example comes from the state of Virginia's Retirement System, or VRS for short. In 1997, the VRS set up a new benefit program for employees covered under the state's public employee retirement system called the "cash match" benefit program. Under

---

[11] William Samuelson and Richard Zeckhauser, "Status Quo Bias in Decision Making," *Journal of Risk and Uncertainty* 1, no. 1 (1988): 7–59.
[12] Richard Thaler and Cass Sunstein, *Nudge: Improving Decisions About Health, Wealth and Happiness* (New York: Penguin, 2008).
[13] See Chapter 19 for additional discussion on libertarian paternalism.

this program, the state matched dollar-for-dollar the contributions of its employees on a pretax basis. For example, if an employee's marginal tax rate is 30 percent, and she contributed $10 to her retirement fund, the state contributed another $10 on her behalf, so she essentially received a $20 contribution for an out-of-pocket cost of $7—a pretty favorable exchange of money now for retirement assets later.

Shockingly, most employees did not take advantage of this deal; in fact, less than 20 percent of new employees joined the program. VRS chalked this up to the status quo effect—that is, not entering the program was the default option, and new employees were loath to change away from it unless they were sure it was better to do so.

So, the VRS Board changed the default option to the maximum cash match option. Sure enough, going forward, 91 percent of new employees took that option. When presented with the options with no action resulting in maximum cash match, only 9 percent of new employees ended up not in the program.

In the same way that it helped explain the endowment effect, prospect theory can help explain the status quo bias as well. Many individuals might consider the default option as their reference point, considering losses and gains from that point in making their decisions. If there is uncertainty around the various options, they might feel that switching could result in a potential gain but could also result in a potential loss from the reference point, and the potential for losses will weigh heavier than the potential benefit from gains due to loss aversion.

Sticking with the default option also helps avoid regret, which prospect theory itself cannot explain.[14] If actively choosing away from the default option terminates in a poor outcome for the individual, it would be hard to argue that they did not make a mistake and hence the feeling of regret would be hard to avoid. However, if they were simply passive and never committed to an option themselves one way or another, it is easier to think that the government or even fate made the choice for them and hence it was not their fault that things went awry.[15] Consequently, these individuals may feel safer sticking with the default choice unless they are relatively certain that moving away from it is the best option.

---

[14] A point that Kahneman sees as an important weakness of prospect theory. See Kahneman, 287–288.

[15] See Chapter 9 for a broader discussion of prospect theory and regret.

DISPOSITION EFFECT

Another effect, closely related to the endowment effect and status quo bias listed earlier as well as the sunk-cost bias discussed in Chapter 10, is the *disposition effect*. Consider the example from the Sunk-Cost Bias section of Chapter 10. You have paid $200 for a ticket to an event you no longer think you will enjoy and have been unable to sell the ticket thus far. Do you attend the event simply because you paid $200 for the right to go? Many people would do just that, even though traditional economic theory would frame this behavior as irrational. In that light, the $200 you paid has been sunk and cannot be recovered, so the only relevant question is whether the event is worth the transportation cost to go and the opportunity cost of the time spent there.

However, most individuals make decisions based on *mental accounting*. In a sense, one has a mental account set up related to this event, and thus far the event has cost $200 on one side of the balance sheet with the corresponding right to attend appearing on the other side. If one were to close the account without going to the event, he or she would be locking in a loss, which is an unpleasant feeling for most people. By attending, the individual could assign some sort of value to the other side of the balance sheet, which is a better feeling—even if the expected value of the event net of transportation and time costs is actually negative.[16]

A similar effect occurs prominently in investing behavior, with important consequences for financial markets. When liquidating investments in order to obtain cash for other uses, investors routinely liquidate stocks that hold paper gains before liquidating stocks that at current prices have lost them money. This is true regardless of the perceived future investment prospects of each stock.

As an example, consider two stocks into each of which an individual had initially invested $10,000, currently facing the following prospects:

- Stock 1 currently has a gain of –$2,000 (i.e., a loss), and going forward has a 50 percent chance of going down $1,000 and a 50 percent chance of going up $2,500.
- Stock 2 currently has a gain of $2,000, and going forward has a 40 percent chance of going down $1,000 and a 60 percent chance of going up $2,500.

The individual needs to close out one position to pay off other debts. Which is he or she more likely to choose? From an investment standpoint,

------

[16] Kahneman, 243.

the current gain or loss is irrelevant—the goal is to maximize the expected return from this point forward, and hence all that matters is the future probability of returns. However, in practice, many close out the winning stock so that they can close that mental account out as a gain, hoping the losing stock will come back up as well, which it has a 50 percent chance of doing, so that they can close that account out as a gain in the future.

This is true despite the tax benefits of closing out losing stocks.[17] The majority of the time, investors close out winners before closing out losers, in every month of the year except one, December, when the tax implications are more on the investors' minds due to saliency.[18] Otherwise, investors are significantly more apt to sell winning stocks than losing ones, even if the winning stocks have better future potential.

Prospect theory provides a clear rationale behind this behavior. The idea of closing out an account and locking in a loss weighs heavily on an investor's mind—so heavy that it often feels better to close out a winner and lock in a gain, even despite the tax benefits, and even if the loser is likely to become an even bigger loser. Losses invoke such a negative emotion that this force outweighs the motivation to invest in such a way as to maximize the expected return.

CONCLUSION

Humans naturally have a tendency to stick with the conditions of their current situations, even in the light of strong motivations to do otherwise. When we are given items that have a potential use to us other than for trade, we place a significantly higher value on these items than we do if we are given currency and asked to buy those items instead. We also have a strong tendency to stick with the default option in a list of options, regardless of which option is labeled as such.

Prospect theory provides an explanation for these behaviors. When we are endowed with an item to start, we adjust our reference point to that particular endowment and feel that giving up the item we were endowed with would entail a loss for us. As prospect theory explains, it would take a higher-than-commensurate gain for us to feel compensated for such a loss due to loss aversion. Similarly, we tend not to move away from a default

---

[17] In the United States, under certain conditions (e.g., the sale is not a wash sale, etc.), investors can write off losses from an investment sale on their tax returns, paying lower taxes overall.

[18] See Chapter 10 for a more extensive discussion of saliency and its effect on behavior.

option, because we think of that option as our reference point, and hence moving away from it carries with it a risk of loss that we often do not feel comfortable bearing.

Prospect theory also provides an explanation for the so-called disposition effect, that investors are more likely to lock in a win by selling a winning stock than they are to sell a losing stock for cash, even if the prospects for the losing stock are less attractive. In our minds, we keep mental accounts of our paper positions; locking in a paper position as a loss carries with it such a negative feeling that it can outweigh the strong incentive we have to maximize our overall portfolio return.

CHAPTER 12

Causality and Statistics

In each of our daily lives, we face a myriad of instances of using data from past observations to draw conclusions about particular hypotheses. From deciding what tie to wear for an interview, or how to approach a friend or colleague to ask a question, or even what to eat for breakfast in the morning, we are taking past data on similar events and trying to ascertain specific details about the given situation.

The process humans use to draw conclusions based on observable data has not evolved in a flawless way. We often overweight particular data points and underweight others in ways that can lead us to draw misinformed conclusions. Some of these mistakes can be rather innocuous, while others can lead to catastrophic outcomes.

In this chapter, we discuss some of the errors people commonly make when drawing conclusions from sets of information, as well as the potential consequences of some of these actions.

REPRESENTATIVENESS

Representativeness reflects the tendency of most people to read too much into stereotypes. As an example, consider the following problem, taken from Kahneman:[1]

Tom W. is a graduate student at the main university of your state. Please rank the following disciplines in order of likelihood that Tom is now a student in each field:

- Business Administration
- Computer Science
- Engineering

---

[1] Daniel Kahneman, *Thinking, Fast and Slow* (New York: Farrar, Straus and Giroux, 2011), 146–154. Example reworded slightly here.

- Humanities and Education
- Law
- Medicine
- Library Science
- Physical and Life Science
- Social Science and Social Work

Most ranked the disciplines in size order of the fields, which is the correct method to rank them without any further information. Subjects were then given the following description and told it was created by a psychologist "on the basis of psychological tests of uncertain validity":[2]

> *Tom W. is of high intelligence, although lacking in true creativity. He has a need for order and clarity, and for neat and tidy systems in which every detail finds its appropriate place. His writing is rather dull and mechanical, occasionally enlivened by somewhat corny puns and flashes of imagination of the sci-fi type. He has a strong drive for competence. He seems to have little feel and little sympathy for other people, and does not enjoy interacting with others. Self-centered, he nonetheless has a deep moral sense.*

This description was designed specifically to conform to specific stereotypes of the departments listed above that tend to be smaller and not to correlate with the characteristics most ascribe to the departments listed above that tend to be larger. For example, one might think this description fits well with computer science but not as well with social science and social work.

The researchers found that individuals completely revamped their ordering of the various disciplines based solely on a simple description by a psychologist, even though they were warned that the description is of uncertain validity. Individuals adjusted their probability estimates far too much in the face of the additional, limited information. Most almost completely reversed their orderings, listing the smallest departments as the most likely, and the largest departments as the least likely.

Mathematically, the task at hand is to calculate the *conditional probability* that Tom W. is a member of each department and then rank those probabilities in order. One approach is to start with the first question's results, the unconditional probabilities that Tom W. is a member of each department, also known as the *base rates*, and then adjust those base rates based on the additional information they receive, namely Tom's personality profile.

---

[2]Kahneman, 147.

However, most respondents adjust their estimates too far—in fact, the evidence shows they shift their estimates almost fully, as if the personality profile is the only information they have, eschewing any knowledge of department size completely.

As an example, if the distribution of all graduate students in the university were as follows:

- Business Administration: 10%
- Computer Science: 5%
- Engineering: 10%
- Humanities and Education: 35%
- Law: 10%
- Medicine: 12%
- Library Science: 3%
- Physical and Life Science: 5%
- Social Science and Social Work: 10%

These probabilities then represent the base rates, or the probabilities that Tom W. is a member of each department unconditional on any information about his personality.

Once we receive his personality assessment, we have additional information we can use to approximate the likelihood Tom is in each department.[3] Let's say the proportion of all grad students in each department that fits this profile are as follows:

- Business Administration: 30%
- Computer Science: 70%
- Engineering: 45%
- Humanities and Education: 20%
- Law: 20%
- Medicine: 15%
- Library Science: 40%
- Physical and Life Science: 30%
- Social Science and Social Work: 5%

To calculate the probability Tom W. is in each department given his personality profile, we must utilize the *law of total probability*, which implies that:

$$P(A|B) = \frac{P(A\&B)}{P(B)} \tag{12.1}$$

---

[3] For the purposes of this example, consider the personality profile reliable.

for two events, A and B, where an event can be any occurrence, such as "it will rain tomorrow" or "the Redskins will win the Super Bowl." The vertical line means that that probability is calculated assuming everything to the right of the line is true. The intuition behind this equation is relatively straightforward—if one wants to know how likely it is to be above 80 degrees given that it is raining, he or she just needs to look at all the times in which it is raining at all and see what fraction of those times it is above 80 degrees in addition.

Here, the event A is that a specific grad student is in a particular department, and the event B is that a specific grad student has the listed personality profile. To calculate the proportion of all grad students that both have Tom's personality and are in a particular department, we simply multiply the unconditional probability of attendance in a department by the proportion of grad students in that department that have the given personality. For example, if 10 percent of grad students are in business administration, and 30 percent of those have the given personality, then 3 percent of all grad students are both in business administration and have the given personality. These percentages for each department are:

- Business Administration: 3%
- Computer Science: 3.5%
- Engineering: 4.5%
- Humanities and Education: 7%
- Law: 2%
- Medicine: 1.8%
- Library Science: 1.2%
- Physical and Life Science: 1.5%
- Social Science and Social Work: 0.5%

To calculate the percentage of grad students in all of these departments that fit Tom's personality profile, we can simply sum these numbers, which yields 25 percent. This is our $P(B)$ from the preceding equation. The last step, then, is to divide the above probabilities by 25 percent. Hence, the conditional probability that a grad student is in each department given he or she has Tom's personality profile is:

- Business Administration: 12%
- Computer Science: 14%
- Engineering: 18%
- Humanities and Education: 28%
- Law: 8%

- Medicine: 7.2%
- Library Science: 4.8%
- Physical and Life Science: 6%
- Social Science and Social Work: 2%

Compare these probabilities with the base rates given earlier. Those for departments that are heavily weighted with students like Tom increased noticeably, whereas departments with a dearth of Tom-like students generally had their probabilities decrease. However, the base rates still weigh heavy in the final outcome. For example, Tom is still twice as likely to come from "Humanities and Education" than from "Computer Science," even though students like Tom occur in the Computer Science department with 3.5 times the frequency they occur in Humanities.

Herein lies the mistake most individuals make. They overweight the effect of these kinds of stereotypes on the original base rates. Most in the survey ranked the departments very closely to the ordering that would exist if only considering the proportion of Tom-like students in each department, ignoring the size of the departments almost entirely.

CONJUNCTION FALLACY

Following on the example from the previous section, assume one is given Tom W.'s personality profile, stated again here:

Tom W. is of high intelligence, although lacking in true creativity. He has a need for order and clarity, and for neat and tidy systems in which every detail finds its appropriate place. His writing is rather dull and mechanical, occasionally enlivened by somewhat corny puns and flashes of imagination of the sci-fi type. He has a strong drive for competence. He seems to have little feel and little sympathy for other people, and does not enjoy interacting with others. Self-centered, he nonetheless has a deep moral sense.

And is asked to rank the following statements in order of likelihood:

- Tom W. is a computer technician.
- In the summers, Tom W. vacations in Maine.
- Tom W. enjoys watching baseball.
- Tom W. is an avid gardener.
- Sometimes Tom W. gets lost in his daydreams.

■ About four times a year, Tom W. gets together with his extended family.
■ Tom W. is an avid gardener and enjoys playing World of Warcraft.

This is very similar to an experiment run by Daniel Kahneman and Amos Tversky in the early 1980s.[4] The fourth and seventh statements are all the experimenters are interested in; the others serve only to make the similarity between these statements less obvious. It is impossible for the latter statement to be more likely than the former. The latter is a subset of the former, and hence any instance of the latter (that Tom W. is both an avid gardener and enjoys playing World of Warcraft) is also an instance of the former (that Tom W. is an avid gardener). However, most participants ranked the last statement as more likely than the fourth.

This persisted even when the subjects were asked to rank only the following statements:

■ Tom W. is an avid gardener.
■ Tom W. is an avid gardener and enjoys playing World of Warcraft.

What is going on here? From the description, individuals find it unlikely that Tom would be an avid gardener, so when they read the former statement, they simply think it is improbable. But when this statement is put in conjunction with a statement they think is likely, that Tom enjoys World of Warcraft, they ignore the conjunction and focus on the part of the sentence they think is likely, incorrectly rating this statement more likely than the former. Kahneman and Tversky termed this phenomenon *conjunction bias*.

This has important implications for financial markets. In the case of financial markets, imagine that a particular stock has exhibited a very high rate of return recently. From which of the following groups of stocks is that stock most likely a member?

■ All common stocks.
■ Technology stocks with very strong earnings.

If the conjunction bias were to come into play, we might find investors picking the latter group as more likely than the former, which includes it.

---

[4] Amos Tversky and Daniel Kahneman, "Extensional versus Intuitive Reasoning: The Conjunction Fallacy in Probability Judgment," *Psychological Review* 90 (1983): 293–315. Discussed extensively in Kahneman (2011), pp. 156–165.

READING INTO RANDOMNESS

Your friend decides to flip a coin ten times and track the results. If we call each landing of heads "H" and each landing of tails "T," which of the following results seems most likely to occur?

- HT HT HT HT HT
- HH HH HH HH HH
- TT TT TT TT TT
- HT TH HH HT HH

The answer seems obvious to many—the first three results appear highly unlikely to happen, whereas the last seems more indicative of the random process. After all, the chances that 10 coin flips come out all heads, all tails, or alternates between heads and tails 5 times seems to be virtually zero, whereas a random pattern as in the last case could easily occur.

That logic is incorrect. There are 1,024 possible outcomes to this experiment, and each of them is equally likely, including all four of the outcomes listed above. Intuitively, however, the first three outcomes seem unlikely to be random, since they appear to follow a very clear pattern, whereas the fourth seems to follow no pattern at all and hence appears more random.

This reflects our nature as humans, attempting to find order in a sea of chaos. From an evolutionary standpoint, this outcome makes sense. Consider two gatherers from long ago that come across a dispersal of apple trees across a wide swath of land. One gatherer finds a pattern in the locations and uses that to predict where other apple trees might be, and the other does not. If there is a pattern to tree locations, the first is much more likely to find a source of food than the second, and if there is no pattern, the second garners no real benefit from having been right. Consequently, it was to our advantage as a species to err on the side of finding patterns in observable data and draw actionable conclusions from them, even when those patterns might not truly exist.

Those instincts can have disastrous consequences in finance. Many traders execute technical analysis trading strategies by looking for price trends, ceilings and areas of support, and so on.[5] These traders make a living finding patterns in prices and acting on that information. But in this case, the trader that finds a pattern in a random assortment of data may pay a big price for his mistake.

This mistake can be very tempting to make. Returning to our coin flip example, if we assume every landing of heads is a $1 increase in a stock

---

[5] See Chapter 7 for a more detailed discussion of technical analysis.

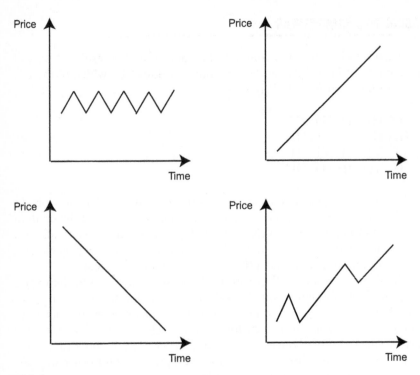

FIGURE 12.1

price, whereas every landing of tails is a $1 decrease in price, our four outcomes correspond to the following four graphs (Figure 12.1).

It is very tempting to say the first three are clearly a function of pattern and the fourth results from a random process, even though all four are equally likely outcomes of the same coin flip experiment.

Another even more costly potential example of reading patterns into randomness in the financial markets involves estimates of the money managers themselves. Many make the argument that some hedge funds must be capable of beating the market because of the track record of those funds over time. One will often hear sentiments such as "they have beaten their threshold return for 10 straight years—they clearly know how to invest money."

Burton Malkiel[6] makes the case that this seeming pattern does not necessarily reflect any innate ability of the fund itself. When considering the number of funds that have failed over the years, if each hedge fund's return

---

[6]Burton Malkiel, *A Random Walk Down Wall Street* (New York: W.W. Norton, 1973).

for the year has a coin flip's chance of beating its threshold, the consequences of such a random process would look a lot like the "pattern" of returns history has witnessed. If 1,024 money managers flip a coin 10 times in a row, one of them is likely to hit heads 10 straight times,[7] and that fund will be the one that survives and makes the news. When people see only that fund's returns, it is very difficult to get away from the thinking that that fund knew what they were doing, more so than every other.

SMALL SAMPLE BIAS

Imagine hearing the following statement: "A disproportionately large number of high-achieving high school senior classes belong to smaller schools." As you hear this statement, it might sound like it represents the result you would expect from smaller schools. Your mind likely floods with reasons why this makes sense—for example, smaller schools are probably able to give their students more attention, or many private schools are smaller than average and these schools probably also have more resources to dedicate to their students than other schools, or perhaps that schools for the gifted tend to be smaller in size and have students that are higher achieving going in.

Now imagine hearing this statement: "A disproportionately large number of low-achieving high school senior classes belong to smaller schools." Had you not heard the first statement, this statement likely would have made perfect sense upon hearing it, and your mind would likely fill with reasons why this is the expected result, such as that smaller schools are more likely to belong to rural areas, where perhaps the quality of both the students and the pool of potential teachers are lower.

Of course, a below-average school size cannot explain students being both high-achieving and low-achieving. However, both statements are in fact true.[8] This might seem extraordinary, but it is a simple consequence of statistics.

To illustrate the cause, consider an experimenter flipping a coin four times. If one ran this experiment and reported a result of all heads, this result might be met with mild surprise, but it would not seem terribly unlikely. In fact, this has a 1 in 16, or approximately 6 percent, chance of occurring.

Now consider running the same experiment, but with 20 coin flips. A result of all heads would be met with a much larger element of surprise—in fact, one would probably doubt the results. Such an extreme result is

---

[7] The probability that 10 fair coin flips will result in 10 heads in a row is 1 in 1,024.
[8] Kahneman, 117.

significantly less likely with so many trials; the chance of all heads with 20 flips is about one in a million.

The natural intuition in these cases reflects a simple mathematical reality: extreme results are much less likely to occur as the sample size increases. If one thinks of each school as a number of draws from an urn with a large number of balls, some labeled "high-achieving," some "average," and some "low-achieving," the chance of getting a large majority of high-achieving draws is smaller when the overall number of draws increases. Conversely, the chance of getting a large majority of low-achieving draws is also smaller the larger the number of draws. This is because the probability of getting a large number of draws of any one given type goes down as the number of draws increases.

Returning to our example, it is not the size of the school that is causing or even correlated with factors that cause the students in those schools to be high or low achieving. It is simply the nature of having fewer students that makes the average achievement in these schools more variable—meaning smaller schools will have more extreme results for average achievement than larger schools will, in both directions. However, individuals tend to put more stock into the observations of a small sample of data than is warranted. Kahneman and Tversky dubbed this phenomenon the "law of small numbers."[9]

This statistical phenomenon has consequences for the scientists running experiments as well—consequences that the scientists often do not realize. One of the most important components of designing an experiment is determining how many data points to collect. The more data points collected, the lower the variance in the results and the more confidence the experimenter can have that the data acquired represents the population. But a larger data set also requires more time and resources to procure.

Consequently, before running an experiment, the scientist faces a trade-off between cost and improved accuracy of results and must determine the optimal data set size based on his or her estimation of the benefit of more data. Unfortunately, studies have shown that scientists are not very good at estimating the informational cost of having a small sample size. In a 1962 study,[10] Jacob Cohen showed that researchers commonly picked sample sizes so small that they undertook a 50 percent chance of having their true hypotheses appear false. Kahneman and Tversky found a similar result in an informal survey of their colleagues.[11]

[9] Amos Tverksy and Daniel Kahneman, "Belief in the Law of Small Numbers," *Psychological Bulletin* 76, no. 2 (1971): 105–110.

[10] Jacob Cohen, "The Statistical Power of Abnormal-Social Psychological Research: A Review," *Journal of Abnormal and Social Psychology* 65 (1962): 145–153.

[11] Kahneman, 113.

These studies show that scientists routinely overestimate the conclusive power of small sample sizes. If professional researchers make such errors, surely laypeople make similar mistakes in everyday life. This result has consequences for financial markets as traders continuously are making decisions on trading strategies based on historical data. Consider a trader determining whether to execute a trading strategy of buying a particular stock after the company releases positive earnings announcements. Suppose that this company releases positive and negative announcements equally as often. The trader could very well think that 10 years of data is a substantial data set. Such a data set would provide only 20 positive earnings announcements[12] from which to derive an opinion. The trader would be putting too much stock into such a small data set. A similar problem might exist if the trader looks at the last 10 years of data to see which days of the week the market tends to move up or down, or the past 100 years of data to see which way months tend to trend.[13]

PROBABILITY NEGLECT

When most people are asked questions such as the following:[14]

- Do strokes kill more people each year than accidents?
- What causes more deaths—tornadoes or asthma?
- What is more likely—death by lightning or death by botulism?

they tend to overstate the probability of events for which they have a large bank of relevant memories or stories relative to the probability of other events. In this case, 80 percent of respondents mistakenly believed accidents kill more people than strokes, most thought tornadoes kill more people than asthma even though asthma is 20 times as deadly, and most thought death by lightning is less frequent than death by botulism, even though lightning kills 52 times as many people each year.

In these cases, it is clear that the level of media coverage of the various events is skewing the respondents' perceptions of each event's likelihood. News outlets are significantly more likely to report on the devastation of a tornado than on a local asthmatic episode, so respondents have a larger

---

[12] Earnings estimates are released four times a year.
[13] See Chapter 16 for a discussion of the potential effect of small sample bias on conclusions reached regarding calendar effects.
[14] Kahneman, 138

pool of memories regarding tornado-related deaths than they do deaths by asthma. Hence, the former seems more prevalent.

This manifests itself in a particular way when considering the probability of a specific event such as a potentially tragic one, a phenomenon that Cass Sunstein refers to as *probability neglect*.[15] If one is awaiting the arrival of a loved one's plane after a long trip, and the plane is inexplicably an hour late, the individual's mind might flood with thoughts of horrible plane crashes from past news stories. This might quickly lead to the conclusion that something disastrous has happened. In the ratio representing the probability that a given plane crashes, the number of tragic plane crashes divided by total number of plane flights, one is considering the numerator when recalling past stories of such events while disregarding the denominator entirely, and hence exaggerating the probability that the event actually happened.

CONCLUSION

This chapter explored some of the psychological phenomena encountered when attempting to use an information set to draw statistical inferences or specific conclusions. The process humans use to evaluate conclusions based on observable data is often accurate but is far from perfect. Whether based on previously encountered stereotypes, or reading into patterns, or a misapplication of innate statistical methods, we often overweight certain data points and underweight others, and the mistaken conclusions that are reached can lead to unfortunate consequences. However, knowledge of these phenomena can help us to be cognizant of our own biases, allowing us to adjust or possibly even correct our natural inclinations toward such incorrect conclusions.

---

[15] Kahneman, 144.

CHAPTER 13

Illusions

Our capacity to predict the likelihood of future events relies in part on our ability to draw inferences from past observations. Traditional economic theory assumes that individuals evaluate and learn from past occurrences in an objective fashion. Psychological studies, however, have shown that humans have persistent limitations in their ability to draw conclusions from historical data and hence often derive false conclusions from past experience.

Cognitive illusions, or biases, represent one subset of these limitations. A cognitive bias is a departure in inference or judgment from objective analysis that leads to a distortion in perception or understanding. From a set of observations on how one performs in a specific context, one may believe he or she is more capable at the given task than actually warranted. When comparing one's prediction to an actual outcome of events, one might tend to overstate the impact he or she had on the outcome. These illusions can have an acute impact on financial markets, as evaluations of investment possibilities and choices of professional managers can be affected significantly by them.

ILLUSION OF TALENT

One of the most successful franchises in video game history is Madden NFL, a series of football video games produced by EA Sports. Named after John Madden, a famous National Football League player, coach, and commentator, the label has sold more than 70 million copies across multiple gaming platforms since its inception in 1988. For about a decade, EA Sports decorated the Madden NFL game boxes primarily with a picture of John Madden on its cover. In 1999, the manufacturer shifted its strategy, instead picturing an athlete coming off a stellar year. Every year since, Madden NFL has had one or more popular players gracing the cover of its box.

Within a few years, the public began to notice that athletes who were on the Madden NFL cover suffered from a sharp drop in production the following year. Consistently, these cover athletes would underperform the expectations set by their recent production. In some cases, these athletes suffered injuries as well, causing them to miss playing time and stunt their production even further. Popular folklore recalls several examples of this phenomenon. In 2000, Eddie George of the Tennessee Titans graced the Madden cover. That year, the Titans lost in the playoffs, and his individual production dropped dramatically afterward; he would never have another season like that which earned him the cover.

In 2004, Ray Lewis of the Baltimore Ravens appeared on the cover. He subsequently broke his hand in the 15th week of the 17-week season and recorded no interceptions for the year. Shaun Alexander of the Seattle Seahawks was featured in 2006 as the league's reigning Most Valuable Player. The next season he sustained a foot injury that caused him to miss six games; his production would never return to the same level again.

Rather quickly, this trend gained widespread attention. Fans of the NFL began to fear their favorite players might grace the cover and suffer sharp drops in production or, even worse, become injured. When LaDainian Tomlinson considered appearing on the cover, his fans started the website SaveLTfromMadden.com in an attempt to dissuade him.[1]

Eventually, this trend gained a popular nickname: the Madden Curse. A similar phenomenon was observed for those who appeared on the cover of *Sports Illustrated,* dubbed the *Sports Illustrated* cover jinx.

The Madden Curse is an example of people providing too much attribution of a given observation to an individual's talent and not enough to luck. Each NFL player's output in each year is a function of two things: his skill and luck. A players' skill will not change much from year to year—a running back who has the speed and agility to gain a lot of rushing yards one year likely has the same skills the next. Luck behaves differently. Whether based on the output of his teammates, or themes in the offensive play calling, or how defenses play against him, many factors unrelated to the actual player will affect his performance the next year, and these can change significantly from year to year.

In a league as prominent as the NFL, the player who ends a given year with the most rushing yards is undoubtedly very talented. However, given the number of running backs in the league, it is unlikely he could have finished first without most of the items relating to luck falling his way as well. The next year, his talent will be unchanged, but to reach the same level of

---

[1] Tomlinson decided not to appear on the cover that year, reportedly due to contract disputes.

production, his luck would need to remain unchanged as well, which is very unlikely. Consequently, when one observes a production drop off after a stellar performance, it is more likely the first performance involved an element of luck that is not easily reproducible than it is that some outside force has cursed the athlete's performance the next year.

This is also an example of confirmation bias, the tendency for people to focus on evidence that confirms their beliefs rather than view the entire set of observations objectively. Those who believe in the Madden Curse or *Sports Illustrated* cover jinx ignore the fact that Larry Fitzgerald had a career year after his appearance on the cover and focus instead on the injury sustained by Troy Polamalu, with whom he shared the cover. They ignore the stellar year Drew Brees had the year after his appearance and focus instead on the fact that his team lost in the first round of the playoffs. They ignore the fact that Michael Jordan graced the cover of *Sports Illustrated* a record 49 times and never suffered any measurable disruption to his performance.

The illusion of talent is closely related to our tendency to see patterns in the outcomes of random processes discussed in Chapter 12. Human nature desires to see more order than may exist in chaotic processes, whether it is attempting to discern predictability in a set of random numbers or attempting to assign causation to a random trend of luck over time. Evidence that argues against these conclusions gets mentally discarded in favor of observations that jive with the desired results.

Kahneman[2] reports a similar finding with professional athletes in golf. Consider a golf tournament in which the average participant shot par in the first round. A golfer who shot six under par on that day is likely more talented than his average competitor, but it is also likely that he enjoyed above-average luck on that day. If asked to predict his score the next day, one would expect he would still have above-average talent, but there is no reason to expect he would have above-average luck again. Consequently, the best guess of his second-round score is slightly better than the average competitor, but not by as much as it was in the first round. The same logic would apply to golfers that had below-average scores the first day—they are likely less talented than their competitors, but also likely had below-average luck, so the best guesses of their second-round scores would be slightly worse than the mean but not by as much as on the first day.

That is exactly what one finds. Golf scores tend to regress to the mean as one moves from day one to day two. One might argue that this tendency

---

[2] Daniel Kahneman, *Thinking, Fast and Slow* (New York: Farrar, Straus and Giroux, 2011), 177–178.

arises for other reasons, such as overconfidence from having done well the first day or nerves from being atop the leader board. However, if one uses round two scores to try to predict the scores in round one, the same result appears: scores regress to the mean. Golfers with extreme outcomes on day 2 were likely impacted significantly by luck, and they tend to have had less luck on day 1.

ILLUSION OF SKILL

A closely related cognitive bias is the illusion of skill, or the tendency for people to think they have an ability to execute a particular task when the evidence shows they are no better at it than random chance. The classic example of this bias lies with the casual market trader who believes he can pick stocks that will beat the market. The universe of studies demonstrating that asset managers do not, on average, beat the market is voluminous. The most famous treatment of this subject comes from Burton Malkiel. In *A Random Walk Down Wall Street*,[3] Malkiel explores the world of money management and finds that managers are no more likely to beat market thresholds than one is to call the outcome of a coin flip correctly.[4]

One of the most famous studies[5] on how amateur investors perform came from two University of California–Davis researchers, Brad Barber and Terrance Odean. With a data set of trades executed by over 60,000 households over a six-year period, Barber and Odean were able to analyze trading activity over a large cross-section of individuals. On average, each household turned over more than 75 percent of its portfolio annually. In total, their data set spanned over one million trades.

The study found clear evidence of overconfidence in one's ability to invest. One sells stocks when he or she expects the price to drop and buys when he or she expects appreciation. Hence, one measure of investor performance would be a comparison of how stocks that were sold did versus the stocks that were bought. On average, the stocks that individual traders sold outperformed those they bought by 3.2 percent.[6] Overall, households

---

[3] Burton Malkiel, *A Random Walk Down Wall Street* (New York: W.W. Norton, 1973).
[4] See Chapter 12 for additional discussion on Malkiel's argument.
[5] Brad M. Barber and Terrance Odean, "Trading Is Hazardous to Your Wealth: The Common Stock Investment Performance of Individual Investors," *Journal of Finance* 55, no. 2 (2000): 773–806.
[6] Kahneman, 213.

that traded the most frequently earned 11.4 percent annualized, versus 17.9 percent earned by the market over the same time span.[7]

Another measure of whether or not individuals have a skill in a given capacity is consistency of performance over time. Using the framework discussed earlier, if output is ability plus luck, output would be somewhat consistent if it is mainly a function of ability, whereas if it is rather sporadic over time, it is likely mainly luck. Kahneman[8] analyzed performance data on 25 wealth managers at a given firm over eight consecutive years. Ranking these managers each year, Kahneman calculated the correlation between the rankings in each year and every other year, yielding 28 pairwise comparisons overall. The average correlation across years was approximately zero; in other words, there was no performance persistence across time for these managers.

When he brought this to the firm's attention, his results were met with avoidance and self-delusion. The firm's managers yielded no reaction and continued along the same path of action as they had previously. The investment managers themselves reacted more strongly, though with only frustration and annoyance at the results. This is the nature of the illusion. Those who have dedicated themselves to a particular profession are loath to realize their success is a function of luck rather than their hard work and skill, which can be a dangerous mindset for market traders to have. It is much easier to conclude that the hours one has spent poring over company financials and analyst reports has yielded an expected return benefit than it is to decide the impact of one's investment decisions are still no less random than the roll of a die.

ILLUSION OF SUPERIORITY

The consequences of the last section are especially intriguing given the view of most traders on the market. Investment professionals tend to believe that most people cannot beat the market. But these same investment professions tend to believe that they are among the few who can. This is an example of the illusion of superiority, which can be summed up as follows: "the average person thinks he or she is above average."

People tend to associate positive attributes with themselves overwhelmingly more so than negative ones, and they rate themselves more favorably and less negatively than a hypothetical generalized individual such as "the average college student." This tendency is so pervasive that it even affects the

---

[7] Barber and Odean, 774.
[8] Kahneman, 215–216.

process of memory. Positive personality information is recalled much more easily than negative personality information, which most find more difficult to process, and information regarding prior successes is more easily recalled than that relating to past failures.

These tendencies also affect perceptions. The aspects of oneself that he or she finds negative are judged to be both more common and less important than the aspects he or she finds positive. Similar findings exist for the tasks at which one is proficient versus tasks at which one has no actual skill. Individuals even create the illusion of improvement in areas that are thought to be important, even when no discernible improvement exists.[9]

Comparison with others' perceptions of a given individual confirm the tendency to overestimate one's abilities. A group of researchers[10] had individuals perform tasks involving group interaction while other individuals observed these interactions. The observers were then asked to rate the participants on a variety of metrics while the individuals rated themselves on the same metrics. Individuals consistently saw themselves more favorably than the observing group did.

This phenomenon has been broadly recognized in the academic literature and is discussed under a number of monikers, including the above average effect, the leniency effect, the primer inter pares effect, and the Lake Wobegon effect, named after the fictional town created by Garrison Keillor in which "all the women are strong, all the men are good looking, and all the children are above average." This tendency has broad implications for financial markets, where one wins simply by performing above average. If an asset manager can demonstrate above average results for years running, he or she would have little trouble raising a large pool of assets to manage. Conversely, if one believes he or she will perform above average consistently over time, he or she will unwarrantedly invest a sizeable amount of assets in their own abilities, likely with disastrous results. Based on the evidence reported by Burton Malkiel and others, many professional investment managers are likely suffering from this illusion.

[9] See Shelley E. Taylor, and Jonathan D. Brown, "Illusion and Well-Being: A Social Psychological Perspective on Mental Health," *Psychological Bulletin* 103, no. 2 (1988): 193–210; and C. Randall Colvin and Jack Block, "Overly Positive Self-Evaluations and Personality: Negative Implications for Mental Health," *Journal of Personality and Social Psychology* 68, no. 6 (1995): 1152–1162 for reviews on the literature on this topic.

[10] P. M. Lewinsohn, W. Mischel, W. Chaplin, and R. Barton, "Social Competence and Depression: The Role of Illusory Self-Perceptions," *Journal of Abnormal Psychology* 89 (1980): 203–212.

ILLUSION OF VALIDITY

Kahneman[11] relays a tale from his days in the Israeli military in which he was tasked with identifying promising individuals for officer training from a pool of potential candidates. He and a colleague watched these candidates perform a task in which they were all stripped of symbols of rank and were asked to use a log to scale a six-foot-high wall without allowing the log to touch either the ground or the wall itself. If the log touched either item, the soldiers were to call it out and restart the exercise.

As the two evaluators watched these men interact, they saw a myriad of emotional cues to help ascertain how they reacted under pressure. Some men got angry when their ideas were challenged, some got increasingly frustrated as they grew physically tired, some decreased their own individual effort when their ideas were rejected by the group, some stepped up and took the reins to lead when the group was fatigued and frustrated. These observations gave Kahneman and his colleague a clear picture of what each soldier was like and his prospective chances of success in officer training. Whether a given candidate was rated very likely to succeed, very unlikely to succeed, or somewhere in between, the two observers were sure their conclusions were correct.

Several months later, the military gathered the data on how the candidates actually did in officer training and compared it to the evaluators' projections. They found that the projections were, at best, marginally predictive in separating good candidates from bad. In other words, the evaluations were barely more likely to be correct than a coin flip would have been. After the analysis was presented, the two evaluators went back to observe more candidates. Despite the clear evidence just presented to them, as each evaluated future candidates, they were again sure that their predictions would be right every time.

As Kahneman termed it, he and his colleague were suffering from the "illusion of validity." Individuals tend to believe the conclusions they draw from a brief set of observables are more likely to be valid than they actually are, and this tendency holds true even in the face of clear evidence to the contrary. This phenomenon closely resembles the representativeness heuristic presented in Chapter 12. Each candidate has a base rate of success, representing the candidate's likelihood of success unconditional on any observation from the exercise. As the evaluators collected observations during the exercise, to the extent that these observations are predictive (which itself is debatable), they should adjust the base rates, but not by much. People tend to change the base rates by more than they should because they put too much faith in the power of their observations.

---

[11] Kahneman, 209–211.

This tendency is also closely related to the *illusion of control*. Individuals tend to believe they have more control over the outcome of random events than they actually have, even when the events are explicitly constructed as random. For example, people believe they have greater control over the outcome of a dice roll if they personally roll the dice rather than having someone else throw them. When anticipating a certain outcome occurring from a random process, if that outcome actually does occur, people tend to overestimate their contribution to its occurrence.[12]

Conversely, when individuals reflect on incorrect predictions they have made, they overestimate the effect of random chance on the outcome and underestimate their personal contribution to the error. Both situations reflect the human tendency to overestimate the validity of his or her predictions. Before they are judged by time or if they are judged correct, individuals tend to overestimate their contribution, whereas if they are instead judged incorrect, people create other reasons that caused them to be wrong to reconcile the outcome with their preconceived illusion of validity.

Experts in a specific content area are particularly likely to exhibit this behavior. Philip Tetlock, a psychologist then at University of California–Berkeley, interviewed over 200 people whose professions it was to identify and discuss trends. He asked each to predict the likelihood of specific events occurring in the future, totaling tens of thousands of predictions across individuals. Over time, he found that the experts were less accurate at predicting these events than random guesses would have been. When asked to reconcile the differences between their predictions and observation, experts were also the most likely to create excuses for their errors, such as they were right but had the timing wrong or had been wrong but for the right reasons.[13]

CONCLUSION

Cognitive illusions have a profound potential impact on financial markets. Substantial evidence already exists that traders—both casual and professional—suffer from the illusion of skill, predicting they are likely to pick stocks that beat the market even while thinking that most other people are not. Consequently, individuals overtrade their portfolios, thinking each trade will generate an above-market return. Instead, the stocks these individuals sell generally outperform the ones they buy in exchange.

A casual trader who recognizes this pattern and decides to invest with a professional manager may run into the same problem. Professional managers

---

[12] Taylor and Brown, 196.
[13] Kahneman, 218–220.

are certainly not immune to these tendencies. Compounding the issue, these illusions also make it difficult to pick a successful manager. Differentiating which managers are actually capable from those that have achieved good returns by random chance requires separating talent from luck, which is difficult for most to do. Humans tend to attribute too much of past performance to ability instead of random chance.

Such inaccurate evaluation of past results has real economy effects. Resources may get allocated inefficiently as those with the most talent and most potential lose out to those who happened to strike the best luck in the past. Managers with stellar recent returns, which could just as easily have been caused by luck as by talent, may win out over those with good but more modest returns over a longer time period. The latter are less likely to have performed based on a string of good luck, but human tendencies may keep investors from evaluating performance records correctly, and inferior managers may end up with more assets under management.

A similar phenomenon can occur with stocks, as it did before the dot-com bubble. Technology stocks became the rage with investors because of their remarkable short-term returns. Older, more well-established stocks, or even indexes, which could not match the short-term track record of these new firms but had provided good returns over a longer time period tended to be neglected. Consequently, capital was over-allocated to these dot-com firms even though an objective look at their track records did not warrant such levels of investment.

Serial Correlation

CHAPTER 14

Predictability of Stock Prices: Fama-French Leads the Way

The 1992 article by Eugene Fama and Kenneth French[1] lit a torch to the broad acceptance of the capital asset pricing model (CAPM) and dealt a substantial blow to the widespread support for the efficient market hypothesis (EMH). Fama and French are strongly associated with the EMH and have been two of its staunchest defenders. It was certainly not their intention to cast doubt upon the EMH, but the conclusion that stocks with high book-to-market values perform better than stocks with lower book-to-market values created a near revolution in the way academic finance and professional money management looked upon the EMH.

The simplest random walk version of the EMH, the martingale property of risk-adjusted stock returns, implies that returns are unpredictable. The conclusion from Fama-French ran counter to that and strongly implied that there was, indeed, predictability that could be gleaned from past data. That argument posed a serious threat to the EMH unless it could be found that unknown risk factors were the cause of the predictability, in which case the predictability would resolve itself via the efficient market's routine pricing of risk. In this chapter, we review the Fama-French research and discuss the ramifications for the EMH.

TESTING THE CAPITAL ASSET PRICING MODEL

The Fama-French agenda was to test whether or not the beta of the CAPM was a significant predictor of stock price returns. Earlier research reached mixed results on the role that the CAPM beta played in forecasting future individual stock returns. Fama and French intended to resolve that ambiguity

---

[1] Eugene Fama and Kenneth French, "The Cross-Section of Expected Stock Returns," *Journal of Finance*, 47, no. 2 (June 1992): 427–465.

and to either validate or invalidate the central prediction of the CAPM. In the process of performing the test of beta, Fama and French considered other variables that had been put forth as potential predictors of stock returns. They proceeded to mix and match the variables to see what shook out as important. Recall the definition of beta:

$$\beta_i = \frac{cov(R_i, R_M)}{\sigma_M^2} \qquad (14.1)$$

for any stock i. The definition says that beta is the relationship between the returns of the stock, R_i, and the returns of the broad market, R_M, normalized by dividing by the variance of the return of the broad market. The usual security market line, depicted in Figure14.1, shows the relationship predicted by the CAPM and captured in equation (14.2).

$$E[R_i] - R_f = \beta_i \left(E[R_M] - R_f \right) \qquad (14.2)$$

In this, the simplest description of CAPM, the only determinant of a stock's return is the beta of the stock, assuming one knows the risk free rate R_f and the expected return of the entire market,[2] R_M. It is this proposition that Fama and French wanted to test against actual data.

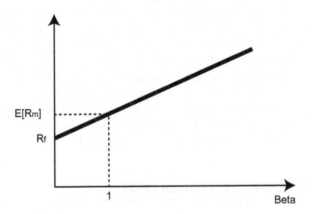

FIGURE 14.1   The Expected Return of Asset i

---

[2] It is somewhat murky as to what is meant by the "entire market." In practice, Fama and French proxied the entire market with well-known market indices. See Richard Roll, "A Possible Explanation of the Small Firm Effect," *Bell Journal of Economics* 36, no. 4 (September 1981): 879-888, for the inherent difficulties associated with the concept of the "entire market."

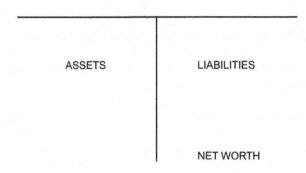

FIGURE 14.2 Balance Sheet as of xx/xx/201x

What Fama and French found was that beta didn't really matter in determining future stock returns, which contradicted CAPM. So what does determine future stock returns?

A PLUG FOR VALUE INVESTING

Fama and French found, as had previous researchers, that size of firm mattered. Smaller firms had better return performance than larger firms. But this size effect was swamped by a relative value effect. The most important finding of Fama and French was that stocks with higher book-to-market ratios had higher stock returns. Book-to-market means *book value* divided by *market value*. Book value is simply the net worth figure taken off of the most recent balance sheet (Figure 14.2).

Derived from the fundamental equation of accounting:

$$\text{Assets} - \text{Liabilities} = \text{Net Worth.}$$

Book value is provided in balance sheet presentations by public companies every three months in the 10-Q filings with the Securities and Exchange Commission (SEC). This data is readily available for all public companies at the SEC's website called EDGAR. Market value is the price per share of the stock multiplied by the number of shares of stock outstanding. Thus the numerator of book-to-market is a number determined from company accounting statements while the market value, the denominator, fluctuates every second of the trading day as the price of the stock fluctuates:

$$\text{Book-to-market} = \frac{\text{Book Value (taken from the Balance Sheet)}}{\text{Market Value}} = \frac{\text{Book Value}}{\text{Stock Price times Number of Shares}} \quad (14.3)$$

The simplest way to think of book-to-market is to think of the numerator as unchanging. Then changes in book-to-market will be determined by changes in the price of the stock. As the stock price rises dramatically, book-to-market falls. As the stock price falls dramatically, book-to-market increases. In practice, net worth on a balance sheet tends to move glacially. This means that stock price movements often dominate changes in the book-to-market ratios by increasing and decreasing the denominator.

Value investors, who trace their lineage back to Graham and Dodd,[3] were cheered by the idea that cheap stocks, interpreted as stocks with high book-to-market ratios, performed better than expensive stocks, interpreted as stocks with low book-to-market ratios. Value investors were skeptics of the EMH and argued that Fama-French was really a denial of it. Undeniably, the Fama-French result implied that stock prices were predictable and in a particularly simple manner. This posed a serious challenge to the EMH unless that predictability carried a risk that was being rewarded with the higher returns. In their 1992 article, Fama and French seemed unperturbed by the predictability of stock prices implied by their research:

> *If our results are more than chance, they have practical implications for portfolio formation and performance evaluation by investors whose primary concern is long-term average returns. If asset-pricing is rational, size and BE/ME must proxy for risk.*[4]

But, what is the risk that book-to-market (BE/ME) is proxying? It has now been two decades since the Fama-French research was published, and we are no closer to discovering the mystery of the undisclosed risk that is attached to high values of book-to-market and its predictability for future stock returns remains in the data.[5]

The Fama-French results, coming from two proponents of the EMH, were unsettling to the then-prevailing consensus supporting it. Their results suggested that some earlier work by De Bondt and Thaler,[6] largely ignored by finance economists, should get a second look. During the two decades following the publication of Fama and French, there was an outpouring of research that suggested other significant return predictability in historical

---

[3] Benjamin Graham and David Dodd, *Security Analysis* (New York: McGraw-Hill, 1934).

[4] Fama and French, 452.

[5] This is not to suggest that no one has tried to find the unknown risk factors that Fama and French allude to. More on this in Chapter 17.

[6] Werner F. M. De Bondt and Richard Thaler, "Does the Stock Market Overreact," *Journal of Finance* 40, no. 3 (July 1985): 793–805.

stock market data. The cumulative effect of this research was to feed upon itself and gradually undermine the long standing consensus support for the efficient market hypothesis.

MEAN REVERSION—THE DE BONDT-THALER RESEARCH

Almost a decade before the publication of the Fama-French research, Werner De Bondt and Richard Thaler presented a paper at the American Finance Association meetings that argued that stocks that had done poorly in the past tended to outperform stocks that had performed well in the past. This came to be known as *reverting to the mean,* or, more simply, *mean reversion.* The actual research used most recent three-year return performance as the variable to predict return performance over the succeeding three-year period.

De Bondt and Thaler described what they found in the data as *over-reaction:*

> *If stock prices systematically overshoot, then their reversal should be predictable from past return data alone, with no use of any accounting data such as earnings. Specifically, two hypotheses are suggested: (1) Extreme movements in stock prices will be followed by subsequent price movements in the opposite direction. (2) The more extreme the initial price movement, the greater will be the subsequent adjustment. Both hypotheses imply a violation of weak-form market efficiency. To repeat, our goal is to test whether the overreaction hypothesis is predictive.*[7]

Their conclusion: "The previous findings are broadly consistent with the predictions of the overreaction hypothesis."

These results seemed to draw little attention until the Fama-French results appeared in 1992. Some wondered if the mean reversion that De Bondt and Thaler found in the data was really nothing but the book-to-market effect found in Fama-French.[8] After all, stocks that have done poorly in recent years could be the stocks with low book-to-market values, if prices fell faster or rose less quickly than book value.

The Reaction to De Bondt-Thaler

De Bondt and Thaler's research was largely ignored by the academic community when it was first published in 1985. Why? If a simple rule—buy

---

[7] De Bondt and Thaler, 795.
[8] See Chapter 17 for a broader discussion on this topic.

three-year losers and sell three-year winners—can lead to such dramatic outperformance in the stock market, why doesn't everyone sit up and pay attention? It is likely that the common view was that, even if De Bondt-Thaler were onto something, once published, the predictability would disappear. Market participants read. As word spread about three-year losers providing better performance, traders would buy three-year losers early. Bidding up the prices of these securities would take away their excess performance. If it's a good idea and people know about it, they will take advantage of it and it will go away. After all, that is what happens in the simplest of arbitrage situations. The early traders win, but the arbitrage closes over time, and one would expect the window of opportunity to be fleeting.

So the results described by De Bondt and Thaler did not make waves and did not spur any new money management businesses organizing to take advantage of the predictability that this research seemed to have uncovered. There are other reasons why De Bondt and Thaler's work fell on deaf ears. There was a strong suspicion that their results depended critically upon the performance of small and/or illiquid stocks.[9] The data on small-capitalization stocks is not generally thought to be as reliable as the data on larger-capitalization stocks, especially if such stocks have very thin trading activity. Thin trading activity means stocks are not as liquid to trade and perhaps don't have reliable daily pricing data from which to construct reliable stock return data. What this would mean is that small stocks may be providing unreliable data or perhaps their illiquidity is a risk in itself that must be priced. In either case, the DeBondt-Thaler results might be illusory. Another possibility may have dampened the enthusiasm for this kind of research: the lurking suspicion that the results may not persist after transaction costs are brought to bear.

WHY FAMA-FRENCH IS A MILESTONE FOR BEHAVIORAL FINANCE

The last thing that Eugene Fama and Kenneth French would have intended was to shake the powerful edifice of the EMH. Far from it. Both Fama and French were defenders of the EMH and many would argue that Fama had codified the EMH concept in his early writings. So why would a paper by two of the EMH faithful serve to undermine the faith? Fama and French implied that stock prices were predictable from use of past data and that

---

[9] De Bondt and Thaler explicitly reject the small stock characterization of their results: "However, the companies in the extreme portfolios do not systematically differ with respect to market capitalization" ("Does the Stock Market Overreact," 804).

such predictability was so strong that money managers could outperform the market by using simple rules relatively easy to implement in practice.

Isn't this precisely what De Bondt and Thaler had said almost a decade earlier: that stock prices are predictable based on past data? But this time it was different. This was not a cry from the wilderness that something is amiss. Instead the trumpet sounded by Fama and French came from within the belly of the beast—from ardent defenders of the EMH. Such a trumpet gave enormous credibility to the idea that stock prices might be predictable after all, as many stock traders had long argued, and that knowledgeable traders might be able to outperform simple indices. Fama and French were making a revolutionary statement, without realizing it, and in doing so would rescue the earlier research of De Bondt and Thaler and others from obscurity.

It seems clear that Fama and French had no inkling that they were on the verge of lighting the spark that would provide momentum to the behavioral finance movement. They were certainly aware that the predictability found in their 1992 article created the possibility of trouble for the EMH:

> *The cross-section of book-to-market ratios might result from market overreaction to the relative prospects of the firms. If overreaction tends to be corrected, BE/ME will predict the cross-section of stock returns.*[10]

But then, in the lines immediately following the above remark, Fama and French would directly confront De Bondt and Thaler:

> *Simple tests do not confirm that the size and book-to-market effects in average returns are due to market overreaction, at least of the type posited by De Bondt and Thaler (1985). One overreaction measure used by De Bondt and Thaler is a stock's most recent 3-year return. Their overreaction story predicts that 3-year losers have strong post-ranking returns relative to 3-year winners. In FM regressions (not shown) for individual stocks, the 3-year lagged returns show no power even when used alone to explain average returns.*[11]

This tells us directly that Fama and French were no friends to the overreaction hypothesis that normally drives the value investing paradigm and underlies mean reversion. They explicitly reject mean reversion. Later

---

[10] Fama and French, 451.
[11] Ibid.

in their famous article they note that: "If asset-pricing is rational, size and BE/ME must proxy for risk."[12]

This is clearly what Fama and French thought to be the case—that far from presenting some kind of anomaly that throws cold water on the EMH, Fama and French felt that their results suggested that the variables they found important, size and book-to-market, were simply proxies for risks that had, as yet, not been identified.

The reality is that Fama and French's results were seen as mainstream confirmation of the previously heretical view that stock markets were predictable. Suddenly, De Bondt and Thaler, as well as other behavioral finance research, assumed much greater importance. It wasn't long before the predictability literature would reach back to research long neglected and provide the spark that would lead to a massive outpouring of research arguing that future stock prices are predictable from currently known data.

---

[12] Fama and French, p. 452.

CHAPTER 15

Fama-French and Mean Reversion: Which Is It?

Contrarian investing has a long history in the stock market. The most famous of the contrarians was Benjamin Graham. Together with David Dodd, Graham pioneered what came to be known as value investing, but could just as easily be labeled contrarian investing.[1] Contrarian investing means, roughly speaking, buying stocks that other people don't like. How do you know other people don't like these stocks? Because they have low prices. But low prices compared to what? Value investors say that you should buy stocks that have low prices compared to their earnings or compared to their book value. This is essentially the Fama-French thesis. A true contrarian investor goes against the crowd. Look for stocks that are performing poorly, buy those stocks, and avoid stocks that have been strong performers. This view is that of De Bondt-Thaler. Are these the same thing? There are some important similarities in the data.

THE MONTH OF JANUARY

Something interesting appeared, buried in the data analysis in the Fama-French study:

> *The average January slopes for ln(BE/ME) are about twice those from February to December. Unlike the size effect, however, the strong relation between book-to-market equity and average return is not special to January . . . there is a January seasonal in the*

---

[1] Benjamin Graham and David Dodd, *Security Analysis* (New York: McGraw-Hill, 1934).

book-to-market equity effect, but the positive relationship between
BE/ME and average return is strong throughout the year.[2]

This was not the first sighting of a "January effect" in the stock price
history literature, but it is striking that January accounted for so much of
the main conclusion of the Fama-French research. Fama and French note
that earlier studies by Roll (1983) and Keim (1983) had found that the "size
effect" was concentrated in January. Fama and French found the same thing
for size. But, even book-to-market was unduly concentrated, though not
exclusively concentrated, in the month of January.

What about mean reversion? According to De Bondt and Thaler: "Sec-
ondly, consistent with previous work on the turn-of-the-year effect and seasonality, most of the excess returns are achieved in January."[3]

They go on to conclude: "However, several aspects of the results
remain without adequate explanation. Most importantly, the extraordinarily large positive excess returns earned by the loser portfolio in
January."[4]

The final paragraph of De Bondt-Thaler is worth repeating here:

[S]everal aspects of the results remain without adequate explana-
tion. Most importantly, the extraordinarily large positive excess
return earned by the loser portfolio in January. Much to our sur-
prise, this effect is observed as late as five years after portfolio
formation.[5]

The "loser portfolio" referred to in the above citations contains the
stocks whose returns were significantly below market averages in prior
periods. The January impact is so pronounced in De Bondt-Thaler that,
absent the month of January, there really is no mean reversion in their
data.

So what is going on here? De Bondt-Thaler uses prior three years returns to establish their winner and loser portfolios and then project these
portfolios forward for three years into the future. Fama and French use a
point in time to establish book-to-market values, assign stocks to deciles
and then project these stocks forward in an effort to predict returns over the

[2]Eugene Fama and Kenneth French, "The Cross-Section of Expected Stock Returns,"
Journal of Finance 47, no. 2 (June 1992): 448.
[3]Werner F. M. De Bondt and Richard Thaler, "Does the Stock Market Overreact,"
Journal of Finance 40, no. 3 (July 1985): 799.
[4]De Bondt and Thaler, 802.
[5]Ibid., 802.

next 12 months. So, strictly speaking, De Bondt-Thaler and Fama-French are doing different things with the data. But, are they picking up the same thing? Or, in fact, is something quite different going on which could be suggested by the "January effect" in the data?[6]

IS THIS JUST ABOUT PRICE?

If the returns of a stock have been well below average in the past three years, that suggests that the stock price itself is the main culprit. Dividends might have been slashed or reduced, but price drops are usually of more significance in declining returns. Book values can drop as well, but book values are certainly not as volatile as stock prices, especially since they are not observed as frequently. If, for whatever reason, book values were constant, then stocks whose prices declined the most would eventually be the stocks with highest book-to-market values. These same stocks would also be the poorest stock return performers over the period as well. We know that book values are not constant, but they are much stickier than stock returns.

THE OVERREACTION THEME

The interpretation of both mean reversion and Fama-French fit the "overreaction hypothesis." The idea is that markets tend to overshoot. The overreaction hypothesis works both ways. When good news hits a stock, especially repeated good news, then the stock becomes somewhat immune to occasional bad news and euphoria reigns. A long enough string of bad news will eventually lead to a dramatic shift in sentiment and the overreaction takes over on the downside.

De Bondt and Thaler see mean reversion as a behavioral finance hypothesis. They are not searching for hidden risk factors. They cite a variety of instances from Kahneman and Tversky and even John Maynard Keynes as lending support to the overreaction hypothesis.[7] A simpler description is that investors may be naive. This type of naïveté was summed up by three authors in a 1994 article that would later lead the three of them to found a very successful money management firm based on the ideas published in the article.

---

[6]We deal explicitly with January effects in Chapter 18.
[7]See De Bondt and Thaler, 793–795.

LAKONISHOK, SHLEIFER, AND VISHNY
ON VALUE VERSUS GROWTH

Josef Lakonishok, Andrei Shleifer, and Robert Vishny (LSV) founded a
money management firm in 1994 that, by the middle of 2011, managed
over $65 billion in institutional funds.[8] Also in 1994, LSV published their re-
search on value versus growth[9] that would provide the ideas that would inform their newly created money management firm. Their fundamental thesis
was to lump Fama and French in together with De Bondt and Thaler as well
as others and to describe all as "value" strategies: "These value strategies
call for buying stocks that have low prices relative to earnings, dividends,
historical prices, book assets, or other measures of value."[10]

In a single sentence, LSV was pushing several different research agendas
into the simple characterization of a value strategy. Stocks that were glamor-
ous[11] were viewed as the exact opposite of a value stock. Over time, stocks
could shift from one category to another, but the paradigm was always the
same. Stocks that did well in the future were likely to be stocks that were out
of favor, for whatever reason, in the present.

LSV explicitly referred to these value strategies as "contrarian" strategies:

> *Value strategies might produce higher returns because they are con-
> trarian to "naïve" strategies followed by other investors. These naïve
> strategies might range from extrapolating past earnings growth too
> far into the future, to assuming a trend in stock prices, to overreact-
> ing to good or bad news, or simply equating a good investment with
> a well-run company irrespective of price. Regardless of the reason,
> some investors tend to get overly excited about stocks that have
> done very well in the past and buy them up, so that these "glamour"
> stocks become overpriced. Similarly, they overreact to stocks that*

---

[8] LSV would not be the only firm that appeared to grow out of contrarian research.
Dimensional Fund Advisory was begun by students of Eugene Fama and Kenneth
French, both of whom became directors of the firm, whose assets under management
exceeded $250 billion by the middle of 2011.
[9] Josef Lakonishok, Andrei Shleifer, and Robert Vishny, "Contrarian Investment, Extrapolation, and Risk," *Journal of Finance* 49, no. 5 (December 1994): 1541–1578.
[10] Ibid., 1541.
[11] The term *glamour stocks* is used synonymously with the term *growth stocks*. Such
stocks are viewed as expensive relative to metrics normally used to value stocks.
Growth suggests that such stocks receive a growth "premium" and trade at a higher
price than their current earnings would normally support because of expectations of
above-normal future earnings growth.

*have done very badly, oversell them, and these out-of-favor "value"
stocks become underpriced. Contrarian investors bet against such
naive investors.*[12]

The LSV agenda was a sweeping one intended to capture all of the various "value" strategies under the same umbrella. The first item on the LSV agenda was to reproduce the results achieved in earlier research by Fama-French, De Bondt-Thaler, and others. The second, more controversial, item was to suggest that value stocks were less risky than glamour, or growth, stocks. There being no universally acceptable notion of risk, LSV examined periods for which the market performed poorly and found that value stocks tended to outperform glamour stocks even in bad markets where the marginal value of an earned investment dollar could be expected to be the highest. This was LSV's way of showing that value stocks were less risky than growth stocks.

The main thrust of the LSV article is that whatever differences there may or may not be, "out-of-favor" stocks, by whatever measure, can be expected to outperform the market. In this sense, Fama and French is being enlisted as supportive of the behavioral finance point of view and consistent, if not identical, with the De Bondt and Thaler argument. The fact that both Fama-French and De Bondt-Thaler provide simple rules to beat the market based upon easily obtainable publicly known data is, for EMH supporters, the haunting similarity between the two.

IS OVERREACTION NOTHING MORE THAN A "SMALL STOCK" EFFECT?

One of the criticisms that was leveled at both Fama-French and De Bondt-Thaler was that their results were mainly confined to stocks with relatively small capitalization. Small-cap stocks generally trade less often, so it is easy to have data problems that might suggest things that aren't really true. Imagine that a small-cap stock has not traded for a month or more, so that there is no recorded price for the stock other than the last trade a month or more ago. It will appear that the price of the stock is unchanged throughout this period. But, that might not be the case. If you own a house and it hasn't been on the market recently that doesn't mean its market price is unchanged. When the stock finally does trade, it may appear that its price has made a significant jump in a single day, when, in fact, it really hasn't. Because a stock doesn't trade that doesn't mean necessarily that its market

---

[12] Lakonishok et al., 1542.

value is unchanged. It may also be unclear what a time series of the value of the stock should look like in this case.

There are efforts to correct for data pricing problems with small-cap stocks by looking at bid-offer spreads.[13] The problem is the size of the bids and the offers. They are typically no more than 100 shares and can be misleading as to where the real market is for a buyer or seller with size. There is no obvious way around the data issues for small stocks with infrequent trading. It is not uncommon for researchers to put minimum limits on trading activity before including a stock in their research. But all of this tends to be relative. Smaller-cap stocks tend to trade less frequently with less liquidity than larger-cap stocks. This fact could introduce problems in interpreting the data.

Related to the small stock issue was the question of return calculations employed by De Bondt and Thaler. Conrad and Kaul[14] argued that De Bondt-Thaler's return calculations were biased in the direction of their main conclusions. Their argument was based upon earlier work by Blume and Stambaugh[15] that demonstrated biases in return compounding. Blume and Stambaugh had argued that holding period returns were not subject to the same biases. Their suggestion was to use holding period returns rather than calculating period returns and then compounding them. The argument was technical but simple.

To see what is happening think about what is involved in calculating a rate of return in a simple situation with no dividends. Let p_t represent the price at the beginning of the period and p_{t+1} the price at the end of the period. Then, the return, R_t, over the period from t to $t+1$ is:

$$R_t = \frac{p_{t+1} - p_t}{p_t} \qquad (15.1)$$

The problem is that one doesn't observe p_t or p_{t+1}. The observation used in De Bondt and Thaler and other studies is a price that either represents the bid side of the market or the offer side of the market. The true price is somewhere in between the bid price and the offer price.

---

[13] The "bid" part of a bid-offer spread is the highest price that anyone is currently bidding for the stock. The "offer" part is the lowest price that a seller is currently willing to accept. The bid and the offer will also specify the number of shares bid for or the number of shares offered for sale.

[14] Jennifer Conrad and Gautam Kaul, "Long Term Overreaction or Biases in Computed Returns," *Journal of Finance* 48, no. 1 (March 1993): 39–63.

[15] Marshall E. Blume and Robert F. Stambaugh, "Biases in Computed Returns: An Application to the Size Effect," *Journal of Financial Economics* 12, no. 3 (November 1983): 387–404.

The bias that can arise is easy to illustrate in a simple example. Suppose that bids are typically 20 percent below the "true price" and that offers are typically 20 percent above the true price and that observing a bid price is exactly as likely as observing an offer price. Call the observed prices p_t^O and p_{t+1}^O. If both p_t^O and p_{t+1}^O are taken at the offer side of the market, then the observed R_t^O is:

$$R_t^O = \frac{p_{t+1}^O - p_t^O}{p_t^O} = \frac{1.2p_{t+1} - 1.2p_t}{1.2p_t} = \frac{p_{t+1} - p_t}{p_t} = R_t \qquad (15.2)$$

and if both are taken at the bid side of the market:

$$R_t^O = \frac{p_{t+1}^O - p_t^O}{p_t^O} = \frac{0.8p_{t+1} - 0.8p_t}{0.8p_t} = \frac{p_{t+1} - p_t}{p_t} = R_t$$

In these cases, there is no bias as all observations are either scaled up by 1.2 or scaled down by 0.8. The problem arises with the other two possibilities. Suppose the beginning of period price is taken at the offer side of the market and the end of period price is taken at the bid side. Then the resulting $^{L}R_t^O$ in this case will be:

$$^{L}R_t^O = \frac{p_{t+1}^O - p_t^O}{p_t^O} = \frac{(.8)p_{t+1} - (1.2)p_t}{(1.2)p_t} = -\frac{1}{3}\frac{p_{t+1}}{p_t} + R_t \qquad (15.3)$$

The final, equally likely situation is when the beginning of period price is taken at the bid side of the market and the end of period price is taken at the offer side. The resulting $^{H}R_t^O$ in this case will be:

$$^{H}R_t^O = \frac{p_{t+1}^O - p_t^O}{p_t^O} = \frac{(1.2)p_{t+1} - (.8)p_t}{(.8)p_t} = \frac{1}{2}\frac{p_{t+1}}{p_t} + R_t \qquad (15.4)$$

All outcomes are equally likely, so the expected observed return is:

$$\frac{^{L}R_t^O + {}^{H}R_t^O + R_t + R_t}{4} = \frac{\left(-\frac{1}{3}\frac{p_{t+1}}{p_t} + R_t\right) + \left(\frac{1}{2}\frac{p_{t+1}}{p_t} + R_t\right) + R_t + R_t}{4}$$

$$= \frac{1}{24}\frac{p_{t+1}}{p_t} + R_t \qquad (15.5)$$

This demonstrates an upward bias. This is an example of Jensen's inequality, which states that a convex function of an expected value cannot exceed the expected value of the same convex function. The form of the bid-ask spread is such that the true return cannot exceed the expected value of the return calculated from the observed prices, causing the upward bias.

This upward bias in simple one-period return calculations is what drives the critique of Conrad and Kaul. This bias would not matter over a long string of periods unless the bias is compounded by averaging future returns instead of the more normal time-weighting procedure. In essence, if one averages future time period returns then the upward bias shown here will show up in every single time period return.

Turning to De Bondt and Thaler's research, it is easy to see Conrad and Kaul's point. De Bondt-Thaler calculate what they call the cumulative average return or CAR by simple unweighted addition of all one period returns. This procedure will produce correct portfolio returns only if portfolios are equally weighted and rebalanced back to equal weights in every period. In De Bondt-Thaler's particular case, the returns are monthly, so that frequent and potentially costly rebalancing is required to reproduce their results. When Conrad and Kaul lengthened the holding periods to three years without rebalancing, they found that the De Bondt and Thaler results no longer held up except for the month of January. January's results, Conrad and Kaul argued, were not attributable to overreaction. Conrad and Kaul also noted that De Bondt and Thaler's "loser" portfolio (the portfolio that would be a winner in future periods) contained a disproportionate number of small cap stocks where the return bias using monthly rebalancing is even worse than for larger cap stocks.

To rescue De Bondt and Thaler from the critique by Conrad and Kaul would require establishing that a monthly rebalanced portfolio of possibly very low priced stocks is implementable in practice by an investor in such a way that transactions costs do not overwhelm the result. As to whether or not the overreaction argument still applies is also not clear, since the more normal interpretation is that you buy and hold over more extended time periods. Why the constant rebalancing would be required by those who believe in the overreaction hypothesis is unclear. The economics of the required rebalancing is not discussed in the De Bondt and Thaler papers, so it remains something of a mystery why this somewhat peculiar method of portfolio construction played such a crucial role for the ultimate results.

Following on heels of the Conrad and Kaul critique, Ball, Kothari, and Shanken[16] argue that De Bondt and Thaler's results are mainly a result of the low absolute prices of the loser stock portfolios.

[16] Ray Ball, S.P. Kothari, and Jay Shanken, "Problems in Measuring Portfolio Performance: An Application to Contrarian Investment Strategies," *Journal of Financial Economics* 38, no. 1 (May 1995): 79–107.

We explore a variety of performance measurement problems, in the context of a De Bondt and Thaler (1985, 1987) contrarian research design. . . . We show that much of the reported profitability of a contrarian strategy is driven by low-priced loser stocks. . . . Loser-stock prices are so low that their subsequent five-year returns are extremely sensitive to even a $1/8 of either mispricing or micro-structure effect.[17]

Ball, Kothari, and Shanken further argue that using December-end data biased the results. They recalculated the De Bondt and Thaler numbers using June-end data and much of the performance advantage of the loser portfolios went away.

Because the December-end evidence is likely to be biased due to the microstructure factors discussed earlier, we give greater credence to the June-end (and similar August-end) results. Whatever the source of the difference, it implies that the De Bondt and Thaler (1985, 1987) estimates of contrarian portfolio performance are far from robust.[18]

The arguments by Conrad and Kaul and by Ball, Kothari, and Shanken are mainly about return measurement problems and the special difficulties involved when the stocks are small cap. Another argument related to small caps is that small caps might be riskier than large caps. If that is so and if De Bondt and Thaler loser portfolios are concentrated among small cap stocks, then Fama's unknown risk factor may come into play. Small stocks might be vulnerable to heightened bankruptcy risks, liquidity risks, or limited information risks. Any one of these could be a priced risk and justify a higher expected return under an efficient market hypothesis (EMH) point of view.

In almost every respect, the attack on De Bondt and Thaler seemed to apply to Fama and French. For example, Fama and French averaged returns in much the same manner as De Bondt and Thaler. Upside return bias should apply to Fama-French in an equal manner. Most of the measurement and risk issues that apply to small stocks are likely to show up for Fama and French as well since size is explicitly a cause of lower return for Fama and French. Strangely, and perhaps it was a matter of timing, the various critiques of contrarian strategies were addressed to De Bondt and Thaler's work but not to that of Fama and French, which continues to be

---

[17] Ball, Kothari, and Shanken, 104.
[18] Ibid., 105.

widely accepted. Book-to-market, the key variable in Fama-French, is now used in addition to other factors in most multifactor asset pricing models, but last three year's performance has not surfaced in these same models.

DANIEL AND TITMAN ON UNPRICED RISK IN FAMA AND FRENCH

A 1997 paper by Daniel and Titman[19] tackled the issue of uncovering the risk factor that might be driving the book-to-market ratios that play such a dominant role in Fama and French. The ongoing debate between Fama and French and Lakonishok, Shliefer, and Vishny was mainly about whether book-to-market represented a risk factor or was a surprise to the market place and resulted from overreaction by market participants. If book-to-market represents a risk factor, such as distress, then Fama and French's results are consistent with the EMH. If LSV are correct that stocks are mispriced and that high book-to-market stocks are incorrectly valued, then Fama and French's results are a violation of the EMH.

What Daniel and Titman proposed was to look at the common characteristics of stocks with high book-to-market and see if they could unearth a risk that was common to this group of stocks. Using factor pricing model techniques, Daniel and Titman observed that high book-to-market had much in common, but an unknown risk factor did not seem to be the element of commonality:

> Our results indicate that (1) there is no discernible separate risk factor associated with high or low book-to-market (characteristic) firms, and (2) there is no return premium associated with any of the three factors identified by Fama and French (1993), suggesting that the high returns related to these portfolios cannot be viewed as compensation for factor risk. To elaborate, we find that although high book-to-market stocks do covary strongly with other high book-to-market stocks, the covariances do not result from there being particular risks associated with distress, but rather reflect the fact that high book-to-market firms have similar properties; e.g., they might be in related lines of businesses, in the same industries, or from the same regions.[20]

---

[19] Kent Daniel and Sheridan Titman, "Evidence on the Characteristics of Cross Sectional Variation in Stock Returns," *Journal of Finance* 52, no. 1 (March 1997): 1–33.
[20] Ibid., 3.

The conclusions of Daniel and Titman reinforce the idea that Fama and French's research is contrary to the EMH, even though Eugene Fama and Kenneth French have never reconciled themselves to that point of view.

SUMMING UP THE CONTRARIAN DEBATE

Without question, the academic literature surrounding contrarian investment had a major impact upon both the academic and the practical worlds of finance. The book-to-market positive relationship to future stock returns seems to be widely accepted, even though it seems to suffer from some of the same critiques that shadow the work of De Bondt and Thaler. In spirit, both seem to undermine the EMH, even though EMH defenders will hear none of it, citing potential risk factors and small stock data problems and biases. Taking the long view, the contrarian debate in the 1990s has resurrected the Graham and Dodd viewpoint that the market often prices assets on incorrect information. That is, in essence, what the contrarian philosophy seems to be saying and it cannot be comforting for those who support the EMH.

Are these two approaches, Fama-French and De Bondt-Thaler, truly different approaches? In philosophy, the answer is yes. Looking at past prices to predict the future is a different exercise than comparing book values to current market prices. Perhaps, that is why researchers have given Fama and French more of a free pass than the treatment afforded De Bondt and Thaler. In the real world, contrarian investors seem to incorporate both approaches, since falling prices can lead to a loser portfolio as well as to a high book-to-market portfolio. Does the reported success of these strategies constitute a violation of the EMH? The evidence seems slightly tilted in the direction of the EMH critics, but future data could easily reverse this conclusion.

CHAPTER **16**

Short-Term Momentum

PRICE AND EARNINGS MOMENTUM

Within a year of the publication of Fama and French's 1992 paper, a research paper[1] surfaced claiming to document another source of stock market price predictability. Wall Street traders had long spoken of a stock's price as *acting well*. Expressions such as "the price action in this stock looks good" usually meant that the price of the stock had been in a short-term uptrend.

Short-term uptrends in prices are sometimes described as *relative strength* or *momentum*. Many traders believed that stocks whose prices had

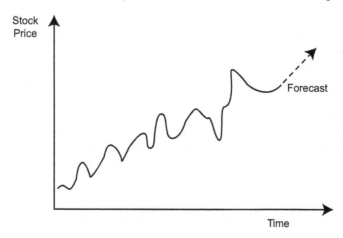

FIGURE 16.1   Short-Term Uptrend in Stock Prices

[1] Narasimhan Jegadeesh and Sheridan Titman, "Returns to Buying Winners and Selling Losers: Implications for Stock Market Efficiency," *Journal of Finance* 48, no. 1 (March 1993): 65–91.

167

performed well would continue that good (relative) performance in the near future. This would seem so important that traders might be heard to say: "Well, while it's true that the stock has good fundamentals and is undervalued, I am still worried about how the stock's price is behaving. It has been lagging the market and that concerns me." In other words, a trader might avoid a stock that is otherwise considered a good buy, from a fundamental point of view, if the price of the stock has not exhibited a recent upward trend. Could there be anything to this?

Narasimhan Jegadeesh and Sheridan Titman[2] argued that stocks that performed well in the past 3 to 12 months tended to perform well over the next three years. The Jegadeesh-Titman (J-T) research concluded that stocks generally continued upward trends. They labeled this phenomenon *price momentum*. Considering a pattern of stock prices exactly opposite of that shown by DeBondt and Thaler, J-T focused on short-term price trends, which echoed the arguments of stock traders that recent uptrends in prices forecast favorable future stock returns. J-T formed winner and loser portfolios based upon the last 12 months and then projected forward to see what happened. Winner stocks in the past tended to be winners in the future and loser stocks in the past tended to be losers in the future. When J-T considered six-month periods only, they found that buying the last six months' winners and holding for six months outperformed market benchmarks by 12 percent annually. What could account for this? How could this momentum be reconciled with its seeming opposite, reversion to the mean?

J-T speculated that these short-term momentum results may hinge on unexpectedly good earnings announcements. The argument is that the market has a tendency to underreact to good earnings news—stock prices rise on good earnings, but not as much as they should. Thus the positive impact of earnings feeds into future stock price performance. To test for this, J-T looked at stock returns surrounding earnings announcements and found confirmation of good stock performance when earnings were announced,[3] but only for a few months, and then the loser portfolio actually begins to eventually outperform the winner portfolio as time passed.

EARNINGS MOMENTUM—BALL AND BROWN

One possible explanation for the results in J-T might be the findings in another neglected paper published in 1968 in an accounting journal by Ray

---

[2] Jegadish and Titman.
[3] Ibid., 86–89.

Ball and Phillip Brown.[4] Ball and Brown (B-B) were interested in whether or not stock prices anticipated favorable and unfavorable earnings announcements. What they found is that "the market begins to anticipate forecast errors early in the twelve months preceding the earnings report . . . and continue for approximately one month after." It is easy to see that this kind of pattern could be what J-T found 25 years later. The stock return behavior seems the same in both J-T and B-B.

B-B developed the concept of "unexpected income changes,"[5] a statistical concept that assumes that the main predictor of a firm's announced income is the average income within their industry. In the actual empirical work, B-B traces the relationship between changes in a firm's reported income and the average of changes in income for all firms in their sample. This relationship is then used to predict future income changes for each firm as a simple linear function of the average change in income for all firms:

$$\Delta I_i = a_i + b_i \Delta M \tag{16.1}$$

where ΔI_i represents change in reported income for firm I and ΔM represents the average change in reported income of all other firms. The estimates for a_i and b_i are used to predict future values of ΔI_i from future values of ΔM. If the actual change in income is different from what would be predicted by this procedure, then the difference is "unexpected income," which can be either positive or negative. B-B looked at the stock price data leading up to and immediately following the date of the announcement of the unexpected income events. B-B's original interest had been to see if the earnings surprises were accurately foreseen by the stock price preceding the announcement.

> *Most of the information contained in reported income is anticipated by the market before the annual report is released. In fact, anticipation is so accurate that the actual income number does not appear to cause any unusual jumps. . . . The drifts upward and downward begin at least 12 months before the report is released (when the portfolios are first constructed) and continue for approximately one month after.*[6]

---

[4] Ray Ball and Phillip Brown, "An Empirical Evaluation of Accounting Income Numbers," *Journal of Accounting Research* 6, no. 2 (Autumn 1968): 159–178.
[5] Ibid., 161.
[6] Ibid., 170.

The key part of the above finding is that the "earnings drift"[7] continued for "approximately one month after." Thus, recent uptrends implied future uptrends. It should be noted that B-B found this tendency in earnings momentum in both directions. Positive surprises produced positive earnings drift; negative surprises produced negative earnings drift.

MEASURING EARNINGS SURPRISES

To know when something is unexpected, you must have some idea what is expected. Ball and Brown solved this problem in a statistical way by predicting earnings from a model that suggested that the main determinant of change in company earnings was the average change in earnings for all companies. That is not a completely satisfying way of defining expected earnings, especially if there are an army of paid research analysts available whose job is to predict future earnings for companies. You would think that a better method of determining the market's expectation of future earnings for a company would be related to what the various Wall Street analysts are predicting for that company. No doubt, Ball and Brown would agree, but at the time of their research, there weren't many Wall Street earnings forecasts being produced for individual companies. That would start to change by the 1980s.

By the mid-1990s, there were enough forecasts from Wall Street research analysts to provide a basis for estimating expected earnings directly from analyst's projections. One of the first articles to use actual analyst predictions was Chan, Narasimhan, and Lakonishok (CJL).[8] CJL's research was one of several research efforts to disentangle earnings momentum from price momentum. Were the two versions of momentum really the same phenomena or were they different? CJL proposed to use three different methods of calculating unexpected earnings. Two of these methods were statistical and similar to that used by Ball and Brown, but the third utilized the newly available data sets containing analyst forecasts. The analyst's forecasts were used in a novel way in the CJL work. CJL calculated a six-month moving average of past analyst earnings revisions scaled by stock price intending to see how quickly such earnings revisions were incorporated into the price of the stock. What they found was that all three measures of earnings

---

[7]The term *earnings drift* apparently was first used by Ball and Brown, but was later used in the literature interchangeably with the term *earnings momentum,* which might normally be suggestive of something very different.

[8]Louis Chan, Jegadeesh Narasimhan, and Josef Lakonishok, "Momentum Strategies," *Journal of Finance* 51, no. 5 (December 1996): 1681–1713.

surprises produced gradual price adjustment consistent with the earnings drift or earnings momentum hypothesis.

The most popular statistical measure of earnings surprise is what is known as the standardized unexpected earnings (SUE):

$$SUE_{it} = \frac{e_{iq} - e_{iq-4}}{\sigma_{it}} \qquad (16.2)$$

where e_{iq} is quarterly earnings per share, announced as of the most recent quarter, q, for stock i, e_{iq-4} is earnings per share four quarters ago, and σ_{it} is the standard deviation of unexpected earnings, $e_{iq} - e_{iq-4}$, over the preceding eight quarters.[9]

SUE is the most common model of earnings expectations in the literature. One reason that SUE is so popular with researchers in this field is that SUE estimates typically perform better, in the sense of predictive power, than measures taken from research analyst estimates of future earnings. CJL's research fit this pattern. SUE performed much better at predicting future price trends, in CJL's research than six-month revisions of analyst earnings estimates.

The use of SUE without reference to analyst forecasts is inconsistent with what market participants would normally think of as "earnings expectations." Expected earnings in a stock market setting is a consensus of analyst estimates for the specific company's earnings, not a statistical procedure involving past earnings trends such as the SUE. The use of SUE would seem to be an inappropriate measure of expected earnings unless it could be demonstrated to relate to consensus earnings estimates that are readily available from analyst forecasts.[10] It is surprising to see a purely statistical measure of earnings estimates used instead of earnings estimates that are used in real world settings. While someone may have tried to make this connection, none of the research cited here seems aware of such a link.

Another measure used in the CJL paper is what they call the "cumulative abnormal stock return," which they call ABR and define in the following manner:

$$ABR_{it} = \sum_{j=-2}^{+1} (r_{ij} - r_{mj}) \qquad (16.3)$$

---

[9]This definition is taken word-for-word from p. 1685 of Louis et al.

[10]This same problem—not reconciling a statistical measure of earnings surprise with analyst forecasts—seems a persistent problem with this literature. See Haigang Zhou and John Qi Zhu, "Jump on the Post-Earnings Announcement Drift," *Financial Analysts Journal* 68, no. 3 (May–June 2012): 63–80. Zhou and Zhu use purely stock price data to arrive at a statistical measure that purports to capture earnings surprise information without attempting to relate their statistical measure to analyst forecasts.

where r_{ij} is stock i's return on day j (with earnings announced on day 0) and r_{mj} is the return on the equally weighted market index.[11] Like the SUE, it is by no means certain that the use of ABR in this context corresponds to what most market participants think of when speaking of earnings surprises.

CJL's main interest was in trying to resolve the issue of whether price momentum or earnings momentum were actually the same. They concluded that the two versions of momentum were empirically distinct in their statistical work. CJL found that price momentum was the much larger effect and its persistence was for longer duration:

> This paper fills in some of the gaps in our understanding of two major unresolved puzzles in the empirical finance literature: why two pieces of publicly available information—a stock's prior six-month return and the most recent earnings surprise—help to predict future returns. The drift in future returns is economically meaningful and lasts for at least six months. For example, sorting stocks by prior six month return yields spreads in returns of 8.8 percent over the subsequent six months. Similarly, ranking stocks by a moving average of past revisions in consensus estimates of earnings produces spreads of 7.7 percent over the next six months.[12]

A decade later, Tarun Chordia and Lakshmanan Shivakumar[13] (C-S) tackled the same issue and obtained results that were very different. C-S conclude that earnings momentum swamps price momentum, while citing an earlier research paper by Hong, Lee, and Swaminathan[14] that concluded that in countries for which earnings momentum seemed absent in the data, there was no evidence of price momentum. SUE is used as the variable for expected earnings in C-S with no reference to analyst expectations. According to C-S:

> Both in time-series and cross-sectional asset pricing tests, we find that the earnings-based zero investment portfolio that is long the

---

[11] Chan et al., 1685. Note that this measure is analogous to the SUE and is a process similar to the Ball and Brown method of determining earnings expectations.

[12] Ibid., 1709.

[13] Tarun Chordia and Lakshmanan Shivakumar, "Earnings and Price Momentum," *Journal of Financial Economics* 80(3)(June 2006): 627–656.

[14] D. Hong, C. Lee, and B. Swaminathan, "Earnings Momentum in International Markets," unpublished working paper, Cornell University, 2003.

highest earnings surprise portfolio and short the lowest earnings sur-
prise portfolio captures the price momentum phenomenon . . . the
above results are consistent with price momentum being primarily
related to the systematic component of earnings momentum.[15]

C-S take their research a step further in an attempt to explain why
earnings momentum should be forecasting future prices. In essence, C-S
examines the characteristics of the portfolio of stocks that are most subject to earnings momentum and finds a systematic relationship between
those characteristics and factors thought to influence future gross domestic
product (GDP) growth. "These results suggest that the PMN portfolio may
be viewed as a risk factor that earns a risk premium."[16]

WHY DOES IT MATTER WHETHER MOMENTUM IS PRICE OR EARNINGS BASED?

Price momentum is based on a historical series of past prices. If there is
price momentum, the weak form of the efficient market hypothesis (EMH)
is false. It is not credible to argue that past price histories can be based upon
some unknown risk factor that the market is pricing. Thus, price momentum, if it exists, is a very serious threat to the EMH. Earnings momentum
is a very different situation. It could be that earnings momentum is capturing something fundamental and that it could, in principle, represent an unpriced risk factor. Thus, earnings momentum is potentially consistent with
the EMH, while price momentum is irreconcilable with it.

C-S show why earnings momentum poses less of a threat. They argue
that the portfolios that they construct with earnings surprise information
have characteristics that could make such surprises an unpriced risk factor.
In their paper, they cite "inflation illusion" as the factor. The argument that
C-S develop regarding the unpriced risk factor of earnings surprise is not
completely convincing, but it does suggest that the EMH has much less to
fear from earnings drift or momentum than price momentum.

Even though earnings momentum could be related to an unpriced risk
factor, the issue is far from settled and until such an unpriced risk factor is
unearthed in a convincing manner, earnings momentum remains a problem
for the EMH.

---

[15] Chordia and Shivakumar, 628.
[16] Ibid., 629.

HEDGE FUNDS AND MOMENTUM STRATEGIES

Price momentum research has never stopped, but much of it has stopped reaching the academic journals. Hedge funds, convinced that there was something to the idea of price momentum, invested their own resources and research efforts into uncovering price patterns in stock price data. So-called "quantitative-based" hedge funds, or *quant funds,* as they are known, are often users of very short-term pricing data in an attempt to undercover profitable trading strategies. It would be useful to know more about the research done by hedge funds on price momentum, but, for obvious reasons, hedge funds do not publish their internal research.

What we do know from casual observation is that much of the price momentum phenomena that hedge funds are adopting as strategies look at very, very short-term trading data. Holding times for strategies are often a matter of minutes or even seconds. One suspects that the research behind these strategies often suffers from data mining considerations. If you run enough regressions, even irrelevant factors will eventually pop up as significant. It is easy to convince others in a hedge fund setting that something that has worked on past data will work in the future. This means that strategies that might not pass academic muster are very likely to be utilized anyway.

Because of the compensation structure of hedge funds, there is an incentive to uncover investment strategies that produce outsize returns but have very large losses with very low probability—so-called tail risk.[17] One suspects that many quantitative investment strategies employing a very short-term version of price momentum fit into this category. In time we will learn more about the short-term pricing momentum strategies employed in the hedge fund industry.

PRICING AND EARNINGS MOMENTUM—ARE THEY REAL AND DO THEY MATTER?

There seems little doubt the pricing momentum is a feature of stock price data in the manner suggested by Jegadeesh and Titman in their 1993 article that began the academic discussion of stock price momentum. While some studies suggest that past pricing data is a proxy for other things, the very fact that past prices matter is a blow to the EMH that is not easily dismissed, as Fama might suggest, by references to unknown risk factors.

---

[17]The kind of "tail risk" that we are speaking of here is not a property of a normal distribution, so there is some other underlying probability distribution implicitly involved.

The literature on earnings momentum is more confusing. The statistical measures, SUE and ABR, as well as Ball and Brown's model of expected earnings do not seem to correspond to what most real-world market participants define as expected earnings. The normal notion of expected earnings is the consensus estimate, perhaps the "whisper" consensus estimate, that is available for most widely owned stocks prior to the actual announcement of earnings. Hopefully, in future research, we will learn more about the relationship between what we call here "statistical measures of expected earnings" and the consensus earnings expectations published by professional research analysts.

Even if there is nothing to the price or earnings momentum stories, it is a fact that real world traders pay attention to past prices. Price charts are ubiquitous in the finance industry, and television financial reporting regularly features price charts. The real world of trading seems to believe that past prices matter and that fact in itself raises issues for the EMH. If past prices are irrelevant, why do traders pay so much attention to them? Are these traders irrational? This is just one more problem for the EMH.

CHAPTER 17

Calendar Effects

Do markets behave differently on different days of the week? Do returns differ in the beginning of the year as compared to the end of the year? Is the beginning of a trading day different than the end of the trading day? These are questions that involve whether the calendar itself has an impact on stock returns. Absent a compelling explanation, seasonal- or calendar-based return patterns would seem to violate the efficient market hypothesis (EMH), since it would suggest investment strategies that could benefit from past data.

Like many aspects of behavioral finance, calendar effects arose from Wall Street lore and the casual observations of traders. "Blue Monday" suggested that returns might be lower on Mondays, which is what traders seemed to think. As the weekend approached, traders got happier and returns were better at the end of the week, according to them. Is any of this true? And, if so, are simple explanations like expectations of the coming weekend really enough to move markets?

The most famous of all calendar effects is the "January effect," discussed in Chapter 15. January seems to be different. Stock returns are higher in January than in the rest of the year. Another January effect also exists. If January returns are above normal, then the stock returns for the rest of the year seem to be above normal. Major research conclusions from such landmark works as Fama-French, De Bondt-Thaler, and Jegadeesh-Titman all find that something strange happens in the January data. It is rare to see any major econometric work on U.S. stock markets that doesn't single January out as significant.

JANUARY EFFECTS

Richard Thaler brought attention to calendar effects in his book *The Winner's Curse*.[1] Regarding January, Thaler cited a 1976 paper by Rozeff and Kinney[2] that documented extraordinary January returns for an equally-weighted index of stocks. Since no such pattern was observed for the Dow Jones Industrial Average,[3] Thaler concluded that "the January effect is primarily a small firm effect." This conclusion was updated by Lakonishok and Smidt[4] in their survey of seasonal anomalies published in 1988. They conclude that "from prior research we know that there is a very high January return for small companies but no such pattern for large U.S. companies."[5]

In 1996, Haugen and Jorion[6] revisited the January effect to see if it could still be found in the data. Given the large size of the January effect, Haugen and Jorion argue that "one would expect to see the January effect slide into the preceding year until it utterly disappears." They seem surprised to find that even decades after first being publicly reported, the January effect remained as strong as ever. "We examined the monthly returns to New York Stock Exchange firms from 1926 through 1993 and documented the existence of the January effect throughout this period. More important, there has been no significant reduction in the magnitude of the effect since its rediscovery in 1976."[7] Hansen and Lunde[8] considered 27 different stock exchanges in 10 countries (Denmark, France, Germany, Hong Kong, Italy, Japan, Norway, Sweden, the United Kingdom, and the United States) and concluded that year-end calendar effects are present but confined mostly to small-capitalization stocks.

---

[1] Richard Thaler, *The Winner's Curse* (New York: Free Press, 1992). See Chapter 11, "Calendar Effects in the Stock Market."

[2] Michael S. Rozeff and William R. Kinney, Jr., "Capital Market Seasonality: The Case of Stock Returns," *Journal of Financial Economics* 3, no. 4 (October 1976): 379–402.

[3] The Dow Jones Industrial Average (DJIA) is composed of 30 large-capitalization stocks, so the absence of a January effect for the DJIA suggests that it doesn't apply to large-cap stocks.

[4] Josef Lakonishok and Seymour Smidt, "Are Seasonal Anomalies Real? A Ninety-Year Perspective," *Review of Financial Studies* 1, no. 4 (Winter 1988): 403–425.

[5] Ibid., 407.

[6] Robert A. Haugen and Philippe Jorion, "The January Effect: Still There After All These Years," *Financial Analysts Journal* 52, no. 1 (January–February 1996): 27–31.

[7] Ibid., 28.

[8] Peter Reinhard Hansen and Asger Lunde, "Testing the Significance of Calendar Effects," Brown University Working Paper No. 2003-03, January 2003.

It seems generally agreed that January is different. The question is why is January different? One potential answer is tax considerations. Selling a stock at a loss can be of benefit to a taxpayer by reducing their taxable income by all or part of the loss.[9] Much of that selling is likely to take place at year-end. Thus, tax selling might occur in December, pushing stocks that had declined in price to even larger price declines. Once the new year arrives, the selling abates and now these same stocks begin to recover. The idea is that these stocks gain more than the market because artificial tax-induced selling has forced them to much lower prices than were warranted. Thus, once the year is over, these stocks are poised to do better that the market.

It is not easy to get data that can confirm or reject the tax-induced January effect suggested in the preceding paragraph. In the United States, taxpayers cannot take the tax loss if they repurchase the stock within the next six months. In the small country of Finland, there is no such wash sale[10] requirement. Finland is a country whose stock market does decidedly better in January than in other months of the year. Using a panel of taxpayer data, Grinblatt and Keloharju[11] reported that not only do Finnish investors engage in tax-loss selling at year-end, but frequently repurchase those same stocks in January with a pronounced emphasis on repurchasing stocks sustaining the largest losses.

A study by Odean in 1998[12] revealed that December was unusual in the high proportion of stocks sold with capital losses compared to stocks sold with capital gains. Due to the "disposition effect,"[13] stock sales are more likely to involve stocks where investors have gains than where investors have losses. But December is different in that the proportions are more nearly even than in other months. Along similar lines, D'Mello, Ferris, and Hwang[14] found evidence for abnormal selling pressure at year-end for

---

[9]Assuming capital gains are taxable and that capital losses can be deducted against capital gains and/or other forms of taxable income.

[10]The term *wash sale* refers to any sale of stock that is followed by a repurchase of that stock within six months. A taxpayer in the United States can deduct, subject to certain limitations, losses from a sale of stock in the year in which it is sold so long as the sale is not a wash sale.

[11]Mark Grinblatt and Matti Keloharju, "Tax-Loss Trading and Wash Sales," *Journal of Financial Economics* 71, no. 1 (January 2004): 51–76.

[12]Terrance Odean, "Are Investors Reluctant to Realize Their Losses?" *Journal of Finance* 53, no. 5 (October 1998): 1775–1798.

[13]The "disposition effect" refers to the tendency of investors to sell winners and hang on to losers. See Chapter 11 for more information.

[14]Ranjan D'Mello, Stephen P. Ferris, and Chuan Yang Hwang, "The Tax-Loss Selling Hypothesis, Market Liquidity, and Price Pressure Around the Turn-of-the-Year," *Journal of Financial Markets* 6, no. 1 (January 2003):73–98.

stocks with large capital losses in the current year and a significant decrease in the average size of the trade. This suggests that individuals, not institutions, may have been behind the abnormal selling pressure and is suggestive that tax-induced selling pressure may provide the motive.

A different rationale for the January effect is the idea that fund managers, those who are ahead of their benchmarks, tend to move their portfolios to more nearly match their benchmarks as the year comes to a close. This would suggest that some stocks that are attractively priced may not get purchased until after the new year begins. As Grinblatt and Moskowitz[15] note, if "window dressing"[16] is the cause of the January effect, the effect would not be concentrated among small-cap stocks.

Thaler had noted earlier that tax loss selling can't be the only explanation for the January effect because such an effect shows up in countries without tax loss considerations and countries whose taxable year ends at a different time. The Chinese stock markets were the subject of a 2005 study by Gao and Kling.[17] China's year-end is generally in January or February, not December. Gao and Kling were interested to see if there was a March effect in Chinese stock market data. This would be especially interesting considering the absence of capital gains taxes in China. There was a pronounced March effect in Chinese data that seemed to reduce over time and gradually slide back into February, as had been predicted by Haugen and Jorion for U.S. data. No such effect, however, has yet been observed in U.S. data. So far, the conclusion that the January effect would slide back into December has yet to be observed in other countries.

THE OTHER JANUARY EFFECT

The "other January effect" is an expression coined by Cooper, McConnell, and Ovtchinnikov[18] (CMO) in their 2006 article to describe the effect that says returns in January are positively related to returns over the next eleven

---

[15] Mark Grinblatt and Tobias J. Moskowitz, "Predicting Stock Price Movements From Past Returns: The Role of Consistency and Tax-Loss Selling," *Journal of Financial Economics* 71, no. 3 (March 2004): 541–579.

[16] "Window dressing" is the action taken by professional managers to change their portfolios to look more like the market as a whole (or to sell stocks whose recent reputation is poor and purchase stocks that have recently done well).

[17] Lei Gao and Gerhard Kling, "Calendar Effects in Chinese Stock Market," *Annals of Economics and Finance* 6, no. 1 (January 2005): 75–88.

[18] Michael J. Cooper, John J. McConnell, and Alexei V. Ovtchinnikov, "The Other January Effect," *Journal of Financial Economics* 82, no. 2 (November 2006): 315–341.

months of the year. Examining data from 1940 to 2003, CMO conclude that "January returns have predictive power for market returns over the next 11 months of the year. . . . In sum, the market return in January appears to contain information about market returns for the remainder of the year: Street lore has been confirmed." As CMO note, the conjecture by security traders had been around for over a century and a half before academics tackled the issue.

Both January effects seem confirmed by the data even long after the first publicly known reports of their existence. Why such effects remain and what they mean are still an object of curiosity.

THE WEEKEND EFFECT

The weekend effect is the idea that early in the trading week, returns are abnormally low, and later in the trading week, returns are abnormally high. U.S. data show negative average returns on Mondays, making Monday the worst day of the week. After 1952, the highest returns for U.S. stocks were posted on Fridays. Prior to 1952, U.S. stocks traded on Saturdays as well, and the data show that Saturdays exhibited the best returns of the week in the pre-1952 data.[19] What could possibly account for this? The weekend?

What would one expect from an EMH point of view? Since the market, on average, earns a positive return, you would expect every trading day to have a positive average return. Given that Monday comes after two days when the market is not open for trading, you would expect Monday to have three times the average return of every other trading day. But, in fact, Monday has a negative return on average and the worst return of any trading day in the week. Unless there is some transparent institutional reason for gloomy Mondays, this would seem to violate EMH.

Is it Monday or is it the weekend? In order to answer this question, one needs to compare the prices at the opening on Monday with the close on Friday to see if the weekend is the culprit. Rogalski in 1984[20] reported that the weekend was the losing period and that market returns were actually positive on average from Monday's opening trade to Monday's closing trade. According to Rogalski, the returns from Friday's close to Monday's opening trade were negative. So why should weekends exhibit negative returns?

---

[19] See Lakonishok and Smidt.
[20] Richard J. Rogalski, "New Findings Regarding Day-of-the-Week Returns over Trading and Non-Trading Periods: A Note," *Journal of Finance* 39, no. 5 (December 1984): 1603–1614.

Research done on data from other countries yields mixed results. Holden, Thompson, and Ruangrit[21] confirm weekend effects similar to that in the United States for Thailand. Using data from 1988 to 2002 from Hong Kong, Indonesia, Japan, Malaysia, Singapore, Taiwan, and Thailand, Lean, Smyth, and Wong[22] confirm the existence of weekend effects. A 2011 paper by Anwar and Mulyadi,[23] looking at stock market data from Indonesia, Singapore, and Malaysia, reported no Monday effect at all and Friday effects in Indonesia and Malaysia, but not Singapore. Similar lack of confirmation of weekend effects had been reported earlier for five Southeast Asian stock markets by Brooks and Persand.[24] Tonchev and Kim[25] rejected significant calendar effects for stock markets in the Czech Republic, Slovakia, and Slovenia. Some research reported only bad Mondays, but not necessarily great Fridays. Reporting on Malaysian data in 2007, Lim, Ho, and Dollery[26] found negative Mondays, but the best day of the week was Wednesday, not Friday.

What reasons could there be for bad Mondays? Is it the back-to-work blues spilling over into the stock market? Are weekends depressing for some reason? Or is it that people are so ebullient on Fridays that they bid the market to excess that must be corrected over the weekend? No one seems to know the answer to this puzzle.

PREHOLIDAY EFFECTS

Market returns seem to be abnormally high on trading days preceding holidays. This is consistent with Fridays having the highest returns of the

[21] Ken Holden, John Thompson, and Yuphin Ruangrit, "The Asian Crisis and Calendar Effects on Stock Returns in Thailand," *European Journal of Operational Research* 163, no. 1 (May 2005): 242–252.

[22] Hooi Hooi Lean, Russell Smyth, and Wing-Keung Wong, "Revisiting Calendar Anomalies in Asian Stock Market Using a Stochastic Dominance Approach," *Journal of Multinational Financial Management* 17, no. 2 (April 2007): 125–141.

[23] Yunita Anwar and Martin Surya Mulyadi, "Analysis of Calendar Effects: Day-of-the-Week Effects in Indonesia, Singapore, and Malaysia Stock Markets," *African Journal of Business Management* 6, no. 11 (March 2012): 3880–3887.

[24] Chris Brooks and Gita Persand, "Seasonality in Southeast Asian Stock Markets: Some New Evidence on Day-of-the-Week Effects," *Applied Economic Letters* 8, no. 3 (March 2001): 155–158.

[25] Dimitar Tonchev and Tae-Hwan Kim, "Calendar Effects in Eastern European Financial Markets," *Applied Financial Economics* 14, no. 14 (August 2004): 1035–1043.

[26] Shiok Ye Lim, Chong Mun Ho, and Brian Dollery, "Stock Market Calendar Anomalies: The Case of Malaysia," University of New England Working Paper No. 2007-5 (2007): 1–26.

week, leading into the weekend. Lakonishok and Smidt calculate that the "preholiday rate of return is 23 times larger than the regular daily rate of return and holidays account for about 50 percent of the price increase in the DJIA."[27] This is a surprisingly large effect and there is no apparent explanation, though there have been numerous efforts.[28] Reporting on data from the United States, the United Kingdom, and Hong Kong, Chong, Hudson, Keasey, and Littler[29] (CHKL) conclude that the preholiday effect has all but disappeared in the U.S. data since 1991, but remains in the data for the United Kingdom and Hong Kong.

There is an interesting further analysis in CHKL. They note that the preholiday abnormal positive return became an abnormal negative return in the 1991–1997 data and after 1997 disappeared entirely. This could be the result of market participants arbitraging away the preholiday effect, or, more likely, the effect may have been illusory in the first place for reasons given in the concluding section of this chapter.

SULLIVAN, TIMMERMANN, AND WHITE

One of the most interesting studies of calendar effects was a methodological study designed to ask whether the various calendar effect anomalies were simply the outcome of too many investigations of a limited data set. This study was done by Sullivan, Timmermann, and White[30] (STW) and the results published in 2001. STW formally raise the question of data mining.[31] Statistical procedures suggest that if enough different hypotheses are thrown at the same data set, then even if all of the hypotheses are false, some will appear to be true. A 95 percent significance test carries with it a 5 percent chance of a Type I error, rejecting the null hypothesis when it is, in fact, true. If one runs enough tests on the same data, sooner or later the null hypothesis will be falsely rejected.

---

[27]Lakonishok and Smidt, 411.

[28]Ryan Chong, Robert Hudson, Kevin Keasey, and Kevin Littler, "Pre-Holiday Effects: International Evidence on the Decline and Reversal of a Stock Market Anomaly," *Journal of International Money and Finance* 24, no. 8 (December 2005): 1228–1229.

[29]Ibid., 1226–1236.

[30]Ryan Sullivan, Allan Timmermann, and Halbert White, "Dangers of Data Mining: The Case of Calendar Effects in Stock Returns," *Journal of Econometrics* 105, no. 1 (November 2001):249–286.

[31]*Data mining* refers to the practice of subjecting a single data set to repeated statistical tests.

Sullivan, Timmermann, and White performed a number of statistical procedures directly related to calendar effects. They conclude that because the data has been reworked so often in the search for calendar rules, the resulting calendar rules that appear significant are not really significant. In their words:

> We find that although nominal p-values for individual calendar rules are extremely significant, once evaluated in the context of the full universe from which such rules were drawn, calendar effects no longer remain significant.[32]

CONCLUSION

The jury is still out on calendar effects. While the evidence for Monday is strong and shows up in countries other than the United States, the Sullivan, Timmermann, and White research casts some doubt that calendar effects are more than a natural result of extensive data mining. Out of sample tests using non-U.S. data, will help resolve this issue. Experimental economics may also be able to shed light on beginning-of-period and end-of-period pathologies. But no definite conclusion prevails based on current knowledge.

---

[32] Sullivan et al., 249.

Other Topics

CHAPTER 18

The Equity Premium Puzzle

A riskless asset should have the lowest market yield. Taxes can distort this simple proposition, but the tax treatment between three-month U.S. Treasury bills and common stock is the same, so that it is natural to expect that three-month U.S. Treasury bills will return, over time, much less for its owner than a diversified portfolio of common stocks. If an individual stock has an expected return of Π, while three month treasuries have an expected return of ρ, then we define the risk premium of a single stock as:

$$\text{Risk Premium for a Single Stock} = \Pi - \rho \qquad (18.1)$$

If we now consider an index[1] of all stocks taken together, we can define the expected return of the index as δ, and the equity premium is defined as:

$$\text{Equity Premium} = \delta - \rho \qquad (18.2)$$

In other words, the equity premium is how much a diversified portfolio of stocks is expected to earn above and beyond the returns expected from a risk-free asset.

MEHRA AND PRESCOTT

In 1985, Mehra and Prescott[2] combined empiricism and economic theory to conclude that the equity premium observed in historical stock prices was

---

[1] Any index will do. The most popular index of U.S. stocks, though not necessarily the best or most complete, is the capitalization-weighted Standard & Poor's (S&P) 500 Index.

[2] Rajnish Mehra and Edward C. Prescott, "The Equity Premium: A Puzzle," *Journal of Monetary Economics* 15, no. 2 (March 1985): 145–161.

simply too large. Mehra and Prescott looked at a 90-year period of stock returns, 1889 to 1978, and estimated the average stock return, corrected for inflation, to be 6.98 percent. Similarly, they calculated that an "average real return on relatively riskless, short-term securities over the 1889–1978 period was 0.80 percent."[3] This made the equity risk premium found in their data to be 6.18 percent in real terms.[4] The question they posed: is 6.18 percent too high, too low, or just about right?

Stocks are risky. When compared to relatively low risk assets, why should anyone own stocks unless they are compensated for that risk? So, the fact that there is an equity premium is not the issue. Stocks should produce higher returns than relatively riskless securities. The question is: how much higher?

To answer this question, Mehra and Prescott noted that the decision to shift a marginal dollar from relatively safe assets to stocks would depend upon the marginal consumption benefit for some future date when the return from the stock would be realized. That future marginal consumption benefit must be weighed against the marginal loss in consumption today, since that secure dollar would no longer be available for current consumption. If individuals are risk averse, they will effectively discount the future higher than if they were not risk averse.

So the simple answer to the puzzle might be that individuals are very risk averse and prefer present to future consumption by a wide margin. They therefore see no reason to take on the risk of stocks and are satisfied with the much lower returns from relatively safe securities. But as Mehra and Prescott dug deeper, they concluded that the size of the premium was inconsistent with the usual economic parameters that had been observed in other studies. A commonly used utility function[5] is the following:

$$E_0\left\{\sum_{t=0}^{\infty}\beta^t U(C_t)\right\}, 0 < \beta < 1 \qquad (18.3)$$

---

[3] Mehra and Prescott, 155.

[4] In the 27 years following the data set used by Mehra and Prescott, the equity premium was even higher—8.1 percent—using the same definition and data sources as used by Mehra and Prescott. See Elroy Dimson, Paul Marsh, and Mike Staunton, "The Worldwide Equity Premium: A Smaller Puzzle," London Business School Working Paper, April 2006.

[5] This utility function discussion is largely taken directly from Mehra and Prescott, 150, 154.

Where C_t is per capita consumption, β is the subjective time discount factor,[6] and E_0 is the expected value operator. A frequently used special case of this utility formulation is the constant relative risk aversion class of utility functions:

$$U(C,\alpha) = \frac{C^{1-\alpha} - 1}{1-\alpha}, \ 0 < \alpha < \infty \qquad (18.4)$$

With α as the constant of relative risk aversion. Mehra and Prescott cite a number of previous studies that suggest that (1) α is likely to be constant, so that this formulation is generally applicable; and (2) that the empirical value of α is likely to lie between zero and 2 for most applications. Based on these previous studies, Mehra and Prescott impose the condition that α be less than 10, which seemed a conservative approach. Using values of β that vary between zero and 1 and values of α that varied between zero and 10, Mehra and Prescott calculated the largest equity premium that would be consistent with those values. The result was 0.35 percent—a far cry from 6.18 percent.[7]

Mehra revisited the equity premium puzzle in 2003[8] and reported that the puzzle remained a puzzle and that the same puzzle appeared in data for the United Kingdom, Germany, Japan, and France as well. After reviewing the various efforts to either dismiss or explain the equity premium puzzle, Mehra concludes: "Over the long term, the equity premium is likely to be similar to what it has been in the past and returns to investment in equity will continue to substantially dominate returns to investment in T-bills for investors with a long planning horizon."

The equity premium puzzle that Mehra and Prescott brought to the attention of the academic community spawned a very large literature designed to either debunk the puzzle or to explain it. While this discussion is not over, there are two important strands of research that seem promising. The first is behavioral and the second is more global in character.

---

[6] If β = 1, then there is no discounting and utility is derived by simply adding up the expected consumption utility in each period. More typically, β is less than 1, reflecting a preference for current utility over future utility. The closer β is to 1, the less prevalent that preference becomes.

[7] Mehra noted 18 years later that Fischer Black had suggested in 1981, probably tongue in cheek, that an α = 55 would solve the puzzle. See Rajnish Mehra, "The Equity Premium: Why Is It a Puzzle?" *Financial Analysts Journal* 59, no. 1 (January/ February 2003): 54–69.

[8] Ibid., 67.

WHAT ABOUT LOSS AVERSION?

If people are loss averse, then they may avoid assets that create many painful situations. On the majority of trading days, stock returns are positive, but not on all trading days. If you derive limited pleasure when your stocks go up, but encounter an enormous amount of pain when they go down, you may avoid stocks because, even if the long run returns are outstanding, you can't take the pain along the way. The path to riches is too hard to endure. It isn't enough to know that there is a pot of gold at the end of the rainbow if the road to that pot of gold is too painful to traverse.

Overall pleasure and pain could turn on the number of times an investor observes the value of her portfolio. If you check the value of your portfolio every 10 years, you are not likely to feel pain very often. But, if you check your portfolio every five minutes, there are many more observations that are painful, even if stocks are generally moving up. If the observations of portfolio loss, less frequent though they may be, are much more painful than the pleasure of the more numerous observations of portfolio gain, the overall pain from observing the losses may just be too much. The investor can't take the pain and retreats to the safe asset, regaining peace of mind. This happens even though the investor's risky asset portfolio may have been increasing in value over time. Not paying attention would have made him or her a better investor.

If loss aversion is an apt description of most individuals, then there will be significantly less stock ownership than one would expect from simple risk aversion, which is something entirely different. Someone who is loss averse displays risk aversion when contemplating potential gains and its opposite—risk preference—when contemplating potential losses. Extreme loss aversion can make individuals avoid the stock market altogether. Thus, loss aversion could account for equity returns that seem too high by other measures.

Why is it that Mehra ignored loss aversion in his 2003 update of the controversy? The problem for Mehra and others of accepting the loss aversion explanation is that one would no longer have a utility function available that is a function of levels of wealth and consumption, which are central to existing economic theory. Having a path-dependent utility function would create problems for much of economic theory and finance theory in particular. This would be throwing the proverbial baby out with the bath water.

But since loss aversion is well documented in the psychology literature and would seem to account for the equity premium puzzle, it is difficult to see why it should not be considered. Thus far, it seems the most reasonable of the explanations offered.

COULD THIS BE SURVIVOR BIAS?

Survivor bias means that the data sample that is used leaves out some data that has not "survived" for one reason or another. A surprisingly large number of hedge funds go out of business in a typical year. If you ask how hedge funds performed in any given year, do you include the data for the ones who went out of business? If you look only at hedge funds that survived for the entire year, your data would be biased. The hedge funds that folded are not likely to have superior performance. Leaving out the nonsurvivors creates a biased sample that will bias the average performance upward, because the nonsurvivors are more likely to have poor performance records than the survivors.

So what does survivor bias have to do with the equity premium puzzle? In 1999, Jorion and Goetzmann[9] reported results of investment performance that looked at global data. They argued that the proper portfolio for a rational investor is a global portfolio, not a home-biased domestic stock portfolio. According to Jorion and Goetzmann, "the high equity premium obtained for U.S. equities appears to be the exception rather than the rule."[10] If an investor owned a truly global portfolio, then the equity returns would not be as impressive as the data that Mehra and Prescott cite. Every other country had lower equity performance on average and several countries' stock markets simply ceased functioning in some periods during the twentieth century. Using data from 1921 to 1996, Jorion and Goetzmann estimated a median real return of 0.8 percent annually for the countries in their study versus a 4.3 percent[11] real return for the U.S. stock market over the same period.

Jorion and Goetzmann constructed what they called a "world market appreciation index"[12] that would serve as a proxy for a fully diversified global portfolio. Lacking market capitalization for most of the early years in their data sample, Jorion and Goetzmann used gross domestic product (GDP) to weight the returns of individual countries in their world market appreciation index. Over the period of their data set, larger-GDP countries had better stock market performance than smaller-GDP countries. The performance of the world market appreciation index was estimated to be 4.0 percent, still large enough to remain an equity premium puzzle. They concluded that there is an

---

[9] Philippe Jorion and William N. Goetzmann, "Global Stock Markets in the Twentieth Century," *Journal of Finance* 54, no. 3 (June 1999): 953–980.

[10] Ibid., 953.

[11] Mehra and Prescott had a 6.98 percent real return estimate for the slightly longer period of 1889 to 1978.

[12] Jorion and Goetzmann, 955.

upward bias if you leave out the rest of the world's countries when considering stock returns. But does this solve the puzzle? It doesn't, because even a diversified global portfolio has extraordinarily high equity returns due to the high capitalization weights of the best performing countries.

OTHER EXPLANATIONS

Some argue that there is no equity premium puzzle—that the future is not going to be the same as the past and that future stock returns will be much lower than past returns. These arguments usually turn on an updated Malthusian type of argument where resource limitations come into play. Another potential explanation is the status quo bias. This is based on the fact that individuals rarely alter their asset allocation decisions made early in life. Early decisions to place tax-deferred assets into safe securities are not revisited with any frequency over an individual's lifetime. Agnew and Szykman (2005)[13] argue that individual investors often follow the "path of least resistance" in making asset allocation decisions. This often works against a high stock exposure in tax-deferred investment accounts.

If, initially, individuals select a heavy concentration of relatively riskless assets, thinking perhaps that they will revisit the situation at a later date, such individuals rarely revisit their allocations. The result is that once you neglect equities, you continue to neglect equities over time due to the status quo bias. Since a significant number of tax-deferred investors choose low risk investments initially, this causes the long-run equity allocation for such individuals to be lower than optimal for their own personal levels of risk aversion. Agnew, Balduzzi, and Sunden reported on 7,000 retirement accounts during a four-year period from April 1994 to August 1998 and found most asset allocations were extreme (either 100 percent equity or 100 percent relatively safe assets). They also found inertia in asset allocations over time.[14]

The issue of whether status quo bias can account for some or all of the equity premium puzzle is muddled by data problems as well as conceptual issues. Looking at the data for a single individual and seeing only their tax-deferred accounts leaves a lot to be desired. Does the individual have other assets? What are these other assets and do they offset what seems to be happening in the tax-deferred accounts? Does the individual have a spouse with

[13] Julie R. Agnew and Lisa R. Szykman, "Asset Allocation and Information Overload: The Influence of Information Display, Asset Choice and Investor Experience," *Journal of Behavioral Finance* 6, no. 2 (2005): 57–70.
[14] Julie R. Agnew, Pierluigi Balduzzi, and Annika Sunden, "Portfolio Choice and Trading in a Large 401(k) Plan," *American Economic Review* 93, no. 1 (March 2003): 193–215.

assets? Parents with assets? Children with assets? It is not clear that panel studies of retirement accounts necessarily present the full picture of the asset allocation that really matters.

ARE EQUITIES ALWAYS THE BEST PORTFOLIO FOR THE LONG RUN?

In 1994, Jeremy Siegel published a book[15] that became the icon for those who believed that long-term investors should own mainly stocks. This book codified what many had long thought: that the risk of owning stocks over a long holding period was less than the risks of holding them over shorter time periods. Siegel makes this point directly in his book:

> *It is very significant that stocks, in contrast to bonds and bills, have never delivered to investors a negative real return over periods of 17 years or more. Although it might appear to be riskier to accumulate wealth in stocks rather than in bonds over long periods of time, precisely the opposite is true: the safest long-term investment for the preservation of purchasing power has clearly been a diversified portfolio of equities.*[16]

An even more optimistic assessment of equities was provided by Glassman and Hassett in 2000,[17] when they forecast that the Dow Jones would soon triple in value. This did not prove to be a good short-term forecast, as their timing coincided with the onset of a decade-long global stagnation in equity prices.

Glassman and Hassett were arguing that stocks were cheap because there was a new world order thanks to the new Internet economy, but Siegel's argument was something different. There had always been a view that long-term investors should choose a different asset allocation with a heavier emphasis on common stocks than shorter horizon investors who should be more fearful of the risks of common stocks. Paul Samuelson famously provided proof that, at least in the context of the capital asset pricing model, long-horizon investors should hold approximately the same portfolio as short-horizon investors.[18]

---

[15] Jeremy Siegel, *Stocks for the Long Run* (New York: McGraw-Hill, 2008).

[16] Ibid., 25.

[17] James Glassman and Kevin Hassett, *Dow 36,000: The New Strategy for Profiting from the Coming Rise in the Stock Market* (New York: Three Rivers Press, 2000).

[18] Paul Samuelson, "Risk and Uncertainty: A Fallacy of Large Numbers," *Scientia* 98, no. 1 (1963): 108-113.

But the case for owning securities can be further buttressed by the following example. Imagine a riskless asset with a 4 percent return and no variance and a risky portfolio with a 12 percent return with a 16 percent variance. What is the likelihood that the risky portfolio will underperform a portfolio consisting only of the riskless asset? Thorley[19] took this example (and more) and provided the answers. The probability of underperformance in one year is 30.9 percent. Over five years, the probability drops to 13.2 percent. The probability of underperformance over 20 years is 1.3 percent and over 40 years is about one-tenth of 1 percent.

Zvi Bodie[20] countered Thorley's example by posing the question of the cost of prepaid insurance that would insure against underperformance by the risky portfolio as the length of the horizon is extended. What Bodie showed was that the value of the prepaid insurance tended, in the limit, to equal the total amount of the original money to be invested. Bodie's argument can be seen as supporting Samuelson's contention that equities look no better over the long haul than they do over the short horizon. Bodie concludes "that the probability of a shortfall is a flawed measure because it completely ignores how large the potential shortfall might be."[21]

IS THE EQUITY PREMIUM RESOLVED?

While loss aversion can explain the equity premium puzzle, it leaves finance theory in a precarious situation, since loss-averse utility functions do not fit neatly into much of existing finance theory. Further, if loss aversion is the true explanation, then EMH is false. People mistakenly own too little equity. They should buy and hold and never check the value of their holdings until they need to access the assets. That would be a better strategy than letting loss aversion push the investors towards an over reliance on lower-variance assets.

It is certainly possible that the equity returns that have been obtained in the past will not recur in the future. That case has been put forward. It is also possible that the Brown and Goetzmann argument of survivor bias may have more force in the future as global capitalizations shift so that a handful of large countries will not dominate the weightings in the future.

But, as yet, the equity premium puzzle remains a puzzle.

---

[19] Stephen R. Thorley, "The Time Diversification Controversy," *Financial Analysts Journal* 51, no. 3 (May–June 1995): 68–76.
[20] Zvi Bodie, "On the Risk of Stocks in The Long Run," *Financial Analysts Journal* 51, no. 3 (May–June 1995): 18–22.
[21] Ibid., 19.

CHAPTER 19

Liquidity

Asset liquidity is concerned with how quickly a collection of assets can be turned into cash and at what cost. Cash is the most liquid asset. Close behind are recently auctioned U.S. Treasury bills. It is relatively easy to buy or sell large numbers of U.S. Treasury bills at a price not much different, if different at all, from the most recent transaction price. That suggests a definition of illiquidity as the difference between the most recent transaction price and the price at which a purchase or sale could take place quickly in which the size of the purchase can vary from small to large.

The problem with this kind of definition is that the most recent transaction price could have occurred a long time ago. Think of selling or purchasing a house. The house may have been last purchased or sold many years before, so the most recent transaction price is likely to be very stale and not very relevant to the current transaction.

As this example indicates, liquidity is one of those things that people talk about, but it is a concept that is difficult to pin down in practice. Large-capitalization stocks are thought to be more liquid than small-capitalization stocks. Recently auctioned U.S. Treasury bills are seen as more liquid than treasury bills that were auctioned at an earlier date. U.S. Treasury securities are deemed to be more liquid than U.S. agency issues. Objects of art are viewed as less liquid than fruits and vegetables.

But what does liquidity mean? How do you define it? Rather than give a definition that is unsatisfactory, it may be best to simply repeat the first sentence of this chapter: Asset liquidity is concerned with how quickly a collection of assets can be turned into cash and at what cost. The reverse is also a notion of liquidity. How quickly and at what cost can cash be used to purchase a collection of assets? Always, implicitly, liquidity involves the notion of a true price versus a transaction price, with the difference providing an estimate of illiquidity.

A SECURITIES MARKET IS A BID-ASK MARKET

If you ask what the current price of an asset is, there is usually no answer. Current price is not a well-defined notion. When people ask what is the current price, the response is usually the most recent transaction price. But that is not a current price. There is a current market, but there is no current price. The current market consists of two prices: a bid price and an ask, or offer, price. The bid price is the highest price that someone is currently willing to pay for the asset. There may be more than one person willing to pay this price.

Suppose we are discussing the market for a stock. The bid price will be for a total number of shares of the stock and cumulates the total amount of shares that potential buyers are willing to bid for at that price. So a bid is something like the following:

Bid: 20¼ bid for 500 shares

The bid might be a single bidder or several bidders accumulated together. There may be many others that are also interested in buying stock, but, by definition of bid, those other potential buyers must not be willing to pay 20¼ for the stock. The ask or offer side of the market is just the reverse. The ask price is the lowest price that anyone is willing to sell stock at the current time:

Ask: 20¾ ask for 1,000 shares

If the ask price is 20¾, then there is no one willing to sell stock below 20¾. There may be more than one seller offering to sell stock at 20¾, but the total amount offered for sale at that price is 1,000 shares in our example. Others may wish to sell stock as well, but by the definition of the ask, those other potential sellers must not be willing to sell for a price as low as 20¾.

We now have enough information to define the current market, which is simply "20¼–20¾, 500 by 1,000." If that is the market and you wanted to purchase 100 shares, then you could transact immediately at 20¾. The new, most recent, transaction price becomes 20¾ and, assuming nothing else has changed, the market becomes "20¼–20¾, 500 by 900." Analogously, a quick sale of 100 shares of stock can be accomplished at 20¼, after which the market becomes "20¼–20¾, 400 by 900." The prices recorded are 20¾ followed by 20¼. Has the market changed? Not really. But the transaction prices make it appear that the stock has fallen one-half point. But, if another buyer wanted 100 shares quickly, the next transaction would be 20¾.

Did the market change? Again, not really, but it appears that the price just went up by one-half.

Suppose we start over with the following current market:

20 bid–21 ask, 500 by 1,000

The difference between this and the first market that we considered is that the bid is lower and the ask is higher. The bid-ask spread, defined as the difference between the bid and the ask, has gone from ½ to 1. Is there a difference in liquidity in these two markets? Can we measure this difference in liquidity?

MEASURING LIQUIDITY

The Qspread

One of the most common measures of liquidity is based upon the bid-ask spread, adjusted for scale. The scale adjustment uses the mid-point of the bid-ask spread, defined as the simple average of the bid and the ask. For a single observation, this liquidity measure is given by:

$$\text{Qspread:}^{[1]} \quad \frac{Ask - Bid}{MP}$$

$$\text{where the MP} = \frac{Ask + Bid}{2} \tag{19.1}$$

Assuming the data are available, a weekly liquidity measure is constructed by calculating the simple average of all the Qspreads observed during the week:

$$\text{Weekly Qspread} = \frac{1}{n}\sum_{i=1}^{n}\frac{Ask_i - Bid_i}{MP_i} \tag{19.2}$$

where n is the number of bid-ask observations during the week.

Daily and monthly Qspreads can be defined in a similar manner. Higher Qspreads are meant to be indicative of less liquidity. How good is Qspread as a measure of liquidity? If every desired purchase or sale involved a small number of shares, then Qspread captures much of what is intended by the concept of

[1]This terminology comes from Robert A. Korajczyk, and Ronnie Sadka, "Pricing the Commonality Across Alternative Measures of Liquidity," *Journal of Financial Economics* 87, no. 1 (January 2008): 49.

liquidity. But what if the buyer or seller wishes to engage in a transaction larger than the size quoted in the bid-ask spread? In that case the bid-ask spread might be inappropriate because it applies only to a smaller size transaction than is intended. If larger buyers and sellers enter the market, one would expect to see the bid-ask spread widen, indicating less liquidity, so it is possible that the Qspread might be sensitive to size, but there is no guarantee of that. Thus, considerations of size may make the Qspread an imperfect measure of liquidity.

Turnover Measure

Turnover calculates the number of shares traded during the period and divides that number by the total outstanding shares[2] at the end of the period. Using this concept, weekly turnover would be defined as:

$$\text{Weekly Turnover} = \frac{\text{Total Volume During the Week}}{\text{Shares Outstanding at the End of the Week}} \quad (19.3)$$

The higher weekly turnover is, the higher the measured liquidity using weekly turnover. So, how good is weekly turnover as a measure of liquidity? At extremes, weekly turnover may be a useful measure. A value of zero would certainly suggest illiquidity and a value of 10 would suggest a large level of liquidity. But what about weekly turnover values in between zero and ten? Does a weekly turnover value of 0.8 mean a stock is more liquid than a stock with a weekly turnover value of 0.75? It might, but it is certainly easy to construct scenarios where this measure rises while what we intuitively think of as liquidity declines over small time intervals.

Order-Imbalance Measure

The order-imbalance measure is constructed from direction indicators. A direction indicator, D, is assigned either a value of +1 or a value of −1, depending on whether the transaction price is above or below the most recent bid-ask midpoint. The idea behind the direction indicator is to suggest whether the transaction is buyer-initiated or seller-initiated. The order-imbalance measure

---

[2]*Outstanding* means freely available to trade. If there is *restricted* stock, meaning stock that cannot be sold due to legal restriction, that stock would not be included in outstanding stock. Also, if there are large concentrations of stock held by a small number of owners, who, there is good reason to believe, would not willingly transact their stock, such stock, if it can be accounted for, would not be included in the total of outstanding stock. The concept of outstanding stock is not the same as the usual notion contained in company Securities and Exchange Commission (SEC) filings.

is calculated by weighting each transaction's direction by the volume involved in that transaction and dividing by the number of shares outstanding.

$$\text{Order-imbalance} = \text{OI} = \frac{\sum_{i=1}^{n} D_i V_i}{SO_i} \qquad (19.4)$$

IS LIQUIDITY A PRICED RISK FOR COMMON STOCKS?

Contrarian investing strategies (Fama-French and De Bondt-Thaler, for example) are frequently associated with small-capitalization stocks, which are likely to be the most illiquid stocks. Thus, if illiquidity carries a risk, the higher returns for the stocks singled out in contrarian strategies might be the result of illiquidity, and the higher market returns for such stocks may be compensation for the risk of illiquidity. But what might the risk of illiquidity be? There are frequently situations where an investor needs to buy or sell quickly. If the stock is illiquid, then there will be costs associated with buying and selling quickly. These costs provide the risks of illiquidity.

There has been some research that suggests that investors can pursue buy and hold strategies with illiquid assets and focus their trading activity on liquid assets to partially offset the illiquidity risk factor. Such models imply that illiquid stocks will not fetch much of a risk premium if investors follow these strategies. Constantinides[3] argued that for a multi-period horizon, small deviations from optimal portfolios have relatively small effects on expected returns. This means that, while liquidity matters, it may not matter much. In Constantinides's theoretical model, investors "trade around" illiquid assets, focusing their trading on more liquid assets. The result is a different optimal portfolio than what would be chosen absent transaction costs. But the illiquidity is a relatively minor problem in Constantinides's model.

In a similar vein, Heaton and Lucas[4] consider transaction costs when there are "idiosyncratic labor income shocks." These shocks make liquidity a real issue because illiquid assets will be difficult to sell to provide consumption during periods of adverse income shocks. What Heaton and Lucas argue, in their theoretical model, is that investors will optimally move their trading

---

[3] George Constantinides, "Capital Market Equilibrium with Transaction Costs," *Journal of Political Economy* 94, no. 4 (August 1986): 842–862.
[4] John Heaton and Deborah J. Lucas, "Evaluating the Effects of Incomplete Markets on Risk Sharing and Asset Pricing," *Journal of Political Economy* 104, no. 3 (June 1996); 443–487.

activity to securities with the lowest transaction costs and trade around the illiquid assets, analogous to what happens in Constantinides's model.

SIGNIFICANCE OF LIQUIDITY RESEARCH

Is liquidity a risk that deserves to be compensated by returns? This question seems to have dominated the research agenda on stock market liquidity for the two decades after 1990. The conclusion reached by this research is that, using a variety of measures of liquidity, liquidity can be seen as a priced risk. Stocks with higher illiquidity, or higher sensitivity to aggregate or commonality factors, have higher equity returns. The effect is not large, but it does appear significant in the statistical research that has appeared.

There is an unsettling sense that liquidity is simply one more attribute of small stocks and that not much mileage is gained by digging down one layer to get to the fact that small stocks are illiquid.[5] We knew that already.

Where liquidity seems to be something new and different is its role in times of crisis. Both in the 1998 Russian default crisis and again in the Lehman bankruptcy crisis of 2008, liquidity became a big issue. What was interesting is that stocks and bonds that were the most liquid were sold, while illiquid stocks and bonds were not. Illiquidity seems to spur a crisis for liquid instruments, as they become the only things available that can be turned into cash quickly.

This process of illiquid securities holding up better than liquid securities during a financial panic is something worth further research. This may be a much more significant issue of liquidity versus illiquidity than whether or not liquidity is a priced risk. Can an illiquidity shock in one market lead to panic selling or margin-call selling in another market? This seems to be a significant aspect of liquidity that needs further study.

While the research on liquidity is far from complete, there remain conceptual issues and data issues. The consensus in the literature to date seems to be that illiquidity is a priced risk, but not large enough to necessarily account for much of the predictability patterns that are observed in stock market data.

---

[5]This argument is applicable not only to common stocks. The pattern of illiquidity in the government securities market where agency issues have slightly higher yields than similar duration treasuries could be another example apart from common stocks, since agency issues are much smaller in outstanding issue. Some have argued that the difference in yield might be the result of a mild credit difference, but that is unlikely.

CHAPTER 20

Neuroeconomics

In Part Three, we reviewed behavioral biases that seem inconsistent with the rationality assumptions of traditional economics. These biases have been documented by psychologists and economists in a large number of studies. What are the sources of these biases? Could we overcome our own biases by learning that we have them and resolving to rid ourselves of the biases that we find harmful to our own interests? Or, more ominously, are these biases innate, possibly genetic? Are these biases attributable to our evolutionary history? Could these biases be culture-bound rather than genetic? The field of neuroeconomics studies the extent to which there is a neurological basis for our emotions and decisions. Research in neuroeconomics began to flourish after the turn of the twenty-first century and was stimulated in part by interest in behavioral finance.

CAPUCHIN MONKEYS

The results of research experiments with capuchin monkeys[1] performed at Yale University seemed to suggest that these monkeys displayed some of the same behavioral tendencies that Kahneman, Tversky, and others had uncovered in humans. The monkeys were confronted with two sellers. One seller would show a single apple slice, but if the monkey were to purchase from that seller, the monkey would receive either one or two apple slices with equal probability. A second seller would show two apple slices but would provide the monkey with the same outcome upon purchase as the first seller—the monkey would receive either one or two apple slices with equal probability. Which seller would the monkeys gravitate toward? The

---

[1] M. Keith Chen, Venkat Lakshminarayanan, and Laurie R. Santos, "How Basic Are Behavioral Biases? Evidence from Capuchin Monkey Trading Behavior," *Journal of Political Economy*, 114, no. 3 (June 2006): 517–537.

first seller represents a potential gain from first appearances, while the second seller represents a potential loss from first appearances.

After a number of trials, the monkeys converged to choosing the first seller, which represented a gain possibility, well over two-thirds of the time. The key to this example is the reference point. The first seller showed a reference point of a single apple slice, while the second seller showed a reference point of two apple slices. While there was no difference whatsoever in the ultimate outcome from each seller, an expected value of one and one-half apple slices in either case, the monkeys decidedly preferred the gain possibility to the loss possibility. A further experiment found monkeys preferred a seller exhibiting a single apple slice to a seller displaying two, even though both sellers provided only a single slice in the actual transaction.

These experiments demonstrated that monkeys were sensitive to reference points in their decisions. The implications for loss aversion are less clear. The authors find loss aversion in the combination of these two experiments due to the fact that the percentages favoring the no-loss choice were higher in the third experiment than in the second experiment. This argument is not completely convincing, and it is certainly conceivable that the loss aversion discussed in Chapter 9 is not precisely the same as the implied definition that emerges from the capuchin monkey experiments.

The study of capuchin monkey behavior is important because capuchin monkeys are thought to be in the evolutionary chain that leads to *Homo sapiens*. If capuchin monkeys are subject to loss aversion and concerned with reference points, then that strongly suggests that human tendencies toward these biases may be innate, genetic in character, and are not either learned behavior or culturally acquired behavior. Innate behavioral biases take on more significance than culturally acquired biases because they are both harder to detect in oneself and should be expected to be more systematic as opposed to idiosyncratic.

Closely related to the innateness argument is the idea that specific parts of the human brain may be responsible for emotions and decisions. This idea first arose by observations of individuals who had suffered brain damage. The loss of functioning in certain parts of the brain appeared to change human emotional reactions to events. This suggested that certain parts of the human brain are responsible for certain emotions and feelings and that some decisions take place in some brain areas while other decisions may take place in other brain areas.

Phineas Gage, an American railroad worker in the mid-nineteenth century, survived an accident that, according to legend, destroyed much of his brain's left frontal lobe. Apparently, Gage's behavior changed dramatically after the accident, and these changes were linked to the damage to his brain. There is some dispute about exactly what Gage was like before and after the accident and, no doubt, the fact that he survived such a serious injury may be his main hold on the imagination of history. Wartime hospitals provided additional examples of particular behavioral changes that seemingly were related to head and brain injuries.

INNATENESS VERSUS CULTURE

Do biases reflect our culture or do biases arise genetically and are part of our anatomical makeup? The answer to this question is important. Cultural biases can be more easily corrected than biases that stem from genetic inheritance. Such biases may also vary from culture to culture and thus may offset one another among a global population. If biases are innate, then they are more likely to be systematic, which suggests more of an economic impact. Even if a bias is innate, it is still possible that learned behavior can supplant an innate tendency, but learning would seem to have more possibilities for correcting biases that are cultural than those that are innate.

Innateness suggests some other possibilities. One often hears that a particular part of the brain is highly activated when two apparently different activities take place. Addiction, for example, seems to be related somehow to the nucleus accumbens[2] part of the brain. It is here that video game players,[3] Wall Street traders,[4] and drug addicts[5] might all find their rewards. Knowing that one has an addictive personality, which might be discoverable if the brain locus is known, could be very useful information. Addictive behavior is not normally viewed as a good thing, so that learning more about the neurological basis for addiction could spur the search for answers to how to control or eliminate such behavior.

DECISIONS ARE MADE BY THE BRAIN

The main impetus behind neuroeconomics is the simple idea that decisions are made by the human brain (and perhaps by the brains of certain animals).

---

[2] M. L. Kringelbach, *The Pleasure Center: Trust Your Animal Instincts* (New York: Oxford University Press, 2009).

[3] Chih-Hung Ko, et. al. "Brain Activities Associated with Gaming Urge of Online Gaming Addictions," *Journal of Psychiatric Research* 43, no. 7 (April 2009): 739–747.

[4] Peter Aldhous, "Happy Traders Take More Risks," *New Scientist* 201, no. 2702 (April 2009): 9.

[5] Gaetano Di Chiara, "Dopamine and Drug Addiction: The Nucleus Accumbens Shell Connection," *Neuropharmacology* 47, Suppl. 1 (2004): 227–241.

By studying the relationship between physical activity in the brain that takes place either before, during, or after humans make decisions, we can better understand human activity, including economic activity. Why is this interesting for economics and finance? Ultimately, the goal of much of this research seems to be prescriptive. How can we improve decision making by better understanding the process that takes place in human brains? For behavioral finance, the point is that if we have biases in our decision-making process and those biases lead us to make incorrect decisions that reduce our welfare or happiness, then perhaps by better understanding the underlying anatomical basis for those biases, we can find corrective measures. Such corrective measures can then lead to improvements in welfare and happiness. In the case of finance, perhaps it can make us wealthier or, at the very least, improve our financial decisions.

Not only are decisions made by the brain, but the evaluation of those decisions seems to be centered in brain activity as well. Whenever we feel good or bad, sense regret or disappointment, feel pleasure or anger, perhaps there is a specific locus in our brain that controls or triggers such feelings. So outcomes, as well as choices, are evaluated by our brains. Our decisions are based on our expectations. Our expectations are presumably conditioned by our experience. But expectations may be very different from experience. It is always possible that individuals want something that, once consumed, they wish they had never consumed. If economic theory is about how preferences become implemented into economic decisions, what if the outcomes thought to be preferred are actually not good outcomes once they have been experienced? Is this a failure of economics, that outcomes are not studied, only the preferences?

Return to our example of addiction. If drug addiction is a bad thing, but a rational individual prefers to consume drugs, what then? You could restrict the choice to legal alternatives. Suppose I prefer big juicy burgers to salads, while we might all agree that salads are better for me. Both burgers and salads can be legally consumed. So when I purchase a burger instead of a salad, I respect my preferences but I might end up with a bad outcome. Imagine a simplified model of the brain, in which one-half of the brain lights up when good outcomes occur and the other half lights up when bad outcomes occur. Shouldn't we be trying to light up the good outcome part of the brain? Admittedly, we do not now know if the brain can be divided in such a convenient way, but who knows? One of the goals of neuroeconomics is to see if such evaluations of outcomes can be accomplished by studying brain activity.

There has been a debate from the earliest discussions of neuroeconomics about whether much will ever be learned about economics from its study. Critics argue that neuroeconomics is more likely to provide information about psychology than about economics. Gul and Pesendorfer[6] have criticized neuroeconomics as an attempt to reinterpret economics into the realm of psychology. They argue that much of the research in neuroeconomics is simply irrelevant to the field of economics, including welfare economics.[7] Camerer[8] has constructed a defense for neuroeconomics that directly counters that of Gul and Pesendorfer. Part of Camerer's argument is that neuroeconomics has "optionality" as a scientific discipline since we may find uses for it in the future.[9] That argument is not compelling, since studying anything at all has optionality in the sense that Camerer is using the term.

DECISIONS VERSUS OUTCOMES

Economists do not normally indulge in the evaluation of outcomes. Are countries with larger gross domestic product (GDP) per capita better off than countries with lower GDP per capita? Who knows? In fact, how would one even begin to answer a question like that? Am I better off consuming what I want, or should someone force me onto a diet? These are not discussions that economists have in their professional roles. But discussions like this are part of the focus of neuroeconomics in their emphasis on experienced utility. Does a particular activity make someone happy? How would you know? Perhaps by studying the brain's response to that activity, we might learn if that activity makes someone happy. Economists generally recoil from this kind of suggestion as if it is not part of their agenda. Neuroeconomics does not recoil from this. Indeed, neuroeconomists are very much interested in whether studying the brain's interaction with outcomes can shed light on whether individuals are happy or unhappy with economic outcomes. Some even argue that outcomes are often obviously not good ones and that decisions should be influenced directly by outside intervention.

---

[6] Faruk Gul and Wolfgang Pesendorfer, "The Case for Mindless Economics," in Andrew Caplin and Andrew Schotter, eds., *The Foundations of Positive and Normative Economics: A Handbook* (New York: Oxford University Press, 2008), Chapter 1.

[7] Here we use the term *welfare economics* as economists use it, describing the allocative efficiency of an economic system. Efficiency can be consistent with grave inequalities and injustices, but involves no wasted resources.

[8] Colin Camerer, "The Case for Mindful Economics," in Caplin and Schotter, eds., Chapter 2.

[9] Ibid., 48.

Thaler and Sunstein[10] have argued that biases can be overcome by "libertarian paternalism," which seeks to influence choices through, among other things, changing default options. A default option is what someone chooses by making no choice. Not choosing the default is known as "opting out" of the default option. A car turn indicator is an example. The default position is that no turn is indicated. If you wish to turn left and use the turn indicator, you would simply move the turn indicator into the left position. By doing so, you would be opting out of the default, the no-turn position.

The status quo bias, discussed in Chapter 11, suggests that individuals will tend to leave the default option in place rather than opting out. Therefore, it is important that the default option is the one that is most appropriate for most situations. This is why turn indicators are normally in the off position in the default mode. Thaler and Sunstein apply this reasoning to investment choices and argue that the defaults for employee investment plans, set by their employers, should be the investment plans that are most appropriate for most of the employees (and not simply the least risky, for example).

The consideration of outcomes is a subject of intense debate in the neuroeconomics field. Some argue that economists should be mainly concerned with outcomes, not preferences. Neuroeconomics can teach us how the brain values outcomes, it is argued. Focusing on preferences might lead us astray. The response to this is that economics is concerned with how individual preferences influence economic behavior and that ultimate outcomes are not relevant.

NEUROECONOMIC MODELING

The heart and soul of neuroeconomic research is the construction of mathematical models of the brain's interaction with emotions. Other factors, such as relative attention and anticipation, play a role in these models as well, but the main focus is on emotions and the effect that emotions have on brain activity. A survey of the simplest models of this type of research was provided by Fehr and Rangel in 2011.[11] In their survey, they lay out the "five key components of the computational model of simple

---

[10]Richard Thaler and Cass Sunstein, *Nudge: Improving Decisions About Health, Wealth and Happiness* (New York: Penguin, 2008).

[11]Ernest Fehr and Antonio Rangel, "Neuroeconomic Foundations of Economic Choices—Recent Advances," *Journal of Economic Perspectives* 25, no. 4 (Fall 2011): 3–30.

choice that arises from the neuroeconomics literature." These five components[12] are:

1. The brain computes a decision value signal for each option at the time of choice.
2. The brain computes an experienced utility signal at the time of consumption.
3. Choices are made by comparing decision values.
4. Decision values are computed by integrating information about the attributes associated with each option and their attractiveness.
5. The computation and comparison of decision values is modulated by attention.

Of these five components, component four is able to summarize the approach that Fehr and Rangel are describing. They cite the following equation[13] as characterizing their approach to neuroeconomics modeling:

$$v(x) = \sum w_i d_i(x) \qquad (20.1)$$

The $v(x)$ is the function that assigns a value, v, to a particular choice, x. It is assumed that there may be more choices available, in which case there is a $v(y)$ where y is some alternative choice that may be available. The function $d_i(x)$ is some characteristic of x, in this case the ith characteristic. For example, if x is eating an apple, the ith characteristic might be any one of "taste, caloric intake, vitamin and mineral regulation, as well as more abstract dimensions such as health or self-image."[14] $v(x)$ provides a weighted average of these dimensions, where the weights, w_i, are specific to the individual trying to make the decision. The research agenda, according to Fehr and Rangel, is to find out what these dimensions are and to attempt to estimate the weights for different individuals.

What we have learned thus far is not clear. Note that experienced utility is very much a part of the research agenda. Fehr and Rangel also discuss fairness as another dimension of valuation. The precise definition of fairness, as well as other concepts, is not obvious. Why are we interested in experienced utility, assuming we know what experienced utility means and can somehow measure it? Is it presumed that an outside party can redirect an individual's consumption pattern so as to achieve higher levels of experienced utility? What about fairness? Is this an individual's conception

---

[12] Fehr and Rangel, 7–13.
[13] Ibid., 12.
[14] Ibid., 12.

of fairness? What if one individual's notion of fairness is not the same as another's? These are issues that continue to cause controversy around the subject of neuroeconomics.

MORE COMPLICATED MODELS OF BRAIN ACTIVITY

Instead of merely computing decision values in the manner described by Fehr and Rangel, some researchers have decided that brain patterns should be analyzed in conjunction with emotions and choices in a more complicated manner. This research was summarized by van Rooij and Van Orden[15] in 2011. Van Rooij and Van Orden argue that simple mathematical models that attempt to assign values to choices in a decision problem are not working and that more "complexity" should be brought to bear. This more complex view uses time series of overall brain activity and employs fractal methods in an effort to unearth patterns of brain activity that correspond to decision making and emotions. Van Rooij and Van Orden describe this approach as generalizing "the linear concepts that preceded it."[16]

THE KAGAN CRITIQUE

Jerome Kagan[17] has produced a critique of psychology that applies with equal force to much of behavioral finance, but especially to neuroeconomics. Kagan contends that there are two major drawbacks to the research on brain reactions to emotions. The first criticism is that the specific emotion under consideration is not well defined. Fear, for example, means very different things in different contexts. The fear that one feels when approached by a lion in the wild is a very different emotion than the fear of losing a point in a tennis match.

The second criticism that Kagan argues is that emotions such as fear, happiness, anger, and joy are not only not well defined but depend on the context. Observing brain activity and brain patterns without taking into account the context of the individual undergoing observation can lead psychologists to make incorrect generalizations about the relationships

---

[15] Martin van Rooij and Guy Van Orden, "It's About Space, It's About Time, Neuroeconomics and the Brain Sublime," *Journal of Economic Perspectives* 25, no. 4 (Fall 2011): 31–56.

[16] Ibid., 50.

[17] Jerome Kagan, *Psychology's Ghosts: The Crisis in the Profession and the Way Back* (New Haven, CT: Yale University Press, 2012).

between brain activity and emotions. Kagan is especially harsh on applications in behavioral economics including behavioral finance.

The Kagan critique is a broadside aimed at experimental psychologists generally and applies with equal force to the process of analyzing decisions in experimental settings, such as those discussed in Part Three of this book. In essence, Kagan is arguing that psychologists are attempting to make generalizations about human behavior that may be inappropriate. The thrust of his critique is that neuroeconomics may lead nowhere if much of human behavior is contextually or culturally bound.

CONCLUSION

The focus on methodology and approach is likely to reflect the paucity of actual results in this area of research. While Camerer and others have high hopes for the future of neuroeconomics, there isn't yet much in the way of hard results. The shortage of hard results and the methodological disputes that plague the young field of neuroeconomics represent a serious challenge. While the study of brain activity may have the potential to open up new vistas of research, one has to wonder whether any of these new vistas will shed much light on economics or behavioral finance.

CHAPTER 21

Experimental Economics

It is common in physical sciences to do a laboratory experiment to test a theory or to unearth a new and interesting hypothesis. The research activities of economics did not involve experimental methods until the second half of the twentieth century. The early work in experimental economics was met with some skepticism and even as the field matured and garnered its first Nobel Prize winner, experimental economics remained something of a stepchild among the various research methods utilized in economics.

The rise of interest in behavioral finance brought new life into experimental economics, which had been mostly devoted in earlier days to market price formation and voting behavior. Behavioral finance suggested a number of other issues to explore using experimental methods—bubbles, inefficient pricing, overconfidence, endowment and status quo effects, and others. Charles Holt distinguishes classroom experiments from economic experiments, where the latter involve actual monetary payments.[1] Since real-world agents are presumed to be motivated by financial considerations only, economic experiments where actual money is involved are viewed as legitimate research experiments. Classroom experiments, where no money is involved, are viewed by Holt as learning experiments, where the students are doing the learning.

So how does an experiment work? Normally, the structure of the experiment is game theoretic. Game theoretic means that there are explicit "players" of the game and the outcome for any individual player is affected by his or her decision as well as the decisions of others involved. Many games are zero-sum games, meaning what one player wins, another player loses. Zero-sum games are not common in economics, and the economy itself is not generally viewed by economists as a zero-sum game, though often the public

---

[1]Charles Holt, *Markets, Games & Strategic Behavior* (Upper Saddle River, NJ: Prentice Hall, 2007), 11.

might see it that way. Most experiments are not zero-sum; often, strategies can provide gains for some players without losses for others.

A market game consists of buyers and sellers who may or may not be aware of the existence of buyers and sellers other than themselves. Market game experiments are the usual environment for studying issues that are suggested from behavioral finance research. One of the most interesting issues studied using experimental methods is that of bubbles and crashes.

BUBBLE EXPERIMENTS

A bubble occurs when the price of an asset rises above its fundamental value, and the gap between price and fundamental value grows over a lengthy period of time. For research purposes, the real world of data does not supply us with an observable fundamental value. Who knows what something is really worth? So how, in practice, can one know if a bubble is taking place or if, instead, fundamental value is increasing rapidly? The inability to observe fundamental value is one of the key reasons that experimental asset markets have proved so useful.

It is relatively easy to define fundamental value in an experimental market. Typically, the value is defined as a combination of a known, certain terminal value of an asset with stochastic dividends along the way, whose expected value is easy to calculate. In most experiments, the participants are given all of the relevant information permitting them to calculate expected values on their own. As if that weren't enough, the participants are often given the expected values directly at the beginning of each trading session.

From the early pioneering work of Vernon Smith, it has been known that asset pricing bubbles occur frequently in experimental asset markets. Initially, it was thought that bubbles arise only when there is considerable uncertainty in the market, but, as the amount of uncertainty was removed, the bubbles remained. Apparently, bubbles do not require uncertainty to be a persistent feature of asset markets according to experimental research. This is somewhat surprising. Even in situations where the details of the asset payoffs are known by the players with absolute certainty, bubbles still occur.

The classic early treatment of bubbles in experimental settings was reported by Smith, Suchanek, and Williams in 1988[2] (SSW). SSW used a procedure that had been common in earlier studies—a "double auction" market. *Double auction* referred to the fact that potential buyers provided

---

[2]Vernon Smith, Gerry Suchanek, and Arlington Williams, "Bubbles, Crashes, and Endogenous Expectations in Experimental Spot Asset Markets," *Econometrica* 56, no. 5 (September 1988): 1119–1151.

bids and potential sellers provided offers. One could view the buyers as one auction and the sellers as another auction, hence the term *double auction*. Holt credits Smith with first using the double auction market.[3]

Participants were given money and/or some amount of the asset in the SSW games. Trading in the asset took place over 15 periods (some experiments involved 30 periods). All participants were given the same information about the asset. Aside from prices of transactions, the main information available to participants regarded expected dividends payable to holders of the assets. Participants were told the different possible dividend payments that the asset might pay at the end of each period and the probability of each specific dividend amount. Then, at the conclusion of each period the amount of the dividend was announced, having been drawn from the probability distribution, about which the participants had been informed.

SSW were interested in two issues. The first issue was to find out if giving all participants identical and correct information would still lead to bubbles. Prior research had suggested that diversity of information was the spark that triggered bubbles. The second issue was to discover if experience mattered. As participants gained experience, would bubbles become more or less likely?

"Of the 22 experiments that did not involve experimenter intervention or inadvertent disruptions, the modal outcome (14 experiments of which 9 used experienced subjects) was a market characterized by a price bubble measured relative to dividend value."[4] Experienced subjects were less likely to produce bubbles in experiments, but bubbles were frequent even with experienced subjects. SSW cautioned that their experiments did not show that rationality was grossly violated but instead revealed "that the predominating characteristic of these experiments is the tendency for expectations and price adjustments to converge to intrinsic value across experiments with increasing subject experience."[5]

There were two other characteristics of the SSW experiments worth noting. First, the mean price in the first period was typically less than the expected value of the dividend stream, suggesting risk aversion early on, prior to the onset of the bubble. Indeed, SSW speculate that early risk aversion may set the prior conditions that provide a breeding ground for bubbles. The second feature of the experiments was a decline in trading volume during crashes and heightened volume during the boom phase of the bubbles. This latter feature seems to correspond with real-world experience, as well as with prospect theory, which predicts people are more likely to sell stocks

---

[3] Holt, 4.
[4] Smith et al., 1148.
[5] Ibid., 1125.

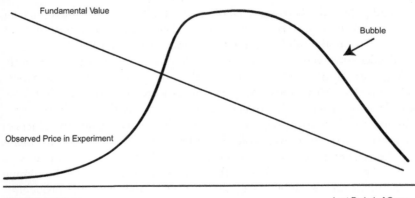

Fundamental Value

Bubble

Observed Price in Experiment

First Period of Game   Last Period of Game

FIGURE 21.1

they perceive as winners than those that feel like losers.[6] The usual pattern of bubbles in experimental situations looks like the pattern described in Figure 21.1.

The conclusion that trading experience reduces the likelihood of bubbles was reinforced by research in the two decades that followed the publication of the SSW results. Dufwenberg, Lindquist, and Moore[7] (DLM) ran a number of experiments controlling for the experience of the participants. Their goal was to learn more about whether bubbles were primarily the result of inexperienced market participants. As they noted in their paper, most experimental economists favored the view that it took only a few inexperienced traders in a market to create a bubble. DLM found just the opposite. Their experiments showed that when at least one-third of the trading participants were experienced, bubbles seemed to no longer take place.

If experience eliminates bubbles, then why do we observe bubbles over time? One potential answer is that inexperienced traders are always entering markets. Markets that are rising in price are precisely the kind of asset markets that attract inexperienced traders. Bubbles are relatively rare in the real world, one might argue, because it takes a lot of newly entering, inexperienced traders to provide the engine that drives the bubble, and most markets do not attract enough inexperienced traders for bubbles to persist. But, once in a while, a sufficient number of inexperienced traders will enter a particular market and that market then becomes a bubble.

---

[6] See Chapter 9 for a more detailed discussion of prospect theory.

[7] Martin Dufwenberg, Tobias Lindquist, and Evan Moore, "Bubbles and Experience: An Experiment," *American Economic Review* 95, no. 5 (December 2005): 1731–1737.

Bubbles could be reduced by the effect of short selling. Both King, Smith, Williams, and Van Boening[8] and Ackert, Charupat, Church, and Deaves[9] found evidence from experimental markets that suggested that bubbles would be less likely if short selling was permitted. Haruvy and Noussair[10] found just the opposite. Huravy and Nussair concluded that "simply adding short-selling capability does not appear to eliminate the trader behavior that underlies bubble formation."[11] Bubbles can be impacted, according to research reported by Porter and Smith,[12] by inserting a futures market that captures directly the price formation applicable to a future date, although the existence of a futures market did not completely eliminate bubbles in their experiments. It simply made them smaller in magnitude.

ENDOWMENT EFFECT AND STATUS QUO BIAS

Experimental methods have been extensively used to demonstrate the endowment effect discussed in Chapter 11. These experiments are similar in design to the experiments that seek to produce asset market bubbles. In Richard Thaler's classic treatment of endowment effects and status quo biases,[13] he notes that status quo biases are the subject of a substantially different type of experiment. Designing both public and private policy defaults is a type of real-world experiment that is based on the idea that most individuals exhibit status quo bias. People tend to accept defaults and not change things. Thus, making defaults produce good outcomes for most people is a policy that Thaler and others have recommended in both public and private settings.[14]

---

[8] Ronald King, Vernon Smith, Arlington Williams, and Mark Van Boening, "The Robustness of Bubbles and Crashes in Experimental Stock Markets," in I. Prigogine, R. Day, and P. Chen, eds., *Nonlinear Dynamics and Evolutionary Economics* (New York: Oxford University Press, 1993).

[9] Lucy F. Ackert, Narat Charupat, Bryan K. Church, and Richard Deaves, "Bubbles in Experimental Asset Markets: Irrational Exhuberance No More," Federal Reserve Bank of Atlanta Working Paper, 2001.

[10] Ernan Haruvy and Charles N. Noussair, "The Effect of Short Selling on Bubbles and Crashes in Experimental Spot Asset Markets," *Journal of Finance* 61, no. 3 (June 2006): 1119–1157.

[11] Ibid., 1121.

[12] David P. Porter and Vernon Smith, "Futures Contracting and Dividend Uncertainty in Experimental Asset Markets," *Journal of Business* 68, no. 4 (October 1995): 509–541.

[13] See Chapter 6 in Richard Thaler, *Winner's Curse* (New York: Free Press, 1992).

[14] Richard Thaler and Cass Sunstein, *Nudge* (New York: Penguin, 2008).

CALENDAR EFFECTS

Calendar effects have been studied using experimental markets. Coursey and Dyl[15] reported results consistent with patterns observed around holidays and weekends by having arbitrary known trading interruptions in experimental markets. Anderson, Gerlach, and DiTraglia[16] studied January effects in experiments that took place separately in December and then in January. They found that prices were bid significantly higher when the experiments took place in January than when the identical experiments took place in the prior month. This could be an area where future research could prove to be very fruitful. Calendar effects remain a puzzling research area and experimental methods may have great potential to add to our understanding of such effects.

CONCLUSION

Experimental economics seems particularly well suited to tackle issues that involve price formation, such as those discussed in this chapter. The fact that experimental markets often conform surprisingly well with actual markets suggests that much will be learned using this research method in the future, especially regarding important issues in behavioral finance.

---

[15]D. L. Coursey and E. A. Dyl, "Price Effects of Trading Interruptions in an Experimental Market," unpublished working paper, University of Wyoming, 1986.

[16]Lisa R. Anderson, Jeffrey R. Gerlach, and Francis J. DiTraglia, "Yes, Wall Street, There Is a January Effect! Evidence from Laboratory Auctions," *Journal of Behavioral Finance* 8, no. 1 (2007): 1–8.

Conclusion

And the Winner Is?

So who is right? Is the market efficient or mostly efficient? Or is it time for a new paradigm entirely that meets the criticisms that have been leveled by the behavioralists? There can be little question that over the past three decades the behavioralists have gained considerable ground and that even the most ardent defenders of the EMH have retreated a bit. Malkiel has kind words for mean-reversion in the latest editions of his classic,[1] and even Fama is willing to admit that there are many open issues. Kahneman urges that the received finance theory not be abandoned, as it holds many truths.[2] Shleifer has, at times, taken the middle ground, even though much of his research has done the efficient market hypothesis (EMH) the most damage.

This is a complicated debate, and the debate is far from over. There remain many different points of dispute. On some issues, the behavioralists seem to have taken the lead, but in other areas, the EMH still seems to reign supreme. In this chapter, we consider various points of contention and try to assess the current scorecard between the EMH and its critics.

THE SEMI-STRONG HYPOTHESIS—PRICES ACCURATELY SUMMARIZE ALL KNOWN PUBLIC INFORMATION

It is commonly accepted that the weak hypothesis (that prices cannot be predicted from past price data) is true. We will probably never have any idea whether the strong hypothesis (that prices accurately summarize all information, public and private) is valid, since traders acting on inside information are not likely to share their performance data with researchers. That leaves us with the semi-strong EMH as the most relevant of the three Fama definitions. The semi-strong hypothesis has been subject to two very different interpretations.

[1] Burton Malkiel, *A Random Walk Down Wall Street* (New York: W. W. Norton, 2003).
[2] Daniel Kahneman, *Thinking, Fast and Slow* (New York: Farrar, Straus and Giroux, 2011). See especially pp. 286–287.

One of the interpretations lends itself to an apparently winning position for the EMH adherents, while the other interpretation favors the critics.

Malkiel's Interpretation of the Semi-Strong Hypothesis

Burton Malkiel has staked his defense of the EMH on the grounds that money managers are unable to beat simple market indices. That is the principal theme of his classic, *A Random Walk Down Wall Street*, and he has updated, but not changed, his position on numerous occasions. Malkiel's argument runs along the following lines. If prices do not accurately summarize all known public information, then some public information could be useful in identifying "underpriced" and "overpriced" assets. Malkiel and others have provided overwhelming documentation that money managers, as a group, fail to beat simple averages, even when fees are neglected.[3]

The argument is that if markets are inefficient and we know it, then smart people can manage money and produce performance that exceeds the returns from simple indices. Why don't they? If managers underperform simple indices, then that suggests it may be impossible to do otherwise with any consistency. What outperformance is observed in the data may be simply the result of the inherent randomness of money management.

Some of the most devastating arguments against manager performance have to do with persistence of good performance. Studies have shown that managers with bad prior performance are as likely to have good future performance as managers with good prior performance.[4] These studies strongly suggest that performance is random, consistent with EMH predictions.

Predictability

If the stock market is efficient, then adjusted stock returns can be represented as a martingale process. This means that future returns are not predictable even if much is known about the mean and variance of the return distribution. This lack of predictability is the same lack of predictability that faces someone rolling a die with six sides. You never know which of the six sides may be the result of the roll, even though you expect each side to have a one-sixth probability as the outcome. Another example is a 50/50 heads-versus-tails coin flip. All of these examples can be construed, with proper

---

[3] There are numerous studies that document that active management does not, in the aggregate, beat simple market indices. A summary of this very large literature can be found in Larry E. Swedore, *The Quest for Alpha* (Hoboken, NJ: John Wiley & Sons, 2011).

[4] Ibid., 82–83.

adjustment, as processes that can be converted into a martingale process, where the next period's return, the next roll of the dice, or the next flip of the coin is not predictable.

But is this what the data show—lack of predictability? The evidence seems to point in the other direction. Mean reversion, price and earnings momentum, and calendar effects are all examples of predictability. The book-to-market effect of Fama and French is a stark example of predictability as well. At first blush, all of these seem to violate the semi-strong hypothesis. EMH defenders retreat to the possibility of a risk that has not been identified but that is responsible for the excess returns from these various simple strategies. But what is that risk? The most common culprits center around the small stock character of much of the predictability evidence. But the evidence is by no means all centered around small stocks.

Even if small stocks are often the dominant players in the predictability literature, that, by itself, is an incomplete defense of the EMH unless there is something about small stocks that either invalidates the basic result, perhaps because of data measurement issues, or points to risks that may be peculiar to small stocks, such as market liquidity. Neither defender nor critic is completely satisfied that this debate is settled and so the debate continues.

It is difficult not to conclude that the critics of the EMH have the upper hand, because mean reversion, momentum, and calendar effects seem to have remained present in stock market data well after such tendencies were first identified in the academic literature. That the strategies are so simple to implement is a feature of the predictability literature that is not easy to dismiss. If simple investment rules such as mean reversion continue to work and no particular risk of any significance is ever advanced after several decades of research, then maybe mean reversion is not going away. That thought is not a comforting one for those defending the EMH.

CAN PRICES CHANGE IF INFORMATION DOESN'T CHANGE?

If information determines prices, then how much wiggle room is there for prices to move around if information seems not be changing? The October 19, 1987, stock market fall of 22.6 percent stands out in sharp relief. Why did a fall in stock prices of this magnitude occur? What information changed? The year 1987 is one of great puzzlement. The year began and ended with the Dow Jones showing little sense of direction. Had you only observed the beginning-of-year and ending-of-year stock market averages, you would have thought 1987 a dull year for stocks. But in the first half of 1987, stock market averages rose nearly 30 percent, then declined, collapsed on a single day in October, and then rallied to approximately where they began the year. Given this pattern, surely there must have been some wild swings in information.

If information did change in 1987 in some systematic way to steer prices in such dramatic fashion, no one has yet to produce any credible evidence of such a pattern of information change. There are numerous explanations for the October 19 crash. Some cite "program trading" or "portfolio insurance" as the culprit for the one-day disaster, but that argument hardly gives much of an explanation for the strange pattern of stock prices for the rest of the year. In any event, mechanical trading activities such as program trading or portfolio insurance presumably would have been known to the market, and market participants would have been prepared to take advantage of any dislocation that such trading could cause. That no such offset appeared is an argument against the EMH.

Either information is driving prices or it isn't. It isn't an adequate defense of the EMH to argue that in the long run, the EMH is true, but in the short run, the EMH may be false. That isn't a satisfactory state of affairs because decisions get made along the way. It is one thing to argue that prices can temporarily deviate by small amounts from efficient prices, quite another to argue that market collapses exceeding 20 percent in a single day can take place with no apparent change in information. If the EMH is consistent with market moves without an information explanation such as the events on October 19, 1987, then the EMH is a theory in trouble. The EMH requires an information-based explanation for 1987 and none has appeared.

The "excess volatility" argument that says stock prices are generally much more volatile than the data that are supposed to determine them—an argument similar in spirit to the puzzling facts of stock market behavior in 1987—throws considerable doubt on the validity and usefulness of the EMH. Linking information changes to asset price changes seems fundamental to any defense of the EMH. So far, that linkage is empirically elusive.

IS THE LAW OF ONE PRICE VALID?

Can substantially identical assets trade at different prices? The answer to this seems to be clearly in the affirmative, unless the assets are fungible. Not only are there a number of empirical examples—Royal Dutch and Shell being the most famous—but Shleifer and others have developed a convincing argument that, because of the limits to arbitrage, absent fungibility, assets with identical fundamental risk can trade at different prices in a free market.[5] This seems to be a clear defeat for the EMH.

---

[5] See Chapter 5 for more information.

Defenders of the EMH would respond that while there may be situations from time to time where the law of one price doesn't seem to hold, these situations are exceptions. But how are we to know that? Numerous examples seem available that suggest otherwise. If the law of one price has trouble, imagine the difficulty for the accurate pricing of similar, though not identical, assets. It is then not much of a stretch to envision important mispricings that lead to bubble episodes that can persist longer than might be suggested by the EMH framework, such as the tech bubble of the late 1990s and the housing bubble in the post-2003 period in the United States.

THREE RESEARCH AGENDAS

Behavioral Finance research can be grouped generally into three separate agendas that correspond to our Parts Two, Three, and Four of this book. The results of these three separate research areas cannot be encouraging to supporters of the EMH.

Noise Trader Research

Noise trader research has not yet reached definitive conclusions, save possibly one conclusion. It seems now well established that there are "limits to arbitrage" that can prevent market prices from settling near the levels suggested by the EMH. The most elegant treatment of the limits to arbitrage argument is that of Shleifer and colleagues cited in Part Two. Much of noise trader research proceeds by assuming that market prices diverge from EMH levels and then working out the results of such divergence. The Shleifer et al. research does not assume the conclusion, but instead provides a convincing logic that undermines the EMH. So, while much of noise trader research does not directly address the underlying logic of the EMH, the Shleifer et al. research is a direct and successful use of the limits to arbitrage argument to undermine the inherent logic of the EMH.

While the theory of bubbles is still a work-in-progress, the recurring bubbles in financial markets over the centuries serve to provide examples of actual market behavior that is difficult to square with the EMH. Research has produced narratives of these bubbles but, thus far, no real theoretical foundations that can explain them.[6]

---

[6]See Carmen Reinhart and Kenneth Rogoff, *This Time Is Different* (Princeton: Princeton University Press, 2009). Rogoff and Reinhart attempt to summarize key features of financial collapses over the past several hundred years, but do not provide a systematic theory of how and why they occur.

Decision Making and Psychology—
The Kahneman-Tversky Agenda

Part Three outlines the decision-making research pioneered by Daniel
Kahneman and Amos Tversky. This research is fascinating and goes beyond
economics and finance. Fama has argued that the various biases that are
demonstrated in this literature act in opposite directions and are probably
canceling each other out in a law-of-large-numbers fashion. Fama has a
point. It is often not clear what the implications for finance are of a particular bias, even if that bias has a strong research footing. Assuming the bias
is typical of human behavior, it is still not obvious that the implications of
any particular bias or collection of biases invalidates any of the predictions
of the EMH. That people do not behave quite as rationally as economics
assumes does not necessarily interfere with the conclusion that an increase
in supply tends to lower a product price or that an increase in demand tends
to increase a product price. More is required than the simple demonstration
that a bias may violate an assumption that underlies a prediction.

Loss aversion is different. If loss aversion is true, then some predictions
of the EMH may be in jeopardy. Loss aversion is a potential answer to
the equity premium puzzle, for example. The EMH provides no generally
agreed-upon explanation for the equity premium puzzle. Loss aversion is especially troublesome because it suggests no obvious way of filling in the gap
that would be left by abandoning traditional decision theory assumptions
embedded in the EMH. Loss aversion is able to account for a number of
other financial data points that are puzzling. The "disposition effect," which
means that individuals are more likely to sell winners than losers, is easily
accounted for by an appeal to loss aversion. Research on capuchin monkeys
has been interpreted, somewhat optimistically as noted earlier, as suggesting
a genetic basis for loss aversion.

Contrarian Investing and Calendar Effects

Serial dependencies in stock market data and simple investment decision
rules that form the core of Part Four provide a wealth of support for the
critics of the EMH. If asset prices can be, even approximately, characterized as a martingale process, then these simple investment rules and data
patterns would not be observed. That such observations persist in the data,
even years after their first public exposure, suggests that something is amiss.
Of what significance is even the weakest form of the EMH if mean reversion and price momentum are persistently available investment strategies to
outperform the market? Yes, there may be an unspecified risk. But what is
it? Anything that risky, given the returns that are achieved, should be easy to
uncover. Thus far, that hasn't happened.

THE CRITICS HOLD THE HIGH GROUND

At the present state of research, the EMH seems to be in serious trouble. Warren Buffett's famous dictum that "in the short run, the market is a voting machine, but in the long run, the market is a weighing machine"[7] doesn't help because short run and long run are not operational concepts. What matters is whether the deviations from EMH predictions are significant enough, occur often enough, and last long enough to make the EMH an inadequate guide to investment activity, to an understanding of financial markets, and to provide a roadmap for government policy.

But if the EMH is in trouble, it is by no means clear what is out there to take its place. Behavioral finance has not provided an alternative paradigm rich enough to be practically useful except in very specific situations. Even the critics of the EMH seem reluctant to completely abandon it. At best, then, one can only conclude that the EMH and its critics continue to duke it out awaiting future research that may lead to a major revision of the EMH or an alternative analytic framework entirely.

WHAT HAVE WE LEARNED?

We have learned a lot from the research program of behavioral finance. Among the things we have learned are the following:

- *Individual decision making can be systematically biased, inconsistent, easy to manipulate, and generally quite different than the traditional utility maximization hypotheses of traditional economics.*

    Behavioral finance has changed our understanding of financial markets in numerous ways. In the popular press, behavioral finance is often understood to suggest that individuals act in pathological or irrational ways. This stems from the popularity of the research ideas that came out of the Kahneman-Tversky tradition. Kahneman and Tversky painstakingly over a span of years showed that human beings do not make decisions in the way that traditional economics has always assumed.

    How humans make decisions and how good those decisions may be is now a subject open for discussion in ways that it was not before the groundbreaking work of Kahneman and Tversky. Thaler and others have broadened the inquiry. Thaler's popular book, *The Winner's Curse* (Princeton: Princeton University Press, 1991), spread the

---

[7] There is no specific citation available for this often-quoted statement attributed to Warren Buffett.

gospel of Kahneman and Tversky to the broader economic readership. Thaler's columns in the *Journal of Economic Perspectives* were the first exposure of behavioralist ideas to the broader economic profession.

Even the world of sports has not been immune to the interests of the behavioralists. The popular book *Moneyball* (New York: W.W. Norton, 2003) broke the ice on professional sports by documenting the poor decisions made by professional baseball teams in the United States. *Moneyball*'s author, Michael Lewis, had the brilliant insight, originally suggested by the famous central banker, Paul Volcker, to study the success of the Oakland Athletics. Oakland was a surprisingly successful baseball team, despite operating on a limited budget. What Lewis discovered is that professional baseball teams had been making consistently bad decisions with their acquisition of players. By making better decisions, Oakland was able to create a winning team without spending much more than a fraction of what several of the high-spending teams were spending.

■ *Some well-known puzzles in finance are easy to explain by decision-making biases that are widespread.*

Finance economists have always puzzled over the fact that individual investors are quick to sell winning stocks but hang on to losers. One of the most famous stock market investors in history, Richard Whitney, was perhaps the most famous investor of all to hold on to a loser. Whitney was president of the New York Stock Exchange from 1930 to 1935. He was a graduate of Harvard University and was thought to be a successful investor. Whitney made history on Black Thursday, October 24, 1929, when he walked onto the floor of the New York Stock Exchange with a large order for U.S. Steel stock, intending by that action to stem the collapse of the stock market. That didn't work, nor was Whitney's investment acumen up to his reputation.

It turns out that Whitney purchased a substantial position in a small stock in the 1920s. The stock declined in price and Whitney increased his purchases. Ultimately, he ran through all of his own assets and what he could borrow from friends. He ended up embezzling from three separate trust funds that he administered and was convicted of embezzlement. He served three years in Sing Sing prison from 1938 to 1941. Whitney's history is an extreme example of an individual's unwillingness to part with a losing investment.

Why are individual investors reluctant to unload stock market losers? Behavioral finance provides an explanation: loss aversion. Behavioral finance is filling a void. The utility functions that are traditionally used in finance theory are not consistent with loss aversion and provide no explanation for the so-called disposition effect, the tendency to sell winners and hold on to losers.

Another long-standing puzzle in academic finance is the equity premium puzzle. If investors feel more pain, relatively, from losses than pleasure from equal dollar gains, then even if stocks have positive returns over time, volatility will produce many painful episodes that may be so painful that investors abandon the long run performance gains to shield themselves from the periodic short term downticks in stock prices. Loss aversion once again comes to the rescue to provide an explanation for something that has long puzzled finance economists.

Saliency provides another example of a behavioralist explanation for something for which traditional finance theory has no apparent rationale. Why do people buy flood insurance only after a flood has recently occurred? Why do people buy flight insurance only at airport kiosks or counters? Why do investors seek safe assets after a market has crashed? All of these apparent irrationalities can be explained by saliency. Out-of-sight, out-of-mind, some things are given zero weight in our decision making unless we have had a recent reminder. Otherwise, even though we may know the correct and accurate probabilities, we still effectively assign a zero weight because we have not had a recent reminder. After a recent reminder, we then have a tendency to overweight the relatively low probability event.

As comforting as it may be to have an explanation provided where previously there was none, it is not so comforting to realize that loss aversion, saliency, and other biases have not, thus far, been embedded in a general framework with which to inform finance theory. If these behavioral biases are true and are inconsistent with our traditional utility formalizations of finance, then the next step would be to revise the traditional formalization of finance to account for these biases. That step has yet to be taken.

■ *Behavioralists would argue that their research helps us explain and understand bubbles and financial crises.*

Bubbles and financial crises have no comfortable resting place in traditional finance theory. Assumptions of rationality and perfect foresight occupy center ground in the traditional theory. Bubbles, which seem to require irrational speculative behavior for their existence, are difficult to reconcile with a world populated mainly with rational investors and traders. This suggests a fertile ground for behavioralists to provide the missing analysis that can lead to an understanding of the formation of market bubbles and, equally as interesting, the factors that lead to the end of bubbles and the resulting catastrophes that follow.

Some progress has been made but not as much as the size of the bubble literature would suggest. We are now convinced that prices of similar assets can become very dissimilar and stay that way for extended periods of time. The limits to arbitrage argument of Shleifer and colleagues has given a satisfactory theoretical underpinning to why this price divergence can take place. It is a short step, then, to see why prices can either be above or below "fundamental" levels. But why should a spiral upward take place?

Traders have long argued that naïve speculators expect current trends to continue and their expectations of future price gains is often a simple extrapolation of past trends. Has the literature proceeded much beyond that? Starting with Shiller's classic paper, the trend has been to assume a price divergence—a divergence between the market price and what the price should be if the price were solely determined by fundamentals—and then postulate some arbitrary growth process of the market price and some arbitrary growth process of the "fundamental price." That provides the dynamics, but, at heart, it is arbitrary and descriptive.

One approach has been to assume that, as time passes, there is a buildup of speculators who fight against the trend until they reach a tipping point and then the crash takes place. There is not much discussion about what happens after the crash begins. The mathematics of all of this is modern and clean, but the economics is not much more enlightening than the descriptions historically provided by real world traders.

We conclude that, while behavioralists have a strong interest in bubbles and financial crises, they have not yet provided much in the way of a theoretical underpinning for these episodes.

■ *Stock market data in stock markets around the world show a surprising level of predictability.*

The jury is still out as to whether contrarian investing and short-term momentum are permanent characteristics of stock market return time-series data. EMH defenders argue that, once exposed, easy to implement return strategies will prove elusive. That may be. But we don't know that yet. What we do know is that a surprising amount of predictability shows up in market data that is consistent with the casual observations of real world market traders.

Data mining is often alleged against some of the findings of predictability, but that charge is hard to level against findings that support the broad consensus of everyday market traders. That market traders believe in short-term momentum and long-term contrarian investing and that such trends are found in the data is remarkable and is a hard won battle for the behavioralists. Winning the war on this point will require future research and more data.

Calendar effects remain a puzzle. While behavioral research has done an excellent job of ferreting out these effects, explanations have fallen short. What is so special about weekends, holidays, year- and month-end, and various times of the day? While a number of explanations have been advanced in the literature, calendar effects still remain something of a mystery. Many of these effects have been found in stock markets outside of the United States, which weakens the charge of data-mining put forth by critics.

WHERE DO WE GO FROM HERE? (WHAT HAVE WE NOT LEARNED?)

If we have learned quite a bit in the past two and a half decades of research, there remains a lot more to learn. Where should behavioral finance go from here? The answer to that question depends partly on which issues one considers important and partly upon which issues are tractable by the research methods currently available to finance economists. Following is our list of things we think should be of highest priority for the future research agenda in behavioral finance.

Bubbles and Financial Collapses

We still have a long way to go toward understanding how bubbles take place, what causes them to end, and what happens after they end. This is of immense practical importance because of the reactions that seem inevitably to accompany financial collapses. The typical reaction to a financial collapse is a reform movement involving substantial new regulation of the financial and other sectors of the economy. This new regulatory regime is designed to prevent future collapses by providing regulations that prevent excesses that are seen to be the ultimate cause of the bubble and the corresponding collapse.

What if there were no bubbles because the regulatory regime is able to successfully snuff them out before they can begin? Not that there is any evidence that postcollapse regulatory initiatives have ever had much success in preventing the recurrence of financial collapses. If bubbles are an endemic and inherent feature of a market economy, how much of the vibrancy and success of market economies would be lost by regulations that rule out the formation of financial bubbles? This is not merely an academic exercise, as the collapses of the 1930s and again in the post-2007 period were characterized by an intense regulatory reaction to the collapse and a correspondingly long and halting economic recovery. Other collapses tended to have quick and strong recoveries by contrast, along with considerably less regulatory "reform."

A number of important issues about financial collapses are not well understood, even though policy makers seem to think that they are:

- *What causes bubbles?* Often, the cause is ascribed to institutions that expanded their activities to support the bubbles, such as the financial intermediaries who supported the housing bubble of 2003–2007. But is this what started the bubble in the first place? That case is rarely made and is not plausible. More likely, something else got the housing bubble started, something as simple as recently rising prices. We need to understand how a bubble gets started and if there are any objective ways of ascertaining when a bubble is taking place.

- *What sustains a bubble?* Bubbles typically are fueled by substantial leverage. Even though every new regulatory regime promises to remove speculative leverage activity from the system, this never seems to work out as planned. When a bubble gets rolling, it always seems to find the financing that will sustain it, regardless of the regulatory regime in place. One answer could be that regulations are too laxly enforced once the bubble takes hold. Another potential answer is other lending institutions come into existence to replace those unavailable because of the regulatory environment. Whatever the truth, future research should try to learn more about the theory and the facts of what sustains a financial bubble.

- *How do bubbles end, and what kind of recovery from a bubble would there be if there were no change in the regulatory regime?* This is a question that rarely gets asked and may not be answerable, since the normal course of affairs is substantial new regulation after a financial collapse. But there are some examples historically where no regulatory activity of substance took place after a financial collapse. It would be worthwhile finding out what happened in some detail in those cases.

Rethinking Decision Theory Foundations of Finance

Loss aversion seems to be a fact of life. One suspects that loss aversion and its implications are no longer controversial. If that is the case, how can we reconcile and incorporate loss aversion into finance theory? At the moment, loss aversion is left in a kind of ad hoc limbo, without being incorporated into a more general approach to decision theory. What role should regret play in decision theory? Much of what is needed is purely theoretical, armchair research into the foundations of decision theory. Behavioral finance has produced convincing evidence that decisions are made in ways that are fundamentally and systematically different from what we assume in financial economics. Is a new synthesis possible?

Do Our Biases Have Welfare Implications?

A recent book by Richard Thaler and Cass Sunstein suggests that our biases have welfare implications and that government policy remedies can improve welfare by taking account of these biases. We need a lot more research in this area. There is a danger that pointing out irrationalities, biases, and mistakes in decision making can be a pretext for increasing the role of government where such an increase may actually reduce welfare, not improve it. This could even be the unintended consequence of Thaler and Sunstein's well-meaning efforts.

Even with traditional utility assumptions of risk aversion, one could argue that if people really are risk averse, they will end up with significantly less wealth in the long run. Maximizing expected value seems a better plan, especially if life consists of many uncorrelated bets. Should one respect expected outcomes or free choice? Sometimes what seems a clearly preferred action may not be if it impinges on an individual's freedom of choice. The freedom to make a mistake is a legitimate one not to be disparaged.

With the appropriate caveats, it nonetheless is important to follow the thread of biases to discover what impact systematic biases have on individual welfare. Maybe a bias helps us, but more often, one suspects, our biases may harm us. Learning the implications may have an educational effect that improves welfare by making such information available to people.

Can Professional Money Management Provide Value?

One might think that this is a settled issue. So much research has confirmed the inability of the average mutual fund and average money manager to beat simple indices that one might think the discussion was over. But, there are new players with not enough data to yet make a complete determination. Hedge funds are the most prominent of the new managers, but private equity managers raise similar performance questions. We need to continue to study the entire money management industry including hedge funds, private equity funds, and other funds in the alternative asset management industry to assess performance.

It is also possible that money management itself is subject to the biases similar to those that have been discovered for individuals. It is worth taking a deeper look into the financial service industry. This is an industry that consumes enormous resources and seems to have a major impact on the global economy. Whether or not firms themselves might be subject to systematic biases and irrationalities is a subject worth exploring.

Feedback Effects

While there have been several attempts in the behavioral finance literature to explore the feedback effects from asset prices back into real productive activities, so far these have not met with great success. If asset prices diverge from fundamental value, do those firms favored with higher than warranted asset pricing end up wasting resources or does something of value occur as a result of the asset mispricing? One suspects the former, not the latter. But perhaps a Schumpeterian type of creative creation takes place. Perhaps things get built that would not have been built and that, for scale reasons, leads to some good outcomes that might not have occurred otherwise.

Even Kahneman suggests that overoptimistic entrepreneurs may actually provide a beneficial impact on the economy. Keynes's animal spirits seem in tune with Kahneman's suggestion. Having prices exceed fundamental value could easily interact with over-optimism and provide some positive effect on the economy. On the other hand, it is certainly possible that mispricing might be generally harmful to economic efficiency, but it still seems worthwhile to explore this issue without assuming the answer in advance.

Experimental Economics May Be One of the Most Useful Laboratories

Our final observation is that experimental economics may be the best laboratory to study some aspects of financial markets. So far, the ability to create bubbles in experimental settings has yielded interesting research results. One suspects that much more can be learned. Economies are finite and few in number, and repeated and controlled experiments are nearly impossible, even in a data-rich world such as finance. There is room for experimental economics to greatly improve our understanding of finance.

A FINAL THOUGHT

Perhaps the best way to think about behavioral finance and the EMH is to use whichever best serves the immediate purpose. If the goal is to understand why people sell winners, not losers, then behavioral finance seems best positioned to provide an answer. However, if one wishes to know why a stock with higher earnings growth commands a higher price/earnings multiple, the EMH seems to provide the best framework for producing an answer. The right tool to use may well depend on the question being posed. This can be disconcerting if what is desired is a grand, overarching theory that explains everything. Hopefully, future research in finance will improve our understanding of these issues.

Index